STUDIES IN CHRISTIAN HISTC

The Forward Movement

STUDIES IN CHRISTIAN HISTORY AND THOUGHT

The Forward Movement

Evangelical Pioneers of 'Social Christianity'

Roger Standing

First published 2015 by Paternoster

Paternoster is an imprint of Authentic Media
52 Presley Way, Crownhill, Milton Keynes, Bucks, MK8 0ES

www.authenticmedia.co.uk
Authentic Media is a division of Koorong UK, a company limited by guarantee

09 08 07 06 05 04 03   8 7 6 5 4 3 2 1

British Library Cataloguing in Publication Data A catalogue record for this book is available from the British Library

ISBN 978–1–84227–803-1

Printed and bound in Great Britain for Paternoster
by Lightning Source, Milton Keynes

For Ross

With gratitude for the formative years at Methodist Central Hall, Liverpool and my introduction to Hugh Price Hughes and the Forward Movement. Who would have thought?

STUDIES IN CHRISTIAN HISTORY AND THOUGHT

Series Preface

This series complements the specialist series of Studies in Evangelical History and Thought and Studies in Baptist History and Thought for which Paternoster is becoming increasingly well known by offering works that cover the wider field of Christian history and thought. It encompasses accounts of Christian witness at various periods, studies of individual Christians and movements, and works which concern the relations of church and society through history, and the history of Christian thought.

The series includes monographs, revised dissertations and theses, and collections of papers by individuals and groups. As well as 'free standing' volumes, works on particular running themes are being commissioned; authors will be engaged for these from around the world and from a variety of Christian traditions.

A high academic standard combined with lively writing will commend the volumes in this series both to scholars and to a wider readership

Series Editors

Contents

Foreword

The popular image of Victorian evangelical Christianity has too often tended to suffer from viewing it through the distorting lenses of later fundamentalist versions of evangelicalism and stereotypes of 'puritanical' kill-joy Nonconformity. This has not done justice to the vigorous and imaginative efforts of late-Victorian Nonconformists to reach those alienated from the churches and to minister to their social as well as spiritual needs. While recognising parallels in other churches and concerns for Nonconformist unity, Dr Standing's study focuses on a welcome re-assessment of the Wesleyan 'Forward Movement' and its main embodiment in Central Halls for a wide-ranging variety of ministries.

While recognising the roots (sometimes unexpected) of some of its leaders in earlier secular reforming movements, he sees its primary motivation as based on an experiential theology inherited from John Wesley but open to contemporary thought and work for social and political change. This was a form of liberal evangelicalism now largely extinct and forgotten and Dr Standing suggests some of the reasons for the breakup of the relationship between evangelicals and the social gospel, particularly stressing the drift away from the earlier experiential theology.

This is a fresh and innovative study of a movement often misunderstood and unjustly disparaged.

Henry Rack,
formerly Bishop Fraser Senior Lecturer in Ecclesiastical History,
University of Manchester, UK

2014

Abbreviations

DCC	J.D. Douglas (ed.), *The New International Dictionary of the Christian Church* (Second edition) (Exeter: Paternoster, 1978)
Minutes	*Minutes of the Wesleyan Methodist Conference*
MR	*The Methodist Recorder*
MT	*The Methodist Times*
MTM	*The Methodist Temperance Magazine*
WMM	*The Wesleyan Methodist Magazine*

Introduction

While I was on the staff of the Liverpool Methodist Mission in the late 1970s we received a request from Don Wright, a lecturer in history at the University of Newcastle in Australia. He was researching the origin of the Sydney Central Methodist Mission and wanted to verify the claim that it was the first in the world to have been established. We located early archive material for the Liverpool Mission in the city library and I set to work on unearthing our history. What I rediscovered was not only Liverpool's historical priority over Sydney but also over the London and Manchester missions as well, a priority which appeared to have been long forgotten. Thus began for me a fascination with the Forward Movement that gave birth to the Central Missions, the work of Charles Garrett who emerged as the 'father' of the movement and Hugh Price Hughes its 'prophetic voice'.

The special emphases of the Forward Movement: its abundant social ministries, political involvement and engagement with contemporary thought became characterised as the core elements of the 'Social Gospel', an approach to mission that was much maligned by evangelicals in the twentieth century. Yet, the leading proponents of this new movement in the nineteenth century, especially within Nonconformity, were also passionate evangelicals. In many ways these pioneers of what they called 'Social Christianity' anticipated the more holistic missiological understanding that was not to be more widely understood and embraced until a century later.

In what follows I will chart the origin and development of this movement, place it within its wider Nonconformist context and explore the relationship between the traditional evangelicalism and the emerging social emphases of the influential leaders and practitioners. My intention was to understand more clearly how the elements of evangelicalism and social gospel were actually held together, and, if possible, why they became detached in the early decades of the twentieth century. To my surprise I discovered an experiential theology that sought to reaffirm a Wesleyan emphasis on entire sanctification, with a particular leaning towards the 'baptism in the Holy Spirit' teaching that was typical of holiness revivalism in America and the 'second blessing' movement.

The Forward Movement itself was never organised and never had a constitution, membership roll or elected leader. It was rather a broad, general stirring and 'movement forward' with Hugh Price Hughes as its recognised voice with in Wesleyanism. This popular leadership places him at the defining centre of the movement. Most often 'forward' ideas were adopted by evangelicals as ministry in needy areas exposed them to the harsher side of Victorian urban life. Typically they would begin to promote the social agencies that were widely practised by others to meet primary local needs. Continued exposure to these needs then tended to begin to politicise them into municipal and national political life.

In looking to more closely explore what the movement stood for, Hughes' weekly leading articles in *The Methodist Times* from its inception in 1885 till the end of 1901, when he died, provide a rich source insight. The paper claimed to be the voice of the movement, subtitling itself, 'A Journal of Religious and Social Movement', and through the subjects chosen, analysis undertaken and commentary offered reveal the week by week substance of their concern and emphasis. Much more than the more selective content of the volumes of published sermons, these leading articles more adequately reflect the substance of the movement and what really mattered to them. Hughes invariably wrote the leaders for his paper, and the testimony of W.M. Crook who met with him weekly while he was the sub-editor, was that in eighteen years he knew of only three that were written by someone else.[1]

David Bebbington's analysis of evangelicalism as consisting of the four special qualities or marks of conversionism, activism, biblicism and crucicentrism has become widely accepted as a defining set of criteria to establish evangelical identity.[2] Across Nonconformity in the late nineteenth century there is no doubt that those who were developing the insights and methods of Social Christianity remained thoroughly orthodox in their evangelicalism according to these criteria.

The term 'Social Gospel' itself has often been regarded as American in origin, but in fact it had no popular usage there either until the twentieth century. David Thompson believes that the origin of the term is obscure, though it may come from Marx's *Communist Manifesto*, where he distinguishes between revolutionary and non-revolutionary socialism.

> [They] wish to attain their ends by peaceful means, and endeavour, by small experiments, necessarily doomed to failure, and by the force of example, to pave the way for the new social Gospel.

It is likely that the first recorded use of the term was in America in 1886 when it was used to refer to the work of Henry George, a theorist whose influence reached across the Atlantic and informed debate in Britain too. The first recorded British use of the term was also in 1886, by B.F. Westcott in a sermon at Westminster

---

1 W.M. Crook, 'An Appreciation of Hugh Price Hughes' (Newspaper cutting marked M.L. 19.11.1902), Dover Methodist Circuit Archive.

2 David W. Bebbington, *Evangelicalism in Modern Britain* (London: Routledge, 1989), pp. 2-17.

Abbey in which he commented that the Abbey, 'proclaims the social Gospel of Christ with the most touching eloquence'. This and other uses of the phrase by the Unitarian, W.C. Coupland, and the Baptist, John Clifford, indicate to Thompson at least that the phrase was not an unfamiliar one in late Victorian Christian circles.[3]

In summary, within late nineteenth century Wesleyanism there was a vigorous attempt to develop the principles of 'Social Christianity'. An analysis of this 'Forward Movement' is not easy, for while the movement was spontaneous and never officially organised, yet its influence and achievements were vast. The principles of the movement were popularly adopted from the mid-1880s, although its antecedents can be traced further back. Its clearest expression was within Wesleyanism where Arminian theology and connexional structure aided both its adoption and the implementation of its agenda, particularly through the Central Mission movement. Similar stirrings also appear within the other Nonconformist churches and further interesting parallels exist with Anglican 'slum priests' and the development of what became the Social Gospel in the United States.

The leaders of the Movement reveal an openness to the progressive social and intellectual movements of the Victorian era, while never departing from their firmly held evangelicalism. The influence of Chartism, the Anti-corn Law League, temperance, the teaching of the mid-century Christian Socialists, the moral philosophy of T.H. Green, Social Darwinism and the work of Spencer, Ruskin, Morris, Mazzini and others can all be clearly seen in varying degrees.

To all intents and purposes the *Methodist Times* was the most influential publication in expressing the sentiments of this growing movement. To understand the relationship between evangelicalism and the developing commitment to Social Christianity in their thought and action, the weekly editorials of Hugh Price Hughes between 1885-1901 enable an analysis that gets beneath the surface of their rhetoric and demonstrates the nature of their ongoing concern.

What is revealed is a spiritual frame of reference that was of primary significance in both their understanding and motivation. They attempted to construct an experiential theology, based on the Wesley's doctrine of entire sanctification, modified by American 'Second Blessing' teaching, and the need for 'baptism in the Holy Spirit' for personal holiness. From this experiential base they desired to engage with contemporary thought and to work for social and political change. This did not blunt their commitment to either evangelism or their own denomination, though it did result in an openness to innovation in both evangelistic method and denominational reconstruction.

Further, a survey of the Nonconformist denominations reveals the breadth of the movement and a widespread commitment to Nonconformist unity. This interrelationship between the denominations means that it would be a distortion to view the work of any single one in isolation. The exchange of pulpits, shared ideas

---

[3] David M. Thompson, 'The Emergence of the Nonconformist Social Gospel in England' in Keith Robbins (ed.). *Studies in Church History, Subsidia 7* (Oxford: Blackwell, 1990), pp. 259-60.

about urban mission strategy and evangelism, the impact of the Nonconformist Conscience and their commitment to Free Church unity are illustrative of this.

The early years of the twentieth century witnessed the rise of the second generation of leaders whose theological underpinning of Social Christianity drifted away from the experiential understanding that had previously firmly embedded it within an evangelical worldview. As a consequence a growing rift developed in the movement between a purely evangelistic proclamation of 'the Gospel' on one side, and the practice of 'the Social Gospel' on the other.

PART ONE. ENGLAND: A CHANGING COUNTRY

Chapter 1

Social Change: Urbanisation and Its Problems

In the autumn of 1883 a brief penny tract was published that was to have a profound impact on Victorian society in general and the evangelical churches in particular. It was a determined attempt to awaken its Christian readers to the desperate conditions of housing, poverty, immorality and irreligion in the heart of London.

> Whilst we have been building our churches and solacing ourselves with our religion and dreaming that the millennium was coming, the poor have been growing poorer, the wretched more miserable, and the immoral more corrupt; the gulf has been daily widening which separates the lowest classes of the community from our churches and chapels, and from all decency and civilisation.[1]

The Bitter Cry of Outcast London was published under the auspices of the London Congregational Union. The Union's Secretary and a former minister in Chelsea, the Rev Andrew Mearns, had been responsible for the research and production of the tract.[2] He used graphic descriptions of the physical realities of open sewers, decaying houses and overcrowding, to point out how these conditions led to sickness, disease and gross immorality. He wrote, 'tens of thousands are crowded together amidst houses which call to mind . . . the middle passage of the slave ship'. Mearns brought before the Victorian public not only the external facts of the appalling environment in which people had to live, but also the consequences for the lives of individuals of that environment. In Victorian England this was unusual as poverty and immorality were commonly held to be the consequences of personal sin, not personal circumstances.

> There can be no question that numbers of habitual criminals would never have become such, had they not by force of circumstances been packed together in these slums with those who were hardened in crime. Who can wonder that every evil flourishes in such hotbeds of vice and disease? . . . Immorality is but the natural outcome of conditions like these. 'Marriage,' it has been said, 'as an institution, is not fashionable in these

---

1 Anthony S. Wohl, *The Bitter Cry of Outcast London by Andrew Mearns with other selections and an introduction by Anthony S. Wohl* (Leicester: Leicester University Press, 1970), p. 55.

2 For a full account of the disputed authorship of *The Bitter Cry of Outcast London*, see Wohl, pp. 13-15.

> districts.' . . . Ask if the men and women living together in these rookeries are married, and your simplicity will cause a smile.[3]

Mearns argued for a concerted effort by the denominations to engage in long neglected evangelism in the poorest neighbourhoods. He also wanted governmental help to change the pitiable conditions in which the poorest had to live, for, 'without State interference nothing effectual can be accomplished upon any large scale'. Society had a responsibility to secure the rights of citizenship for the poorest of its people.[4]

The Bitter Cry was not the first work to bring these facts before the public. Many official reports supplemented by the writing of Mayhew, Dickens, Kingsley, Sims (who had himself published a series of articles in *The Pictorial World* of June 1883 entitled, 'How the Poor Live') and others had all covered similar ground, but had excited little interest in the press or popular imagination.[5] *The Bitter Cry* was different because in the autumn of 1883 it was taken up and serialised by *The Pall Mall Gazette*. It was the first issue to be publicised by the *Gazette's* newly appointed, campaigning editor, W.T. Stead. In his editorials that accompanied *The Bitter Cry*, Stead used his style of popular journalism to elicit greater indignation in his readers. He spoke about 'reeking tenements', 'stunted squalid savages of civilisation', 'the foul ulcer of London' and 'a huge cancer eating into the very heart of the realm'.[6] The Gazette reported in its issue of 2 January 1884 that its message had been sent,

> echoing from one end of England to the other . . . We shall have to go back a long time to discover an agitation on any social question in England which has produced so prompt, so widespread, and, as we believe, so enduring an effect.

Stead's campaigning journalism left his readers in no doubt, London was on 'the verge of moral combustion'.[7] The ensuing agitation even disturbed the consciences of Queen Victoria and the Prince of Wales.[8] Bentley Gilbert believes that *The Bitter Cry* was, 'perhaps the most influential single piece of writing about the poor that England has ever seen'.[9]

The problems of urbanisation were not restricted to London either, although in terms of size and function London was unique in its development. Just as Victorian society was characterised by the growth of cities, so their cities were characterised by the parallel growth of all the associated problems. In Liverpool as early as 1844

---

3 Wohl, *The Bitter Cry*, pp. 60-61.

4 Wohl, *The Bitter Cry*, p. 69.

5 John Rees & Lindsey German, *A People's History of London* (London: Verso, 2012), p. 130-31; A.N. Wilson, *The Victorians* (New York: Arrow, 2003), pp. 442-43.

6 Wohl, *The Bitter Cry*, p. 82.

7 Tristram Hunt, *Building Jerusalem: The Rise and Fall of the Victorian City* (London: Weidenfeld & Nicholson, 2004), p. 292.

8 Wohl, *The Bitter Cry*, p. 13.

9 John D. Beasley, *The Bitter Cry Heard and Heeded (The Story of the South London Mission, 1889-1989)* (London: South London Mission, 1989), p. 11.

the Medical Officer of Health, the first to be appointed in the country, estimated that in the city there were 6,294 cellars which housed 20,168 people, and he continued by describing what he termed a cellar:

> They are 10' – 12' square, generally flagged – but frequently having only bare earth for a floor and sometimes less that 6' high. There is frequently no window, so that light and air can gain access to the cellar only by the doors, the top of which is often not higher than the level of the street. In such cellars ventilation is out of the question. They are of course dark, and through the defective drainage, generally very damp. There is sometimes a back cellar, used as a sleeping apartment, having no direct communication with the external atmosphere, and deriving its scanty supply of light and air solely from the first apartment.[10]

While these cellars were relatively short-lived and the Liverpool Sanitary Amendment Act had given the city power to buy and clear housing declared 'not fit for human habitation', 10,000 people were still confined to pre-legislation housing a generation later. Only £6,000 a year had been budgeted for owner compensation in slum clearance, so the well intentioned Act suffered through under-funding. This lack of finance also hit provision of what was to replace demolished housing stock. Local authorities were not obliged to provide state subsidised residences until the Housing Act of 1919. Authorities that did, like Liverpool and London, were therefore forced to borrow money and run municipal housing schemes on a commercial basis. In Liverpool 2,895 council units were built prior to 1919, but they replaced 11,308 that were demolished. Added to this, the rents for the new properties were relatively high to cover loan charges, and in 1907 the authority made public their policy of looking for a better class of the dispossessed to take up tenancy, namely, those who could pay the rents and conform to the standards of housekeeping demanded by the corporation.[11]

These problems of housing were a direct result of the whole process of urbanisation in the nineteenth century. The facts relating to urban growth are startling and it is not surprising that Engels called the immigration to the cities 'social suicide'.[12] In 1800 there was no place with a population that exceeded 100,000 outside London. By the time Victoria came to the throne in 1837 there were five such cities, and by the end of the century these had grown in number to twenty-three.[13] The decade 1821-1831 was a period of astonishing growth. Leeds, Liverpool, Manchester, Birmingham and Sheffield all increased their population by 40-50%.[14] By the middle of the century England was the most urbanised country in

---

10 Gordon Read & David Jebson, *A Voice in the City* (Liverpool: Liverpool City Mission, 1979), p. 20.

11 Richard Lawton (ed.), *The Rise and Fall of Great Cities: Aspects of Urbanisation in the Western World* (London: Bellhaven, 1989), pp. 37, 103-104 & 128-32.

12 Jeffrey G. Williamson, *Coping with City Growth during the British Industrial Revolution* (Cambridge: CUP, 2002), p. 7.

13 Asa Briggs, *Victorian Cities* (London: Odhams, 1963), p. 57.

14 Briggs, *Victorian Cities*, p. 81.

the world with 80% of the population being urban dwellers according to Lawton.[15] Manchester's growth is illustrative of this phenomenon. In the 1770s the population stood around 30,000; by the time of the first census in 1801 this had risen to 70,000 and thirty years later to 142,000, with a remarkable 45% growth in the decade 1821-1831. The number of houses had increased from 3,500 in 1775 to 22,500 in 1831. The 1911 census recorded a total population of 410,000.[16]

The pressure on available housing became intense. Increasing population added to the substantial demolition for municipal use, railway development and slum clearance schemes meant that many new units were required. However, labourers needed to live near their employment where it was difficult for builders to build. This was because the value of the land for industrial or commercial use made it too costly for inexpensive working-class dwellings. Rising building costs exacerbated the problem. Hence, as the middle classes moved into the suburbs away from the poorer areas, houses were let and sublet until the one-roomed family became commonplace and overcrowding a serious problem.

The links between industrialisation and urban growth are in one sense obvious, and the new cities of the north and midlands were each growing in different ways as a result of various combinations of factors. Manchester grew from an older town based on the developing cotton trade. Middlesbrough was a new town altogether, reliant on coal and iron works. Newcastle, Gateshead, North and South Shields, Wallsend and Jarrow were all old towns that became fused in the new north-eastern urban complex that benefited from a port, raw materials and a ready supply of labour. However, the process of industrialisation and urbanisation was not a smooth or uniform one. Gareth Shaw sees it more in terms of fits and spurts according to the phases of economic development. The first phase, typified by the mid-1820s, saw the development of textiles and metal manufacturing in the northern and midland towns, particularly near ready supplies of coal and water to take advantage of steam power. The second phase towards the middle of the century was a period of consolidation and expansion, incorporating specialised and technical innovations. The third phase from the mid-1880s saw a gradual shift from manufacturing into tertiary activities, particularly in the service and retail sectors.[17] This diversification was the consequence of having been the first country to industrialise. International industrial primacy could not be maintained forever. Thus, in the last quarter of the century the Victorians believed they were going through a great depression as a result of it. The newer competitors, Germany and the United States, had the latest and most efficient equipment, while much British capital was tied up in increasingly obsolete plant.

---

[15] Lawton, *The Rise and Fall of Great Cities*, p. 5.

[16] Josef W. Konvitz, *The Urban Millennium: The City Building Process from the Early Middle Ages to the Present* (Illinois: Southern Illinois University Press, 1985), p. 96; Stephen Halliday, *The Great Filth: Disease, Death and the Victorian City* (Stroud: History Press, 2011), p. 18-19.

[17] Lawton, *The Rise and Fall of Great Cities*, pp. 57-61.

Jones concluded that throughout this period the British economy experienced erratic but continued expansion, sufficient to support continued improvements in mass living standards. However, the growth was accompanied by complex and painful changes in economic structure and shifts of emphasis and investment.[18] During this period of instability the evidence indicates growing rates of unemployment, albeit given to wide and short-term swings, which hit the masses of unskilled workers in the large cities more than anyone else.[19]

This unemployment and poverty was made worse by the inherent problems of the Victorian city. Economic individualism and common civic purpose were difficult to reconcile. High industrial investment meant a low commitment to social provision. Industrial priority meant all other aspects of life were secondary. The sheer weight of numbers in the cities rendered every existing facility for urban living inadequate. Machinery for public health, water supply, drainage, housing, disposal of refuse, care of those in need, education and recreation were all services that in the latter part of the century needed much attention. Given this overall situation it is not surprising that epidemics of typhus, cholera and smallpox were frequent and claimed many lives, especially in the 1840s-50s.[20]

There was also increasing concern about the impact of the urban environment on all who lived there, rich and poor alike. Dr Cantlie, a surgeon and medical educator in the London hospitals, described a condition he called 'urbomorbus' or 'city disease'. In a lecture on 'Degeneration amongst Londoners' (1885), he argued that the air lacked ozone and that most inhabitants could not therefore gain the benefits they needed from vigorous exercise. He said, 'Everyone in the inner conscience knows and believes that town air is bad, that everyone working in it must suffer after a time.'[21]

Other medical experts, such as Fothergill, noted that urban dwellers were small boned, light in muscle and short in stature.[22] Shockingly, the life expectancy in the most deprived areas of Liverpool and Glasgow was the lowest since the time of the Black Death.[23]

Some saw a more positive side to city life. Robert Vaughan summed up the rather more optimistic sentiment of many in 1842 when he declared, 'Our age is pre-eminently the age of great cities', and many agreed with him.[24] They saw the new cities as allowing a greater independence from the old order and consequently

---

[18] Peter d'A. Jones, *The Christian Socialist Revival (1877-1914)* (Princeton: Princeton University Press, 1968), p. 39.

[19] The national unemployment rates during the period were 1.28% (1873); 11.4% (1879); 2.3% (1882); 10.2% (1886). Jones, *Christian Socialist Revival*, p. 33.

[20] P.J. Waller, *Democracy and Sectarianism: A Political and Social History of Liverpool, 1868-1939* (Liverpool: Liverpool University Press, 1981), pp. 84-85.

[21] Andrew Lees, *Cities Perceived: Urban Society in European and American Thought, 1820-1914* (Manchester: Manchester University Press, 1985), p. 137.

[22] Lees, *Cities Perceived*, p. 137.

[23] Hunt, *Building Jerusalem*, p. 29.

[24] Lawton, *The Rise and Fall of Great Cities*, p. 3.

a greater level of personal freedom. Greater size allowed for a wider variety of consumer commodities, entertainment and cultural activities, as well as a genuine transfer of power. Many cities generated a real municipal pride that was followed by new and bold courses of action.

Not everyone was so positive. Men like William Cobbett and Charles Masterman were extremely fearful of the urban masses. It was a new dimension to the fear of the mob. Cobbett said, 'jails, barracks and factories do not corrupt people by their walls, but by their condensed numbers. Populous cities corrupt for the same cause.'[25] The new urban areas became the source of a new threat as a fear of the 'masses' began to trouble the nation.

Briggs identified two contributing elements to this fear.[26] The first was the realisation of how irreligious the large cities were. Engels had noted their 'widespread and almost universal indifference to religion' in 1844,[27] and this, in turn, had been substantiated by the religious census of 1851. Indeed Horace Mann calculated that on the census Sunday fewer than one person in ten attended church or chapel in Birmingham, Liverpool, Manchester, Sheffield and Newcastle.[28]

Non-attendance at worship became an important issue in the churches for the rest of the century. In Liverpool in 1868 a meeting was held to enquire into 'the cause of the prevailing indifference of the working classes to public worship'. The reasons put forward by working-class speakers were: pew rents; lack of suitable clothes; effects of weekday fatigue and opportunities for recreation, pleasure and alcoholic drink. Clerical defects, namely failure to visit or to appreciate working-class problems, were also mentioned, along with dull sermons.[29]

Certainly, as the nineteenth century drew to a close, the Church had to compete with Trades Unions, Friendly Societies and political parties for the allegiance of the working class. Charles Booth tentatively suggested that pleasure, amusement and sport were the most popular alternatives to church, with the church offering no serious challenge.[30] McLeod notes that those within the working class who were either politically or religiously active were more likely to be the prosperous element, who were closer to the middle-class, whose status and power needs were greater than their material requirements. Those at the bottom were too absorbed in the struggle to stay alive to be involved in anything else, and they were even liable to hold God responsible for their predicament.[31]

---

[25] Briggs, *Victorian Cities*, p. 58.

[26] Briggs, *Victorian Cities*, pp. 60-62.

[27] C.E. Gwyther, *The Methodist Social and Political Theory and Practice, 1848-1914; with special reference to The Forward Movement* (Liverpool, 1961: unpublished M.A. thesis), p. 55.

[28] Briggs, *Victorian Cities*, p. 52.

[29] R.B. Walker, 'Religious Change in Liverpool in the Nineteenth Century', *Journal of Ecclesiastical History*, 19 (1968), pp. 208-09.

[30] K.S. Inglis, *Churches and the Working Class in Victorian England* (London: Routledge, 1963), pp. 335-36.

[31] Hugh McLeod, *Class and Religion in the Late Victorian City* (London: Croom Helm,

The second concern that this fear of the masses brought out was a political one. The Victorian urban revolution had resulted in a system of class ghettos in which a more homogeneous group was being born through the similarity in life of urban living, factory-centred work and public elementary education, offered on a large-scale after 1870 and free after 1891. As a result a 'new unionism' emerged in the 1890s amongst the semi and unskilled workers.[32] It was the harbinger of the coming mass labour movement, which was increasingly articulate and well organised. To those in authority it suggested the stirrings of the lower classes.

Growing fear accompanied the occurrence of riots in cities around the world. The Paris uprising of 1871 and the Haymarket riots in Chicago of 1886 were at a comfortable international distance, but they held a foreboding. The latter was the result of a bitterly fought strike that had culminated in the execution and martyrdom of four of the strike leaders. However, 13 October 1887 (Bloody Sunday) brought things to the centre of the empire. After months of marches and rioting the unemployed fought with police in Trafalgar Square and invaded the service at Westminster Abbey. In every city, respectable newspapers contained dire warnings of the breakdown of society.[33]

During the period of public disturbances during the Boer War, Charles Masterman feared the corrupting nature of the Metropolis, talking about mile after mile of mean streets, inhabited by the innumerable multitudes of pent-up, common people. They constituted, in his mind, a potentially volcanic force whose grievances might one day erupt violently. He likened common people emerging from the underground railways to rats coming out of drains and surging through the streets, brushing off the police like elephants dispersing flies.[34] Disraeli suggested that all 'agitation' had its origin in the life of the city, he pointing to the Political Union's origin in the city of Birmingham, the Anti-Corn Law League in Manchester and the 'ubiquitous and amorphous movement of urban protest called Chartism'.[35]

Victorian cities were a mixed blessing. They were essential for the industrial development that had been the engine of Britain's pre-eminence in the world following the industrial revolution. They had their supporters who glowed with municipal pride at their achievements, yet within them there were appalling conditions and scenes of untold human misery. London was the modern 'Babylon', at once invoking the wealth, splendour and refinement of the ancient city alongside alluding to the apocalyptic judgement of the Book of Revelation.[36] Victorian society was, on the whole, shocked and fearful of what was revealed to them about their large cities. It was to these religious, social and political problems that the churches sought to address themselves. As Charles Booth said:

1974), p. 283.

[32] P. Jones, *Christian Socialist Revival*, p. 40.

[33] Lawton, *The Rise and Fall of Great Cities*, p. 20.

[34] Lees, *Cities Perceived*, p. 169.

[35] Briggs, *Victorian Cities*, p. 52.

[36] Lynda Nead, *Victorian Babylon: People, Streets and Images in Nineteenth Century London* (New Haven: Yale University Press, 2005), p. 3.

When we count the 100,000 individuals and the 20,000 families, that lead so pinched a life among the population described, and remember that there are in addition, double that number who, if not actually pressed by want, yet have nothing to spare, we shrink aghast from the picture.[37]

[37] Lees, *Cities Perceived*, p. 114.

Chapter 2

Social Ferment: Attempts at Reform

Industrialisation and urban growth presented Victorian Britain with numerous challenges that required the country to engage in significant social reform. Of course, the nature and focus of the proposed reforms varied according to the convictions and outlook of the prospective reformers. Lord Shaftesbury was pre-eminent among them. His legislative work, though paternalistic, brought basic changes in industrial practice and other areas of national life that had practical benefits for thousands.

Leaders among the working classes had other ideas; they agitated for political reform. Thomas Cooper, Feargus O'Connor and the other Chartist leaders anticipated many of the democratic developments that the next century of political life would bring. However, the middle years of the century proved to be a time for building up a fledgling labour movement through Trades Unions, Co-Operative and Friendly Societies.

The Anti-Corn Law League was a predominantly middle-class, single-issue pressure group that fought for economic reform. Its success was a significant milestone, but nonetheless depended upon a combination of factors.

Temperance, on the other hand, looked for the personal/moral reform of the drunkard. The movement had many different emphases. Moral suasionists argued against the legislative compulsionists. Others fought for absolute abstention in opposition to those who felt that moderation was sufficient. Yet others gave their energies to providing counter-attractions to the public house.

Whatever the success or failure of these movements, they were a part of the reforming spirit of the Victorian age that surrounded evangelical Christianity, and which was to have such a profound effect upon some of them.

Tory Reformers

Anthony Ashley Cooper, the Lord Shaftesbury was a Tory patrician who sponsored reforming legislation, having entered Parliament in 1826. His work resulted in the Lunacy Commission that Parliament established in 1833; the Ten Hours Act (1847); the Factory Act (1874); acts regulating child and female labour in 1864 and 1867; the Climbing Boys Act (1875) protecting young boys who were used to sweep chimneys, as well as promoting legislation to protect milliners and dressmakers.[1] Shaftesbury was a convinced Tory as well as being an aristocrat and substantial landowner and, while he did an enormous amount to alleviate the suffering of the most vulnerable and exploited within society, he was neither a socialist nor a democrat. It is a particular paradox that one of the most celebrated social reformers of the nineteenth century remained implacably opposed to many of the most basic reform movements of his day.[2] The working classes regarded him with suspicion, and though his paternalism led him to work for them, he could not be described as having worked with them.

An Anglican and convert to the evangelical cause following his reading of Philip Doddridge and Thomas Scott, Shaftesbury adopted pre-millennialist convictions under the influence of Edward Bickersteth. For Turnbull this is not insignificant in the light of Shaftesbury's public service, his declining of high public office and his tireless work for evangelical missionary and benevolent societies. Central among which was the London City Mission, for which he was a staunch supporter and advocate for over forty years.[3]

Other Tory reforms during the middle of the century included the Enfranchisement Act (1867) and the Forster Education Act of (1870). This was followed by Disraeli's social reform Parliament that began in 1874. They were also responsible for a Working Class Housing Act (1875); two labour reform acts in 1875 that legalised peaceful picketing and abolished imprisonment for breach of contract; the Plimsoll Act to protect sailors (1876), and a Public Health Act (1878).[4]

Randolph Churchill was instrumental in initiating a return to Disraeli's social reforms in the 1880s through the progressive conservatism that became known as 'Tory Democracy'. His hope was that by extending these reforms the Tories might capture the working-class vote. His resignation from the cabinet in 1886 prematurely terminated his influence.[5]

Chartism

William Lovett, aided by a few Radical Members of Parliament, summarised the needs of the newly formed National Union of Working Classes in a bill intended for Parliament. By August 1838 the six points of 'the People's Charter' had been accepted by a variety of working men's groups, who agreed to merge their agitation into one common struggle. Further to this, at Manchester in August 1840 the National Chartist Association was formed. It became a powerful and comprehensive protest that mobilised much of the radical spirit of the time and caught the popular imagination of the people. The six points of the Charter were:

---

1 DCC, p. 900.

2 Richard Turnbull, *Shaftesbury: the great reformer* (Oxford: Lion, 2010), p. 15.

3 Turnbull, *Shaftesbury*, pp. 34-36, 135-41.

4 Peter d'A. Jones, *The Christian Socialist Revival (1877-1914)* (Princeton: Princeton University Press, 1968), pp. 41-60.

5 Jones, *The Christian Socialist Revival*, p. 42.

1. Universal manhood suffrage.
2. Annual parliaments.
3. Voting by ballot.
4. Equal electoral districts.
5. No property qualification for Members of Parliament.
6. Payment of Members of Parliament.[6]

The difficulties surrounding the People's Parliament that began in February 1839 were illustrative of the tensions present within the diverse coalition of interests that lay behind the Charter. The movement's slogan had been 'Peaceably if we may, forcibly if we must', but in March the issue of violence and ulterior measures swept through the Convention. Disturbances at Devizes only added to a growing sense of unease at the advance of the Chartist cause with those in authority discerning the spectre of insurrection.[7] When their proposals were introduced to Parliament they were soundly defeated by 235 votes to 46. By June 1840 five hundred Chartist leaders were in jail and when in 1841 the proposals were voted on again, this time they were defeated by 287 votes to 59.[8]

Organisation was not the strongest point of the movement, although they did attempt to adopt a vaguely 'Methodist' pattern consisting of class meetings, weekly subscriptions and even camp meetings.[9] Indeed, Lovett himself had been brought up by Cornish Methodists who instilled in him his enthusiasm for self-improvement and a strictly disciplined approach to life.[10] While not the controlling influence, Christianity permeated the whole movement. Speakers often used biblical images and religious language to express themselves. William Hill, the editor of the semi-official Chartist newspaper *Northern Star*, said:

> Every Christian must be a Chartist, and all will be better Chartists for being Christians ... I believe Christianity to be the soul of which Chartism is the body; and I cannot consent to separate them.[11]

One of the issues on which Christians within the movement tended to differ from their non-believing Chartist brothers and sisters, was on the use of force. Violence was rare, but was always rumoured by the authorities as an effective weapon against the movement. There were attempts at violence in Sheffield and Bradford in January 1840, but following this there were no further outbreaks until August

---

[6] Richard Brown, *Chartism: Rise and Demise* (United Kingdom: Authoring History, 2014), p. 71.

[7] Malcolm Chase, *Chartism: a new history* (Manchester: Manchester University Press, 2007), pp. 57-60.

[8] Robert F. Wearmouth, *Methodism and the Working Class Movements of England, 1800-1850* (London: Epworth, 1947), pp. 108-14 & 122-25.

[9] Asa Briggs (ed.), *Chartist Studies* (London: Macmillan, 1962), pp. 308-10.

[10] Brian Harrison, '"Kindness And Reason": William Lovett and Education', *History Today* 37.3 (1987), p. 16.

[11] D. Jones, *Chartism and Chartists* (London: Allen Lane, 1975), pp. 49-50.

1842.[12] While it is doubtful that Feargus O'Connor really wanted physical force to be employed, he always wrote and spoke in a violent and provocative manner. Added to which he explicitly urged violence, should violence be necessary. The majority, though, would have joined with Lovett and other Chartist leaders who looked for peaceful change:

> Then rise, my boys, and fight the foe,
> The arms are truth and reason;
> We'll let the Whigs and Tories know
> That Union is not treason.[13]

Asa Briggs regards O'Connor as the most important of the Chartist leaders.[14] Indeed, his fiery oratory with its flamboyant and extravagant style was a tremendous asset to the movement. The reverse side of this trait was that his colleagues found it difficult to work with him, complaining of his vanity, jealousy, impatience when criticised and his unstable emotions.[15]

Many felt that O'Connor's 'Land Plan' was a real distraction from work towards the Charter. He felt strongly that the answer to arresting regular famines was to put more land under cultivation through small holdings. His conviction was that 'spade husbandry' would increase productivity, and as each man worked his own 'labour field', he would experience independence and develop the grand principle of self-reliance. Thus machinery would be made into man's holiday, not his curse. The Land Plan was peripheral to the Chartist cause, and reflects more of O'Connor's nostalgia to a passing order than the cutting edge of social change.[16]

All Chartists shared the conviction that, 'we are many, they are few'. With this went a belief that in struggling for the Charter they were not rebels, but honest Britons fighting for their birth right. Yet, divisions amongst them became an ever deepening problem. Thomas Cooper declared, 'Antagonisms come up within and without, and have been our greatest curse.'[17] These divisions were the consequence of Chartism being a diverse group, with a broad platform and many different emphases. When their agitation reached its climax in 1848, not one of the original leaders stood by O'Connor's side.

The economic crisis of 1847-48 caused a revival in the movement's fortunes. A mass demonstration was called to begin at Kennington Common on 10 April 1848 to be part of presenting a mass petition to Parliament. Due to a popular fear of violent insurrection occurring at Chartist hands with popular uprisings having occurred earlier that year in France, Austria, Germany and Italy, the Duke of Wellington took command of the defences of London. He exercised every possible

---

12 Wearmouth, *Methodism*, pp. 103-06.
13 Briggs, *Chartists*, p. 294.
14 Briggs, *Chartists*, p. 301.
15 Maldwyn Edwards, *Methodism and England* (London: Epworth, 1944), p. 44.
16 Briggs, *Chartists*, p. 306.
17 Jones, *Chartism*, p. 183.

precaution and 22,853 special constables were sworn for the Metropolitan area.[18] Though declared illegal by the government, organisers went ahead, though on the day while the 250,000 anticipated by the executive did not turn up, a crowd of some 150,000 did assemble.[19] The police persuaded them not to march and heavy rain brought the speeches to an early close. It was later to be known as the 'fiasco of Kennington Common'. The petition did not fare well either. O'Connor had claimed it contained 5,700,000 signatures, but calculations estimated a total of 1,975,496, less a large number that should have been discounted as they were in the same hand, were fictitious names or were women.[20]

Chartism was the child of its age. Wedded to the notion of progress it was presumed that constitutional reform would inexorably lead to social and economic advances too. It is interesting to note that universal manhood suffrage was argued on the grounds of expediency rather than from natural rights and made no attempt to re-enfranchise women, neither was there any attempt to address the reform of the House of Lords.[21] As a movement it was doomed to failure from the beginning for three main reasons. First, its very nature was to suggest measures to a half-reformed House of Commons that the House would never accept. Second, the economic conditions were not right to force the government to concede. Third, there was a lack of agreement within the movement about the means that should be employed to achieve their agreed ends.[22] The inevitability of their failure should not rob the movement of its importance. The Radicals' demand for the Six Points survived the failure of the Chartist attempt to secure them. Though the dream of social democracy lost much of its appeal, it did not disappear. Rather, it lodged in the subconscious of the nation, re-emerging later to become a living reality. As it was, the Chartist activists were scattered by the movement's demise into the various Trades Unions, Co-operative and Friendly Societies that continued to build the growing labour movement and working-class consciousness.

Had the Chartists followed the lead of the Peterloo Meeting of 1819 and linked together their demands for Parliamentary reform with the abolition of the Corn Laws, perhaps the story would have been different. However, O'Connor had poisoned the minds of the Chartists against Cobden, Bright and the Anti-Corn Law League, calling them a 'plague' at a time when the League was looking to the working class for support. However, their campaign developed on a wholly different basis to that of the Chartists and Cobden may not have ultimately been prepared to broaden his platform anyway.

---

[18] Wearmouth, *Methodism*, pp. 105-106.
[19] Chase, *Chartism*, p. 302.
[20] Chase, *Chartism*, p. 312.
[21] Brown, *Chartism*, pp. 3, 74, 510.
[22] Asa Briggs, *The Age of Improvement* (London: Longman, Green, 1957), p. 306.

The Anti-Corn Law League

'I hereby appoint you my Lieutenant-General against those equally vile and silly Corn Laws.'[23] So wrote Lord Brougham to Joseph Sturge on 29 September 1838. In doing so Brougham expressed the conviction of a growing number of people.

The Corn Laws had been introduced in 1815 and prohibited the entry of foreign corn into Britain until the home price reached 80s a quarter. Many people, like the writer William Cobbett, predicted that the measure would fail, as it did. The price fell from 71s 6d to 52s 10d within the year.[24]

The League itself was born on 20 March 1839, when delegates from different groups agitating against the Corn Laws decided to establish a national organisation. They had been in London to lobby Parliament, but their efforts had been in vain.[25] Bizarrely, as they met at the Brown's Hotel in Westminster Palace Yard Chartist delegates for the first Chartist convention arrived only to find the venue double-booked.[26]

Previously their action had been sporadic and localised. The formation of the Anti-Corn Law League would change all that. It was to become a highly organised, and ultimately successful, extra-Parliamentary pressure group. The object was simple and direct - the total repeal of the Corn Laws. The League was shrewd in its refusal to merge this aim with other social reforms, preferring rather to concentrate their energies.

The constituency of opinion to which the Anti-Corn Law League appealed was completely different to that of the Chartists. Richard Cobden acknowledged more than once that their fervour and efficiency as an organisation depended upon the middle classes.[27] The political difference between these two constituencies was significant. The middle classes had been enfranchised by the Reform Act of 1832. Cobden admitted:

> we have carried it on by those means by which the middle class usually carries on its movements. We have had our meetings of dissenting Ministers: we have obtained the co-operation of ladies: we have resorted to tea parties and taken those pacific means for carrying out our views which mark us off as a middle class set of agitators.[28]

The League immediately found that mill owners and industrialists had sympathies with their cause. Highly priced bread meant higher labour costs, which in turn made it difficult for them to capture foreign markets. Such an alliance further alienated the Chartists who were extremely suspicious of 'respectables', 'millocrats', and 'shopocrats'. 'Why do these liberal manufacturers bawl lustily for repeal of the Corn Laws?' demanded the placards at a Chartist meeting on 19 March 1841,

---

23 Norman Longmate, *The Breadstealers* (London: Maurice Temple Smith, 1984), p. 17.
24 Briggs, *Improvement*, pp. 201-203.
25 Longmate, *The Breadstealers*, pp. 32-34.
26 Chase, *Chartism*, p. 59; Brown, *Chartism*, p. 85.
27 Briggs, *Chartism*, p. 299.
28 Edwards, *Methodism*, p. 41.

'Because with the reduced price of corn they will be enabled to reduce the wages of working men.'[29] Public meetings were an integral part of the civic life of Victorian Britain and, while the League was not in competition with the Chartists, it was not unusual for rowdy and boisterous meetings to slip into brawling.[30]

Born at the same moment in history and committed to reform and, at least in some degree appealing to individuals with progressive sympathies, had the League been able to offer a simple and convincing reply to this fear of exploitation, and had Cobden and Bright not been identified as opponents of factory reform, Chartist opposition might not have been so intense. That was not to be, rather they were seen as compromised because of the vested interests of their supporters in business, and even a deliberate diversion sanctioned by Westminster to draw attention away from more radical reform.[31] A League member reported to the *Manchester Guardian* of 2 September 1842, '[we] have not had a meeting where the public were admitted which has not been upset by the Chartists.'[32]

The League's campaign was based primarily around four main points:

1. Repeal would solve the 'condition of England' problem by cheapening goods and allowing regular employment.
2. It would guarantee prosperity for manufacturers by affording outlets for their products.
3. It would encourage agricultural efficiency by stimulating urban demand.
4. Free international trade would lead to fellowship and peace.

Repeal of the Corn Laws meant a strategy to either convert the majority of MPs, or to rouse the members of the electorate to such a pitch that they would in future accept only candidates pledged to repeal. They maintained that the only barrier was the ignorant self-interest of the landlords, 'the bread-taxing oligarchy, unprincipled, unfeeling, rapacious and plundering'.[33] In the hands of Cobden and Bright the League became a moral crusade against the self-interest of a landed Parliament which they often called 'aristocratic misrule'. Cobden saw religion as a powerful agent of progress and viewed co-operation with church leaders as key to their success. League membership cards were printed with the slogan 'Give us this day our daily bread', and when the Anglican clergyman Thomas Spencer publically announced that alleviating the needs of the poor and feeding the hungry were religious duties, the League printed and circulated his views under the title, 'The Repeal of the Corn Laws, A Religious Question.'[34]

---

[29] Longmate, *The Breadstealers*, p. 82.

[30] Chase, *Chartism*, pp. 158-59, 197-98.

[31] Paul A. Pickering & Alex Tyrrell, *The People's Bread, a history of the Anti-Corn Law League* (London: Leicester University Press, 2000), pp. 141-42.

[32] Longmate, *The Breadstealers*, p. 81

[33] Briggs, *Improvement*, p. 314.

[34] Pickering & Tyrrell, *The People's Bread*, p. 88; Richard Francis Spall, 'The Anti-Corn-Law League's opposition to English Church establishment', *Journal of Church & State*, 32.1 (1990), p. 97-123.

In 1841 Cobden contested the election and was returned for Stockport. In July 1843 Bright, a Quaker,[35] joined him as the member for Durham. With the support of merchants and manufacturers the League began to loom large nationally, winning increasing support for its policy of abolition. The failure of the Irish potato crop in 1845 gave an unexpected opportunity. The logic of the situation was obvious to all but the most fanatical protectionists: if the staple food of Ireland was destroyed, to tax the only alternative to it would be both cruel and lunatic.

By late 1845 Shaftesbury had changed his position on abolition, but in advocating what he saw as a middle way he alienated both sides of the debate and, realising he could not represent the views of his Dorset constituency to retain the Corn Laws, he resigned from Parliament.[36] Queen Victoria was also convinced that change was necessary, writing to Robert Peel, the Prime Minister, on 28 November 1845: 'The Queen thinks the time is come when a removal of the restrictions upon the importation of food cannot be successfully resisted.'[37]

After much politicking, Peel brought in a measure to gradually reduce the tax to a nominal tariff of one shilling by 1 February 1849. Cobden later admitted that without the Irish potato famine or without Peel the Corn Laws might not have been repealed as early as they were.[38] On the 2 July 1846 the League ceased to exist.

The Anti-Corn Law League was a successful experiment in the formation and management of national public opinion, with large funds, an efficient central office and a consistency of purpose. It was prepared to work through the system to change the system, whether by lecturing, which Sydney Smith considered the 'great engine of repeal'; by organising petitions, of which 2,758 were submitted containing 1,465,476 names by 1842; by encouraging property ownership to gain the vote; by mobilising the active participation of women, a the Grand Bazaar raised over £25,000 on 8 May 1845; by doorstep canvassing which combined paid overseers with the work of volunteers, or by maintaining a mailing and subscription list that pioneered the use of a card index, colour coded and identified with letters and numbers to indicate the member's area and usual subscription.[39] They even utilised the new 'penny post' to distribute literature. In the early days print runs for tracts were of 10,000; these increased to 50,000 and at the height of the campaign to 500,000. By 1842 they had distributed 5 million tracts and in 1843 they were employing 300 full or part-time workers in packing and distribution in Manchester alone. From 1840 up to three and a half tons of literature a week was being dispatched.[40] In November 1843 *The Times* announced that 'a new power has arisen in the state' and for both their contemporaries and later commentators the

---

[35] Pickering & Tyrrell, *The People's Bread*, p. 100; Anthony Howe, 'Richard Cobden and the Crimean War', *History Today*, 54.6 (2004), p. 46.

[36] Turnbull, *Shaftesbury*, pp. 117-18.

[37] Longmate, *The Breadstealers*, p. 212.

[38] Briggs, *Improvement*, p. 322.

[39] Longmate, *The Breadstealers*, pp.66, 118, 200-201, 97 & 110.

[40] Briggs, *Improvement*, p. 318; Longmate, *The Breadstealers*, pp. 101 & 110.

political machinery devised and adopted by the League was to be admired and copied.[41]

In his resignation speech as Prime Minister Robert Peel paid tribute to Cobden's role in the most successful extra-parliamentary political movement of the nineteenth century.

> The name which ought to be, and will be associated with the success of those measures, is the name of one who, acting, I believe from pure and disinterested motives, has, with untiring eloquence the more to be admired because it was unaffected and unadorned, the name which ought to be chiefly associated with the success of those measures, is the name of Richard Cobden.[42]

Trade Unionism

Of all the movements indigenous to the working-class in the nineteenth century Trade Unionism came to predominate as the century progressed. While at the end of the 1830s there were fewer than 100,000 in Union membership with most of those in the traditional craft industries such as tailoring or shoemaking,[43] by the early 1890s this had risen to 1.5 million, by the turn of the century to 2 million, and by the commencement of the first World War to over 4 million.[44]

It is perhaps impossible not to link the rise of the Trade Unions with the other movements from the same socio-economic background - Radicalism, Chartism, the Friendly and Co-operative Societies and ultimately the birth of the Independent Labour Party. While the relationship between Chartism and unionism has proven to be an issue of some controversy, there is no doubt they intersected at a variety of levels. However, it cannot be concluded that all union members were Chartists, and certainly not that all Chartists were involved in unionism,[45] and that following the Kennington Common disaster what little radicalism had penetrated the Union movement receded still further. The Unions were altogether more practical and down-to-earth in their policies and objectives. This led Engels to write to Marx in 1858, 'The English proletariat is becoming more and more bourgeois.'[46]

During the century the concerns of the labour movement remained essentially the same: patient organisation; developing district and national unions and

---

[41] Pickering & Tyrrell, *The People's Bread*, pp. 14-15, 247-48; Simon Morgan, 'From Warehouse Clerk to Corn Law Celebrity: The Making of a National Hero', in Anthony Howe & Simon Morgan (eds), *Rethinking Nineteenth-Century Liberalism* (Aldershot: Ashgate, 2006), pp. 40-47.

[42] David Eastwood, 'Peel and the Tory party reconsidered', *History Today*, 42.3 (1992), p. 27

[43] A.E. Musson, *Trade Union & Social History* (London: Routledge, 1974), pp. 16-17.

[44] E.H. Hunt, *British Labour History, 1815-1914* (London: Weidenfeld & Nicolson, 1981), pp. 250-51 & 295.

[45] Malcolm Chase, *Early Trade Unionism: Fraternity, Skill and the Politics of Labour* (London: Breviary Stuff, 2012), p. 144; Henry Pelling, *A History of British Trade Unionism* (London: Penguin, 1987), p. 34.

[46] Hunt, *British Labour History*, p. 275.

associations; collective bargaining on wages, hours, apprentices and working conditions, combined with the arrangement of benefits for unemployment, sickness, superannuation and death.

It was the repeal of the Combination Acts in 1824 that was to signal a watershed moment in Trade Union development and it is possible to identify the beginnings of a movement. No longer was it a ground for prosecution under common law to assemble and work together. While a substantial amendment to the repeal measure was enacted in 1825 outlawing the 'molesting and obstructing people at work' and once again subjecting trade disputes to the common law of conspiracy, trade unions were no longer explicitly illegal.[47]

A burst of Union activity between 1829 and 1834 soon floundered, illustrating how early unionisation was typified by this sporadic, localised and short-lived phenomenon. The Government was also anxious to suppress and make examples of any developments that they considered to be particularly worrying. It was this that led to the transportation of six Dorsetshire labourers from Tolpuddle to Australia in 1834.[48]

Unionism rallied in the 1840s, and in 1851 what has been termed the period of 'New Unionism' began with the advent of the Amalgamated Society of Engineers. Musson argues that 'New Unionism' is a misnomer as the characteristics of previous generations of similar activity were preserved. Sectionalism remained entrenched, particularly in the older and established trades that saw themselves as a kind of 'labour aristocracy'. They worked to maintain differentials and their own craft status through apprenticeships and clear demarcation lines and held themselves aloof from attempts at concerted action. Attempts at wider Union co-operation were regularly made, but failed, such as the Co-operative and Trade Union Congress, London, 1833; and the United Kingdom Alliance, Sheffield, 1866.[49] What did begin to develop were combined local initiatives like the London Trades Council which was formed in 1860.[50] In fact it was the Glasgow Trades Council that initiated the first successful political action in 1863 for the reform of the Master and Servant Acts. They gained the support of other councils and called a conference in London for May 1864. A vigorous campaign of lobbying, deputations and petitioning of MPs followed which resulted in a Parliamentary committee being formed in 1865, whose report led to the amendment of the Act of 1867.[51]

Unionism, however, was not universally liked. Public outrage was fuelled by evidence of the pilfering and destruction of tools, violence, and even a few instances of murder which had as their objective the forcing of people to join Trade Unions and obey their regulations. The exploding of a can of gunpowder in the home of a non-Unionist was one of a series of events that precipitated the outcry and call for a

---

[47] Chase, *Unionism*, p. 89; Pelling, *History of British Trade Unionism*, pp. 21-22.

[48] Joyce Marlow, *The Tolpuddle Martyrs* (St. Albans: Panther, 1971); Chase, *Unionism*, pp. 134-41; Pelling, *History of British Trade Unionism*, p. 32.

[49] Musson, *Trade Union*, pp. 24 & 32.

[50] Musson, *Trade Union*, p. 25.

[51] Musson, *Trade Union*, pp. 27-28.

Public Inquiry in October 1866 which was supported by many of the more respectable unions. William Broadhead, the Treasurer of the United Kingdom Alliance, was found to be one of the ringleaders.[52] Added to this popular disquiet, a decision of the Queen's Bench on 16 January 1867 appeared to withdraw the limited legal recognition that the Unions had enjoyed since 1825. The judgement considered that the work of the Unions was an illegal 'restraint of trade'. On top of this the Government also decided to establish a Commission of Inquiry into Trade Unions early in that same year.[53]

A conference was called by the London Working Men's Association to consider the situation in March 1867. They called for legislation to give Trade Unions protection, and permission to send representatives to the Inquiry to conduct the Unions' case.[54] In March 1868 the Manchester and Salford Trades Council made a proposal for a Congress to meet in Manchester in May. Their proposal was for an annual congress, rather than just ad hoc emergency meetings. They actually met in June, and the Trades Union Congress was formed. A second Congress met in Birmingham in 1869 and a third was planned to meet in London at the time of the introduction to Parliament of the Trade Union Bill. This was introduced in February 1871, fulfilling all their fears and dashing all their hopes. Legal recognition was accorded, while 'molesting, obstructing, intimidating, threatening et al' within the work place were still outlawed. Congress met on 6 March with 49 unions representing 289,430 members present. Their lobbying was to no avail and the measure was passed.[55]

Keir Hardie founded the Independent Labour Party in 1893. Fearing eventual Socialist domination of the Congress, the Parliamentary Committee resolved to change the standing orders to guard against this. Voting was to be proportional to a Union's strength, and only full-time Union officials, or bona fide representatives working at their trade were allowed to be delegates. This did little to staunch the flow of the new born socialism that was to become the ascendant power in the twentieth century, displacing the radical Liberal tradition of the nineteenth century.[56]

By comparison with 1825, the situation in 1914 was vastly different. The work-force was more numerous, achieved greater productivity and was better paid. Fewer children were at work and the balance of the population had shifted to urban areas where they worked in industrial and tertiary employment. The working week was shorter, the work-place less dangerous and the urban environment much healthier. At the time of the repeal of the Combination Acts there were few Trade Unionists in the working class and they had little political influence. By 1914

---

[52] Musson, *Trade Union*, pp. 33-36.
[53] Musson, *Trade Union*, p. 34.
[54] Musson, *Trade Union*, p. 36.
[55] Musson, *Trade Union*, pp. 40-56.
[56] Hunt, *British Labour History*, p. 309.

almost 25% of the labour force was organised, most workmen had the vote and the Labour Party had begun to make its presence felt at Westminster.

The changing perspective on trade unionism was well articulated in 1860 by Sir Archibald Alison, a Scottish Sheriff who had previously been viewed as a relentless adversary of the movement. Addressing a National Association for the Promotion of Social Science conference he acknowledged that while employers viewed the unions as a great social evil, he had come to see them as necessary for the balance of the fabric of society by restraining the power of capital and ensuring that workers were not beaten down.[57]

Temperance

> 'Drink has been the cause of a curse more terrible, because more continuous, than war, pestilence, and famine combined.' W.E. Gladstone.[58]

Temperance and teetotalism were certainly more widespread than almost any other social movement of the Victorian era. In the early days they were also popularly associated with radical politics. A young Charles Garrett, later to become a national temperance leader, was warned by a Wesleyan Class Leader that abstaining from drink was, 'a Manchester trick to upset the Throne . . . a scheme of those Radicals; you don't know what these men are up to; you had better have nothing to do with it'.[59]

In many ways Garrett's Class Leader had a clear-sighted perception. Many of the temperance advocates were also involved in agitation for other social reform too. Temperance Chartists were not unusual with itinerant advocates like Henry Vincent,[60] and Josephine Butler - who campaigned later in the century for the repeal of the Contagious Diseases Acts - related her experience that:

> temperance men almost always lead in this matter - abstainers, steady men, and to a great extent members of chapels and churches, and many of them are men who have been engaged in the anti-slavery movement and the abolition of the Corn Law movement. They are the leaders in good social movements, men who have had to do with political reform in times past.[61]

There was also a good deal of traffic between the Anti-Corn Law League and the temperance movement. Richard Cobden declared: 'Every day's experience tends more to confirm me in my opinion that the temperance cause lies at the foundation of all social and political reform.'[62]

---

[57] Chase, *Unionism*, p. 202.
[58] S.E. Keeble (ed.), *The Citizen of To-morrow* (London: C.H. Kelly, 1906), p. 173.
[59] James W. Broadbent, *The People's Life of Charles Garrett* (Leeds: James Broadbent, 1900), p. 7.
[60] Lilian Lewis Shiman, *Crusade Against Drink in Victorian England* (London: St. Martin's, 1988), pp. 32-33.
[61] Brian Harrison, *Drink and the Victorians* (London: Faber & Faber, 1971), p. 26.
[62] Shiman, *Crusade Against Drink*, p. 9.

John Bright was one of several leaders of the League who lectured for the temperance societies. Teetotallers often provided the League with hospitality and the audience at their rural meetings. The relationship was reciprocal. Joseph Livesey, the teetotal pioneer from Preston, was an ardent supporter of the League mainly because of the failure of teetotalism to tackle poverty. However, according to Harrison, the affinity between the movements was never complete as only 10% of teetotal leaders were members of the League.[63]

Lilian Shiman sees four main phases to the temperance movement in Britain:

1. The early 1830s. Temperance was the preserve of clergymen, middle class moralists and upper class social reformers. These were given to helping their lesser brethren fight their intemperance.
2. The mid 1830s - mid 1870s. The working class teetotallers predominated in what became a movement for self-help. 'Moral suasion' rather than 'legal compulsion' remained dominant. The 1870s saw the arrival of 'gospel temperance', the fusion of teetotalism with large tracts of evangelical Christianity.
3. The 1880s - 1890s. Many old teetotallers were now firmly established in local political circles, holding offices of both status and power. Their political influence was officially recognised by the inclusion of 'The Local Option' into the Newcastle Programme of the Liberal Party in 1891.
4. The rejection of the Newcastle Programme by the electorate in 1895 was blamed on the temperance proposals, and as the denominations never came to require teetotalism as a condition of membership, the movement began its inexorable decline.[64]

The roots of temperance can be traced back to the campaign for working-class sobriety in the 1750s-90s through the anti-spirits movement. These campaigns sprang up in several places at the same time and were still exerting their influence for sobriety in the 1820s. The Temperance Movement, as a nineteenth-century phenomenon, originated in 1828 and was first associated with abstinence from spirits. Teetotal societies soon grew out of this movement in the early 1830s and various pledges of total abstinence - what many regarded as the cornerstone of the movement - had been adopted by some as early as the end of the decade. In the early days of teetotalism, voluntary abstinence and education were the means to their end. Although similar developments were happening in many places the birth of teetotalism is usually recognised to be at Preston on 1 September 1832 when seven men signed an experimental teetotal pledge for a year. One of these men was Joseph Livesey, who was later to become one of the most prominent of the national leaders within the teetotal movement.[65]

---

[63] Harrison, *Drink and the Victorians*, pp. 174 & 176.
[64] Shiman, *Crusade Against Drink*, pp.3-5.
[65] Edwards, *Methodism*, pp. 103-104.

The pressure for actual prohibition did not begin until 1853 when the United Kingdom Alliance was founded under the inspiration of the Maine Law agitation in America. It was then that the teetotal camp was divided into two groups, the 'moral suasionists' and the 'legislative compulsionists'. Livesey maintained that drink was the enemy, not the drink traffic. He wanted to educate people and convert them to abstinence. *The British Weekly* voiced a common concern that legislation dealt merely with outward circumstances, not with the individual that needed help and moral strength.[66] Monsignor Nugent of Liverpool did just that, pointing out the differences between the drunkard and the abstainer in his home, marriage and family life. He also taught women domestic economy to help encourage their men to stay at home.[67] Replying to the charge that, 'You cannot make men good by Act of Parliament' and that to legislate is to, 'interfere with the liberty of the subject', *The Methodist Temperance Magazine* compared the drunkard with the murderer, thief, forger and libeller who did have their liberty restricted by Act of Parliament as a way of restraining them from their vice.[68] The Alliance was of the conviction that twenty years of moral suasion had achieved only a relatively small amount. For them, the environment hindered action and therefore the environment must be changed. Livesey countered that no constituency would return a teetotaller or prohibitionist to political office and the claim that individuals were longing for the protection of the prohibitionists seemed to him patently absurd. Following on from the publicity surrounding problems that had been encountered in Maine, the United Kingdom Alliance made its only compromise when it adopted 'The Local Option' proposals that the Liberals were to take up in the mid-1890s.

The most practical branch of the temperance cause issued from those who were described as the 'counter-attractionists'. As early as 1840 the Pamphilion in london was serving cold meat and coffee at midday. Philanthropists in Dundee were the first to provide public houses to serve coffee and snacks, and this idea rapidly spread. The first British Workman Public House was launched in Leeds in 1867, and it was in Liverpool in 1875 after the visit of D.L. Moody that it was first decided to run a number of these houses on a commercial basis - The British Workman Public House Co. Ltd. or 'Cocoa Rooms'.[69] In Liverpool by 1907, 69 Cocoa Rooms; 7 cafes; 7 kiosks & 1 Coffee Cart were in operation. 25% of the Cocoa rooms also provided accommodation.[70] These various provisions all helped to begin to change the working man's environment.

Churchmen were some of the most committed of the temperance men. Livesey himself was a Baptist, having been baptised in 1811. However, Christian opposition

---

[66] John Briggs & Ian Sellers, *Victorian Nonconformity* (London: Edward Arnold, 1973), p. 69.

[67] Harrison, *Drink and the Victorians*, p. 321

[68] MTM, July 1892, p. 106.

[69] R.G. Milne, *The History of the British Workman Public House Company Ltd. (The Liverpool 'Cocoa Rooms')* (unpublishhed Dip. Local History, Liverpool University, Dept. Extra-Mural Studies, 1982); Harrison, *Drink and the Victorians*, pp. 303-304.

[70] Milne, *History of the British Workman Public House Company Ltd*, p. 5.

in the early days of the movement took him outside the church for the rest of his life.[71] A list from 1866 reveals that of 2,760 teetotal ministers, 22% were Anglican, 19% were Congregationalist while only 7% were Wesleyan. [72] Leading Nonconformist teetotallers at this time were John Clifford and C.H. Spurgeon (Baptists), Charles Garrett and J.R. Ray (Wesleyans).

What is particularly interesting to note is the Wesleyan reluctance to wholeheartedly join the temperance movement, especially considering John Wesley's own lead on the abstinence from spirits. In fact, the Wesleyans were hostile to the movement and in 1841 four hundred Cornish members separated from the Connexion with their minister and formed the Teetotal Wesleyans.[73] Even candidates for the ministry were turned down at this time for being teetotallers.[74] However, as the century progressed, the mood within Wesleyanism changed, and by 1882 when Charles Garrett was elected President of the Conference and Hugh Price Hughes was elected the Secretary of the Temperance Committee, the substantial view within the denomination had shifted.

Whether the temperance movement actually affected consumption of alcohol is debatable, since during the period when the movement was strongest consumption increased and, when the movement was declining, so was consumption. The advocates of the movement claim that the reduction in consumption was due to the decades of temperance work that preceded it, as well as the importance of regulating drink outlets.

Criticisms of the movement are searching. Their widespread conviction that social ills flowed from moral failure meant that rarely did they ask why people drank or open themselves to explore other environmental or personal factors that might lead to excessive drinking. Individuals, like Wesleyan minister Samuel Keeble, were few and far between in their encouragement of a debate about causal influences of drunkenness that was 'free from prejudice, wishful to know the truth'.[75]

Another criticism that has been levelled is that in the early days the movement was slow to finance the counter attractions, indeed some complained that teetotallers were too narrow in their concern and were 'men of one issue'. Yet a detailed look at Joseph Livesey's life shows him to be a man who sought the material, social, intellectual and moral good of his neighbour.[76] Livesey, like many who had been involved in the Anti-Corn Law League and its success, had learned the importance of concentration on the single chief evil and its eradication. Therein lay the difference between the League and the Chartists, and why Livesey, Garrett, Sturge and others were wholly committed to temperance as the century progressed.

---

[71] Charles Garrett, *Loving Counsels* (London: Charles H. Kelly, 1887), p. 178-79.
[72] Harrison, *Drink and the Victorians*, p. 181.
[73] Edwards, *Methodism*, pp. 102-103.
[74] Cyril J. Davey, *The Methodist Story* (London: Epworth, 1955), p. 140.
[75] Keeble, *To-morrow*, pp. 173-84.
[76] Garrett, *Loving Counsels*, pp. 176-205.

Charles Kingsley was opposed to teetotalism because he believed that it generated, 'that subtlest of sins, spiritual pride'.[77] This may be true of some, yet many leading statesmen, social reformers and churchmen were truly motivated by an altruistic desire to improve the circumstances of those who they knew were in desperate need.

Summary

British society was changing in the nineteenth century. The movements briefly outlined above were some of the most important catalysts in realising progress and instituting many of the reforms and changes that by the twentieth century were taken for granted.

These movements proved to be particularly important for evangelicalism. Men who came to denominational leadership in the 1880s-1890s had been profoundly affected by what they witnessed and did during the earlier years of the century. Garrett was employed by the Anti-Corn Law League and worked voluntarily with the Chartists. He was also converted to teetotalism in his youth under the oratory of John Cassell. The founder of the Salvation Army, William Booth, had been drawn into Chartism under the oratory of Feargus O'Connor and by the spectacle of bitter poverty, as had Baptist John Clifford in Nottingham. Joseph Parker, the Congregational Minister at the City Temple, was inspired by the Chartist poet, Thomas Cooper, as a boy and Thomas Champness also had sympathies with the Chartists having witnessed the riots in Manchester at first hand.[78] Many were also committed to temperance, if not teetotalism, and were greatly influenced by the public utterances of John Bright as the century progressed.

The influence of the Trade Unions is perhaps less marked, although the participation of the Methodists in particular has been well documented by Wearmouth, and is illustrated by the Tolpuddle Martyrs, four of the six being Methodists; of Joseph Arch, the Primitive Methodist leader of the National Agricultural Labourers Union from the Midlands and his Primitive Methodist brothers in the mining unions of County Durham.[79]

---

[77] Harrison, *Drink and the Victorians*, p. 136.

[78] On Garrett, see Broadbent, *The People's Life*, p. 1; on Booth, see Inglis, *Churches and the Working Class*, p. 177; on Clifford, see James Marchant, *Dr. John Clifford: Life, Letters and Reminiscences* (London: Cassell, 1924), p. 1; on Parker, see Joseph Parker, *A Preacher's Life* (London: Hodder & Stoughton, 1899), p. 56.

[79] Wearmouth, *Methodism*, pp. 179-94.

Chapter 3

Social Thinkers: Influential Ideas for a New Generation

Late nineteenth-century evangelicals did not minister in an ideological or philosophical vacuum. The melting-pot of social and theological ideas that surrounded them helped to shape their understanding and practice. As they articulated their convictions some sources clearly emerge as particularly influential. The four sketches that follow are representative of those sources of thinking that key influencers within the Forward Movement found inspirational. They help to fill out the cultural context with which they were interacting but are not meant to be exhaustive, either in scope or depth, rather to provide a more defined impression of the richness of the wider worldview they inhabited.

The Christian Socialists

Three men are particularly associated with this small and short-lived group that was to have a profound effect on many Christian leaders later in the century. F.D. Maurice was the thinker of the trio, having been appointed Professor of Theology at King's College, London in 1846. Charles Kingsley was a country parson from Eversley, Hampshire, and was the great populist of their ideas through his novels. The lawyer, J.M. Ludlow, a much neglected figure was the leader and activist of the group. They conceived of their task as one of initiating a revival of Christian influence. This would be accomplished by restating Christian principles in a way that was relevant to contemporary social relations and problems.[1]

The events surrounding the demise of Chartism at Kennington Common on 10 April 1848 were the immediate catalyst that brought them together. They were fearful of the priorities that the working classes were being encouraged to adopt by the Chartist leaders. Maurice volunteered to be a special constable and Kingsley came to London ready to give a speech that he hoped would deter bloodshed.[2] Maurice was turned down by the authorities on the ground that he was a clergyman and Kingsley arrived at Waterloo Bridge with Ludlow only to find that the meeting had ended prematurely. In conversation that evening the foundations for their

---

1 E.R. Norman, *Victorian Christian Socialists* (Cambridge: CUP, 1987), p. 56; DCC, pp. 643-44 & 608.

2 Florence Higham, *Frederick Denison Maurice* (London: SCM, 1947), p. 58; Norman, *Victorian Christian Socialists*, p. 44.

Christian Socialist group were laid. The following day Kingsley erected a poster addressed to the 'Workmen of England', sympathising with their cause, but proclaiming that the Charter by itself would not set things right. 'Jesus Christ, the poor man who died for poor men, will bring you freedom,' he declared.[3]

Ludlow's experience in Paris during the revolution of February 1848, and of the earlier revolution of 1830 when he was a child, convinced him of the need to do something in England before the working class became a revolutionary threat there too.[4] His knowledge of French socialism and Louis Blanc's experiments with co-operative workshops in Paris led him to suggest to Maurice the need to Christianise socialism.[5] Maurice expressed the same sentiment back to Ludlow in a letter of 1850, discussing the title of what was to become, *Tracts on Christian Socialism*:

> [I]t seems to me, the only title which will define our object, and will commit us at once to the conflict we must engage in sooner or later with the unsocial Christians and the unchristian Socialists.[6]

They opted for the term 'socialist' to avoid some of the odium attached to 'co-operative' which they preferred. In fact Maurice did not particularly like the term 'socialist' either.[7] Under his influence the political element was expunged and what little of genuine socialism was left resulted from Ludlow's French connection. Of course, the socialism of this time bears no resemblance to the modern post-Marxian era, indeed, while Maurice and Marx were contemporaries it is unlikely that they read or were even aware of each other's writing.[8] Producers' cooperatives rather than state ownership of the means of production were the radical innovations of their philosophy.

Maurice was no practical activist but he had a very clear understanding of his own role, 'I'm not a builder, but one who uncovers foundations for building on.'[9] The foundations that he uncovered were theological. He believed that Christianity had erred when it made man's sin the starting point of Christian faith. He preferred to begin by reasserting the truth of God's absolute Fatherly love and the incarnation. Where evangelicals insisted on the 'dead-weight' of human depravity and the division between the elect and the damned, Maurice removed all this and

---

3 Olive J. Brose, *Frederick Denison Maurice* (Ohio: Ohio University Press, 1971), p. 181; Jeremy Morris (ed.), *To Build Christ's Kingdom: F.D. Maurice & his Writings*, (Norwich: Canterbury, 2007), p. 15.

4 Una Pope Hennessey, *Canon Charles Kingsley* (London: Chatto & Windus, 1948), p. 73.

5 Higham, *Frederick Denison Maurice*, p. 57.

6 John F. Porter & William J. Wolf, *Towards the Recovery of Unity* (New York: Seabury, 1964), p. 151.

7 Norman, *Victorian Christian Socialists*, p. 31.

8 Jeremy Morris, *F.D. Maurice and the Crisis of Christian Authority* (Oxford: OUP, 2008), pp. 138-39.

9 Norman, *Victorian Christian Socialists*, p. 80.

concentrated on the Kingdom of Christ which encompassed the whole human race. Sin was that which divided men off from the purposes of creation that God had intended. Maurice believed that 'every man is in Christ' the condemnation of every man is that he will not own the truth. In this sense the Kingdom of Christ is already a reality, awaiting its discovery and recognition.[10] Believing, too, that the gospel was addressed to society as a whole as well as to the individual, working for the realisation of the Kingdom on earth was a Christian responsibility.[11]

This theology made a development into socialist concern an inevitable consequence. Because all were 'in Christ', even if they failed to recognise it, there was a brotherhood of man under the Fatherhood of God. Indeed, as a loving Father of all, God was intimately bound up with his concern for all people.[12] Therefore, competitive economic practice which allowed poverty and insanitary conditions was a blasphemy, a denial of the intention of God for his creatures. Ludlow maintained that if Christians learnt of such conditions, as:

> all earthly society is the work of God and not of man . . . we have to . . . endeavour to understand them; having understood them to endeavour to remedy them; and God will help us in so doing, if to Him we look for help.[13]

The lynchpin of Maurice's understanding was the doctrine of the incarnation. God makes himself known in a person, through whom the believer is invited into a relationship with God. The incarnation of the Word then becomes the interpretive key for the whole of human history as all history and society have their origin in the incarnation.[14]

This kind of theological thinking was revolutionary. One of Maurice's most unsympathetic contemporaries complained, 'In reading Maurice one had to learn not so much a new set of facts as a new way of thinking.'[15] So new and uncomfortable was this fresh way of thinking that the Council of King's College dismissed their Professor in October 1853 following the publication of his, *Theological Essays*. His apparent denial of the eternal punishment and the suspicion of him being a universalist led to the Council of the College concluding that the essays were, 'of dangerous tendency and calculated to unsettle the minds of the theological students'.[16]

The theological, spiritual and biblical foundation of the group was the heart which sustained them. Ludlow suggested they hold a weekly Bible study with Maurice, which was to become the centre of the fellowship life of the circle.[17]

---

[10] Gilbert Clive Binyon, *The Christian Socialist Movement in England* (London: SPCK, 1931), p. 88; Norman, *Victorian Christian Socialists*, pp. 7-8.

[11] Morris, *To Build Christ's Kingdom*, p. 124.

[12] Morris, *To Build Christ's Kingdom*, p. 18.

[13] Norman, *Victorian Christian Socialists*, pp. 8 & 60.

[14] Morris, *To Build Christ's Kingdom*, pp. 18-19.

[15] Porter & Wolf, *Towards the Recovery of Unity*, p. 11.

[16] Higham, *Frederick Denison Maurice*, p. 92; Jeremy Morris, *Authority*, pp. 160-61.

[17] Norman, *Victorian Christian Socialists*, p. 62.

Their social conviction that the goodwill engendered by co-operation and association would be the means of changing society, not revolution or legislation, flowed from Ludlow's insights of the French, 'Associations Ouvrieres'. Competition engendered a struggle to get for oneself at the expense of another. Co-operative workshops and enterprise on the other hand would eliminate class attrition and produce fellowship in its place. Class interdependence and harmony would be the result.

Adult education, popular literature, sanitary improvements and health reforms were also objects of their concern, particularly through the writing and activity of Kingsley. His outraged sensibilities caused him to be an effective disseminator of the ideals of Christian Socialism. Maurice, however, only participated in the educative activities. His abhorrence of systems and programmes led him to keep at a distance from the other more practical elements of their work. With Kingsley, he also had a dislike for extending the franchise. They felt that the British worker was unfit for political democracy. Years of education and spiritual uplift were needed to elevate them. With this view went an understanding that socialism did not imply a changed relationship between master and servant. Social conservatism meant that levelling was positively dangerous. Maurice opposed strikes on the basis that they were contemptuous of the authority of employers and gave the workers a dangerous sense of their own power. The monarch and the aristocracy held their authority from God, and were intended to rule and guide the land.[18]

Ludlow differed with them at this point, believing that democracy was always the necessary accompaniment of socialism. But he had always been in advance of Maurice and Kingsley and was always prepared to disagree with them. He had previously been an active member of the Anti-Corn Law League, which had horrified his friends. Ludlow remained convinced that mere social transformation was not enough in itself to set men free. They needed the change of heart and inward cleansing of the soul that Christianity preached. Then they could truly serve their brothers.[19]

It was the anti-democratic views of Maurice and Kingsley that attracted the attention of the working classes who suspected them to be Tory Paternalists. The Manchester Radicals said of Kingsley: 'These Christian Socialists are a set of medieval parsons, who want to hinder the independence and self-help of men, and bring them back to absolute feudal maxims.'[20] Kingsley would not have disagreed: 'I would, if I could, restore the feudal system, the highest form of civilisation - in ideal, not in practice - which Europe has ever seen.'[21] In effect they had made Christian Socialism a matter of adult education, self-help, economic enterprise and

[18] Peter d'A. Jones, *The Christian Socialist Revival (1877-1914)* (Princeton: Princeton University Press, 1968), pp. 23-25; Norman, *Victorian Christian Socialists*, pp. 17-19 & 23.

[19] Norman, *Victorian Christian Socialists*, pp. 69 & 64.

[20] Norman, *Victorian Christian Socialists*, p. 39.

[21] Norman, *Victorian Christian Socialists*, p. 53.

a general exhortation to mutual respect between the social classes. All hint of political content had been long since removed.

By 1854 Maurice had withdrawn from the movement, disillusioned, giving himself more fully to the work of adult education. Kingsley's impulsive enthusiasm was diminishing and by 1859 it had all but disappeared, though he never renounced his earlier opinions. Ludlow carried on the work undaunted. He fought for public crèches for working mothers and while initially suspicious of Trade Unions, came to see them as the most effective school for teaching working men, 'Those paths of organisation which, when rightly controlled and directed, make the will of the mass, the will of one.'[22]

Though short-lived, the circle of mid-century Christian Socialists that clustered around Maurice, Kingsley and Ludlow was far from being insignificant. Their immediate impact was as a fillip to the Co-operative movement, but their abiding contribution was a theological one.[23] 'The Fatherhood of God and the brotherhood of man' was to become a clarion cry of a new generation of Christian leaders in the closing decades of the century. Ironically, the teaching of Maurice and Kingsley became the theological platform for the political involvement and democracy they abhorred. The Christian Socialism they believed to be ethical and educative was later to be used to justify the forays into the political struggle of their successors.

The Manchester School

It was Disraeli who coined the phrase, 'The Manchester School' in February 1846. By it he meant to disparage what he perceived to be the extreme political views and activities that were still associated with the names of Richard Cobden and John Bright.[24] For after the repeal of the Corn Laws they had both remained very active in politics.

Cobden and Bright readily adopted the name for the group that was gathered around them, though it often had little to do with Manchester. It embraced merchants, manufacturers and businessmen from all parts of the country who supported free trade to benefit their profits; philanthropic Radicals who supported free trade on the grounds of political economy; pacifists (especially Quakers) who supported free trade for moral and religious reasons; and various individuals who mixed all three in varying combinations.

The political and economic agreement between Cobden and Bright was extensive, although never complete. Of the two, it was Cobden who was the more radical. Both were powerful speakers, Cobden because of his quiet and reasonable appeal to the logic of the question, Bright because of his impassioned oratory. Writing for the *New York Daily Tribune* in November 1858 Karl Marx observed: 'John Bright is not only one of the most gifted orators that England has ever

---

[22] Norman, *Victorian Christian Socialists*, p. 79.

[23] Morris, *Authority*, p. 145.

[24] Donald Read, *Cobden and Bright: A Victorian Political Partnership* (London: Edward Arnold, 1967), p. 103.

produced; but he is at this moment the leader of the Radical members of the House of Commons.'[25]

Their platform of concern remained surprisingly consistent in their years of political leadership. Underlying their concerns was an absolute commitment to free trade and an acceptance of Adam Smith's principles laid out in *The Wealth of Nations*.

Cobden was a calico printer who had set up in partnership with friends at Manchester in 1828. Bright was a Quaker from Rochdale who had taken over running the family cotton mill at 27 when his father retired in 1839.[26] Both men advocated reforms as middle-class employers rather than working-class activists. They were both well read in politics and economics, as well as being widely travelled.

Cobden's international travel was part of a growing mid-nineteenth century cosmopolitan sociability that confirmed to him the importance of free trade and its importance for peace through the friendship of nations.[27] Cobden's first pamphlet, *England, Ireland and America*, following a visit to the United States in June 1835, is a good example of this. Britain was preoccupied with concern over the Russian aggression towards Turkey. Cobden felt that it was really American economic aggression that should be the prime concern. British business was at an artificial disadvantage because of Imperial protectionism and an aristocratic foreign policy of interventionism that resulted in heavy taxation and debt: 'Economic strength makes a country truly great, not military conquest.'[28]

Adam Smith had concluded that overseas possessions were always expensive to defend and gather the benefits from. So free trade implied withdrawing from the colonies and developing markets in their place. Increased demand would strengthen and stabilise industry, create international interdependence, which in turn would result in peace and fellowship. War would be against the national self-interest.

In the 1850s this stance led Cobden and Bright to oppose the Crimean War, and therefore to be labelled as unpatriotic.[29] Parliamentary colleagues were also suspicious of their proposed plan for settling international disputes by arbitration. In addition their approval of the American system led to gibes in the House of Commons being directed at them as, 'the two members for the United States'.[30]

At home they saw that reform was necessary to remove vested interest and allow unfettered trade. This was the rationale of the Anti-Corn Law League and the later reforms they advocated. Religious and political privilege was part of the system that

---

[25] Bill Cash, *John Bright* (London: I.B. Tauris, 2012), p. xxv.

[26] Norman Longmate, *The Breadstealers* (London: Maurice Temple Smith, 1984), pp. 137-44.

[27] Anthony Howe & Simon Morgan, *Rethinking Nineteenth-Century Liberalism* (Aldershot: Ashgate, 2006), pp. 14-15.

[28] Read, *Cobden and Bright*, pp. 12-14.

[29] Anthony Howe, 'Richard Cobden and the Crimean War', *History Today*, 54.6 (2004), p. 46.

[30] Read, *Cobden and Bright*, p. 280.

was designed to further the interests of the landed aristocracy. Bright's first success in Parliament was in securing a Select Committee to inquire into the working of the Game Laws. These compelled farmers to suffer continuous damage to their crops and pasture by game-birds and animals that were preserved by law for the sport of gentry.[31]

Ridding the system of privilege and making a freer and more open society was also the moving force behind their desire to extend the franchise; reform the House of Lords; disestablish the Anglican Church and develop a national system of education. While Cobden's honesty and decency made him an attractive figure, his staunch opposition and denunciation of the landed elite meant that he was not universally admired.

> For Cobden, all of Britain's evils stemmed from the fact that 'we are a servile, aristocracy-loving, lord-ridden people,' mesmerised and immiserated by 'armorial hocus-pocus, primogeniture, and pageantry'.[32]

Bright had always considered that after the repeal of the Corn Laws all other reforms would flow from the extension of the franchise. He could not understand why the Chartists and the working class radicals kept on attacking capital, machinery and manufacturers. He felt that these were the 'only materials of democracy'. Yet they largely left the aristocracy and state church alone, 'which are the materials of oligarchical despotism under which they are suffering'.[33]

In 1848 he spoke alongside Cobden in favour of household suffrage, only because he felt that this was all that was likely to be achieved in his lifetime. Later, he sponsored a bill that would have enacted these proposals as well as the disenfranchisement of 86 boroughs and withdrawing one representative from a further 34. These seats were then to be redistributed to centres of population. However, the bill was lost due to the dissolution of Parliament. But when Gladstone made his famous comment in May 1864 that, 'Every man was morally entitled to come within the pale of the constitution', Bright forecast that this would mark a new era in the reform question.[34]

Combined with extending the franchise, reform of the House of Lords and disestablishment of the Anglican Church were policies that Cobden had advocated since his election as Member of Parliament for Stockport in 1841. The Lords was the stronghold of the landed aristocracy and needed to more fairly represent the proper influence of manufacturing interests and its demands for equality and economy. The established church was a further plank in the system of privilege, especially with the system of church rates, and in no small way contributed to the

---

[31] Read, *Cobden and Bright*, p. 94.

[32] Linda Colley, 'Invader', *London Review of Books* 9.13 (July 1987), pp. 20-22.

[33] Read, *Cobden and Bright*, p. 36.

[34] Read, *Cobden and Bright*, pp. 165-67.

problems in 'catholic' Ireland. Cobden's views were advanced for a committed member of the Church of England.[35]

As a Quaker, Bright had been brought up with daily Bible reading with his father at the breakfast table.[36] Always true to his upbringing he was sharply aware of the disadvantaged position of the Dissenting denominations. He had cut his teeth in a Church Rates dispute with the new vicar of Rochdale in 1840. Standing on a tombstone he had declared:

> The New Testament teems with passages inculcating peace, brotherly love, mutual forbearance, charity, and disregard of the filthy lucre, and devotedness to the welfare of our fellow men. In the exaction of Church Rates . . . in the imprisonment of those who refuse to pay . . . a clergyman violates the precepts he is paid to preach.[37]

It is important to remember the contribution of their Christian faith to their principled radicalism. Cobden was an Anglican whose sincere faith in a beneficent God was tested by the premature death of his only son at 15.[38] He believed that the moral and religious code applied as much to the market-place as to the church. He challenged a young Gladstone to a public debate, and promised to show him that the Corn Laws were, 'an interference with the disposition of Divine Providence as proven by the revealed Word of God', amongst other things. He believed that the people's 'veneration of God shall be our leverage to upset their reverence for the aristocracy'. Free trade was 'the international law of the Almighty', a 'natural law' of economic science similar to the natural laws of physical science. God, in his wisdom, had made peace-keeping through the international interdependence of trade, both morally right and materially advantageous.[39]

A system of national education was another significant element to their thinking. They were convinced that Britain failed to prepare people for the role they had to play in an industrial and constitutional country. Elementary reading, writing and arithmetic were essential for a happy and prosperous nation. Education would also have the benefit of reducing that part of poverty which was the result of ignorance rather than vice; overcoming social cleavages and divisions by raising the lower classes nearer to those above them. The mixing of the lower classes with the middle classes in education would also drive away thoughts of revolution. Cobden believed that education not only taught men the rights of free citizens, but that it also qualified them to possess them.[40]

In their own terms, Cobden and Bright were failures. Free Trade depended upon international peace, yet the British proved again and again that their xenophobia against the French, Americans and Russians made this an impossible dream. Yet they could be proud of the contribution to free trade that they had made. Repeal of

---

[35] Read, *Cobden and Bright*, p. 16.
[36] Cash, *John Bright*, p. 3.
[37] Read, *Cobden and Bright*, p. 81.
[38] Howe & Morgan, *Rethinking Nineteenth-Century Liberalism*, p. 5.
[39] Read, *Cobden and Bright*, pp. 31-32, 35 & 110.
[40] Read, *Cobden and Bright*, pp. 177-78.

the Corn Laws; the secret ballot; the extension of suffrage; the redistribution of Parliamentary seats; the weakening of the power of the great landowners; educational reform and the disestablishment of the Church of Ireland all bore the imprint of their agitation. In a very real way the contribution of the 'Manchester School' was one of the first practical attempts to embed the 'Enlightenment Project' in the life of the nation.[41]

T.H. Green

Thomas Hill Green was born into the home of an evangelical Anglican clergyman in Yorkshire in 1836. During his youth he attended Rugby School, before going up to Oxford. While at University he obtained a name for himself as a radical when he addressed the Oxford Union in defence of John Bright. He discovered at the end of the debate that he was in a minority of two. Twenty years later, in 1878, he was appointed Whyte's Professor of Philosophy at Oxford University.[42]

Essentially there are three main elements to Green's life: his Moral Philosophy, his Christian faith and his involvement in reforming politics. In the discussions of his life and work the relative importance of each has been examined. Richter sees his faith as being the controlling influence, Cacoullos his concern for rights and Thomas his philosophy itself. These differing opinions perhaps illustrate how well integrated these three elements were within Green.[43] Indeed, his analysis of the problems of his own day was rooted in what he referred to as a lack of a 'philosophy of life'. This inadequate 'popular philosophy' subsequently had a detrimental effect on life that manifested itself in moral conduct, politics, religion and epistemology. Helping to address this lack of a 'philosophy of life' Green saw contemplative poetry and religious faith as important sources for fostering genuine moral beliefs.[44]

His faith was primarily experiential rather than a traditional acceptance of dogmatic creeds. Thomas believes that he discerns the influence of F.D. Maurice in this. Indeed, it is true that Green's faith had a high view of divine immanence:

> No eye can see or ear hear Him. Any assertion that He exists, cannot be verified like any other matter of fact. But what if that be not because He is so far off, but because He is near? You cannot know Him as you know a particular fact related to you, but neither can you so know yourself, and it is yourself, not as you are, but as in seeking Him you become, that is His revelation.[45]

---

[41] Howe & Morgan, *Rethinking Nineteenth-Century Liberalism*, p. 1.

[42] Herman Ausubel, *John Bright, Victorian Reformer* (London: John Wiley, 1966), pp. 240-41.

[43] Ann R. Cacoullos, *Thomas Hill Green: Philosopher of Rights* (New York: Twayne, 1975), pp. 13, 26 & 44.

[44] Ben Wempe, *T.H. Green's theory of positive freedom* (Exeter: Imprint Academic, 2004), pp. 4-5.

[45] Cacoullos, *Thomas Hill Green*, p. 17; Melvin Richter, *The Politics of Conscience: T.H. Green and his Age* (Cambridge: Harvard University Press, 1964), pp. 26-27; Geoffrey Thomas, *The Moral Philosophy of T.H. Green* (Oxford: OUP, 1987), p. 18.

In the two lay sermons that he preached at Balliol he revealed that for him, faith was independent of the historical evidence for the birth, death and resurrection of Jesus. Rather, it rested on the living presence of God working in the individual.[46] In the 1878 sermon he defined faith, 'As conviction issuing in disposition', and so it was for him.[47] At one point he seriously considered becoming a Nonconformist preacher,[48] but his disposition of faith ultimately issued in his being actively involved in working out the principles of that faith and his moral philosophy in the community in which he lived. He remained a deeply religious person who provided spiritual inspiration to many who sat under his teaching, though his faith was somewhat unorthodox.[49] Leighton believes that he was the last great thinker in the Liberal Tradition to see the positive value of 'Christian Principles' for individual and social development.[50]

Nicholson holds that his ideas are only properly understood in in relation to the eternal consciousness and, in an age when scholars are wary of faith and metaphysics Dimova-Cookson and Mander make the observation that if Green's ethical and political ideas are attractive then there is no need for embarrassment by his doctrine of the eternal consciousness, indeed support for it is drawn from sociological, theological and metaphysical perspectives.[51]

At Oxford he served on the School Board from 1874 and helped to establish a Grammar School for boys that drew pupils from the Elementary Schools of the town; he was the first Fellow to be elected to the Town Council by the rate-payers and not the University; as a teetotaller he campaigned for the temperance cause while it was almost unheard of at the University, being personally convinced by the appropriateness of 'The Local Option'. In national life he followed the example of Cobden and Bright, whom he much admired, by opposing the Crimean War. He also served as Assistant Commissioner for the Schools Inquiry Commission that was established in 1864.[52]

Green's philosophy, British Idealism, represents this integration and divides distinctly into two steps: from metaphysics to ethics, and from ethics to politics. Beneath his thinking lies the experiential question, 'What should I do?' With Green this develops into, 'What should I be?' Which more precisely becomes a quest for 'What kind of person do I need to become if I want to achieve "self-satisfaction"?'[53]

---

[46] Cacoullos, *Thomas Hill Green*, pp. 43-44.

[47] Cacoullos, *Thomas Hill Green*, p. 43; Thomas, *The Moral Philosophy*, p. 13.

[48] I.M. Greengarten, *Thomas Hill Green and the Development of Liberal-Democratic Thought* (Toronto: University of Toronto Press, 1981), pp. 6-7.

[49] David O. Brink, *Perfectionism and the Common Good* (Oxford: Clarendon, 2007), p. 6.

[50] Denys P. Leighton, *The Greenian Moment: T.H. Green, Religion and Political Argument in Victorian Britain* (Exeter: Imprint Academic, 2004), p. 318.

[51] Maria Dimova-Cookson & William J. Mander, *T.H. Green* (Oxford: Clarendon, 2006), pp. 3 & 158.

[52] Greengarten, p. 4; Thomas, *The Moral Philosophy*, pp. 19-21; Cacoullos, *Thomas Hill Green*, pp. 30 & 40-41.

[53] Thomas, *The Moral Philosophy*, pp. 369 & 313.

His starting point is an attempt to provide a metaphysical framework for his moral and political concepts. He posits that, just as in our own experience our intelligence unifies the objects of our experience while distinguishing ourselves from them, so the objects of nature, being real, must be unified by some principle analogous to that of our own understanding. Nature, therefore, in its reality, implies an all-uniting agency which is not natural, but a thinking self-distinguishing consciousness like our own, the Divine Mind. The immanence of this Divine Mind thus becomes the ultimate end of rational conduct, the self-realisation of that Divine Mind which is gradually reproducing itself in the human soul.[54]

Cacoullos and Thomas both believe that the metaphysics are little more than a marginal, historical sideshow on Green's work. They maintain that they can be detached from the rest of his work without loss. Richter, on the other hand, believes that Green intended, through his philosophy, to provide an unassailable foundation for Christian belief that was increasingly under siege to science, the theory of evolution and higher Biblical criticism.[55] Leighton goes further and concludes that the reluctance of many scholars to acknowledge the place of religious belief in Green has hindered a proper understanding of his ideas and an inappropriate avoidance of him and the British Idealism of which he was apart.[56]

Green believed that there was a dual nature within human beings that seeks both the fulfilment of needs, as well as self-fulfilment, arguing that the latter is the ultimate end of humanity. This is the reproduction of the eternal consciousness in the individual. It is accomplished by the active and creative exercise and fulfilment of the individual's powers and capacities. However, the selfish pursuit of pleasure and material well-being is looking for self-satisfaction where it cannot be found.

Furthermore, Green sees this ultimate end of humanity to be both unexclusive and non-competitive - a common good, which, in being achieved by individuals, represents their greatest possible contribution to the general good. Community is then the context in which all people are ends in themselves, and not merely the means to the selfish ends of others.

Cocoullos maintains that a sense of the importance of 'koinonia' or community dominates Green's social and political theory. Self-fulfilment is achieved only by the individual's participation in communal affairs.[57] It is his exploration of community that was to provide the step from ethics to politics.

Green maintained that individual rights do not exist only in law (positivists), but that there are also natural rights. These, however, are not innate to all at birth (Locke), but rather are the commonly held precepts of what is fundamental and of value. Rights are made by men. The existence of them in a community becomes the measure of that community's moral and social development.

---

[54] Henry Sedgwick, *Lectures on the Ethics of T.H. Green, Mr. Herbert Spencer and J. Martineau* (London: Macmillan, 1902), pp. 2-10.

[55] Cacoullos, *Thomas Hill Green*, p. 45; Thomas, *The Moral Philosophy*, p. 18; Richter, *The Politics of Conscience*, pp. 26-27.

[56] Leighton, *The Greenian moment*, p. 34.

[57] Cacoullos, *Thomas Hill Green*, pp. 19-20.

While he never used his philosophy to form the basis of a political programme, Green had a clear vision of the role of government. It was to provide the conditions for moral life in which every citizen could achieve self-realisation.

> Our modern legislation . . . is justified on the ground that it is the business of the State, not indeed directly to promote moral goodness, for that, by the very nature of moral goodness, it cannot do, but to maintain the conditions without which a free exercise of the human faculties is impossible.[58]

The philosophical school of 'British Idealism' which he launched was to become a major influence on British thought and public policy in the closing decades of the nineteenth century and the opening years of the twentieth. The key themes of the common good, positive freedom, equality of opportunity, and the state as an enabling agency were used by later idealists to justify ethical socialism.[59] It is hardly surprising that Green was branded with the label of the 'New Liberalism' as he practically supported many of those issues associated with it. Added to which the social legislation passed by the Liberal governments of 1906-1916 clearly bears the imprint of his thought.

His impact on British historiography has been minimised by his premature death, the difficult style in which he wrote, the rising star of Marxism and the prodigious volumes of John Stuart Mill. Yet his contribution was very significant in itself and has been much neglected. Indeed Carter maps Green's legacy as his followers expand and develop his ideas, providing the intellectual and moral tradition that was to shape Tawney's socialism, an influence that Tawney readily acknowledged.[60] In addition, his personal integration of faith, philosophy and politics was a rare combination, but one that was not lost on contemporary evangelical leaders like Hugh Price Hughes, not least because of the strand of perfectionist thinking in Green that was concerned with the motives of action and their political application had strong resonances with Wesleyan holiness teaching and Hughes' own social activism.[61]

Henry George

Sympathetic rumblings throughout the world followed the publication of *Progress and Poverty* in 1879 by the American, Henry George. Such rumblings indicated that he had touched an issue that was widely perceived to be important. The book was actually translated into ten languages and sold seven million copies.[62]

---

[58] Cacoullos, *Thomas Hill Green*, p. 37.

[59] Matt Carter, *T.H. Green and the development of ethical socialism* (Exeter: Imprint Academic, 2003), pp. 3, 7, 21-27, 76.

[60] Carter, *T.H. Green*, pp. 168-70.

[61] Brink, *Perfectionism*, p. 70; Leighton, *The Greenian moment*, p. 272.

[62] Robert V. Andelson, *Critics of Henry George: A Centenary Appraisal of Their Strictures on Progress and Poverty* (London: Associated University Presses, 1979), p. 29; Jones, *Socialist*, p. 49.

George was concerned at the widespread poverty that he observed in America. He was convinced that industrial development meant that the prospect of material welfare of all was a real possibility. The use of machine technology, expanded production and cheaper costs should result in the increase of everyone's gross income. What he saw, however, was that wherever industry flourished it served to enhance the contrast between rich and poor. *Progress and Poverty* was his attempt to rectify this.

His thesis was disarmingly simple and rooted in an analysis of the production of goods and services. He saw there being three component parts to production: land, labour and capital. Whilst labour and capital participate in the provision of goods and services, land is a wholly passive agent, yet, the income from production has to be apportioned into three shares.

In their role as rent receivers, George believed that landlords performed no useful function. Rent was simply a toll levied by monopoly. Moreover, as the value of the land increases, so the tribute to the landowner increases, reducing the gains of labour and capital through improved technology and productivity. Here, George's reasoning was based on Ricardo's 'law of rent': that is, rent is determined by the difference between what can be produced on good land, compared with marginal land, with the same application of labour.[63] George uses the term 'rent' in a very precise way that indicates the value of the 'raw land' without improvement or facility.

In the process of production, therefore, George sees no inherent conflict between labour and capital, for capital is just another form of labour. The real enemy to production and free trade is the landowner. He argued that as the value of a piece of raw land is determined by the community, and that without a population to occupy an area, cultivate, build and utilise it, land has no value. A landowner is merely the title-holder for he has no control over the process of land value creation; that value belongs to the community that produces it. 'The value of land expresses in exact attachable form the right of the community in land held by an individual.'[64]

As George believed that each individual should receive the full benefits of their labour, it also followed that there was no right to receive that for which one had not worked. Ownership of land (which one did not create) and the benefit of rent (for which one did not work) were therefore unethical. As the rental value was generated by the community he proposed to recapture this value through the 100% taxation of the rent on raw land. This neither meant dispossession by purchase or confiscation:

> I do not propose either to purchase or to confiscate private property. The first would be unjust; the second, needless. . . . let them continue to call it their land. Let them buy and

[63] Steven B. Cord, *Henry George: Dreamer or Realist?* (Philadelphia: University of Pennsylvania Press, 1965), pp. 23-24.

[64] Andelson, *Critics of Henry George*, p. 34.

> sell, bequeath it and divide it . . . it is not necessary to confiscate land; it is only necessary to confiscate rent.[65]

George's calculations indicated that this single tax would thereby eliminate the need for any taxes on productive enterprise. Each man could therefore benefit from the full reward for his labour. The heaviest burden of taxation via the land rent would fall upon those who do the least to generate wealth.

He did cede that a percentage of the rental value could be retained if landowners acted as collecting agents for government, as long as this percentage was less than the cost of public collection. He also believed that the scheme should be introduced in stages to aid its adoption.[66]

George tested his proposals against the four canons of taxation: that it falls as lightly as possible on production; that it is simply and inexpensively collected; that it is certain in its incidence and that it bears equally upon all. He found the land value tax to be confirmed in each case.[67] In consequence, he foresaw the prices of goods, services and property falling as they were relieved from the burden of taxation. However, labourers and capitalists alike would then enjoy the full benefits of their labours, free from direct taxation, as a more complete system of free trade was in place.[68] George's work was published in Britain in 1880, and *The Times* wrote in review: '*Progress and Poverty* well merits perusal for it contains many shrewd suggestions and some criticisms of economic doctrines which future writers on political economy must either refute or accept.'[69]

George visited Britain six times between 1881-90 where he found new intellectual challenges in meeting with Herbert Spencer and an exacting debate with Arnold Toynbee at Oxford.[70] Following the visit of 1889 his programme was taken up by Liberal and radical politicians.[71] A monthly newspaper, *The Single Tax*, was issued for the first time in 1894, and had established a circulation of 5,000 by February 1896.[72]

Almost from the day of its creation in 1889 the London County Council pledged itself to local taxation of land values. A bill the Council introduced to Parliament in 1897 was unsuccessful. By 1907, 518 local authorities were pledged to the reform, and between 1891 and 1905 no fewer than fourteen bills and resolutions had been placed before Parliament.[73]

---

65 Andelson, *Critics of Henry George*, p. 15.
66 Andelson, *Critics of Henry George*, pp. 36-37.
67 Andelson, *Critics of Henry George*, p. 37.
68 Andelson, *Critics of Henry George*, pp. 38-40.
69 Charles A. Barker, *Henry George* (Oxford: OUP, 1955), p. 374.
70 Eileen W. Lindner, 'The redemptive politic of Henry George: a legacy to the Social Gospel', *Union Seminary Quarterly Review*, 42.3 (1988), p. 3.
71 Jones, *Socialist*, p. 54; E.P. Lawrence, *Henry George in the British Isles* (Michigan: Michigan State University Press, 1957), p. 111.
72 Lawrence, *Henry George*, pp. 112-13.
73 Lawrence, *Henry George*, pp. 118-19 & 123.

The Liberal victory of 1906 led to a Land Values (Scotland) Bill, but this was rejected by the Lords. It was reintroduced in 1908 and emasculated by them through amendment. It was introduced a third time as a budget measure in 1909 causing a constitutional crisis. Thus, before the measure was passed it took two years, two general elections and a Liberal threat to create enough peers to secure the passage of the Parliament Bill before the Conservatives finally recognised the popular mandate, having to accept George's land tax, and reform of the House of Lords too.[74]

Those who followed George in Britain were, in fact, very rarely 'single taxers'. Indeed, his name and any mention of the single tax had to be played down because of the widespread opposition they engendered.

George's ultimate concern was to reduce poverty by enabling men and women to realise their intellectual and moral capacities by enjoying the full benefit of their labour. Ethically he felt that his proposals enshrined natural justice in every way, especially because as all men are created equal they must have equal right to be supported by nature, air, sea and land. For this the Episcopalian in him was happy to appeal to divine sanction: 'We are all here by equal permission of the Creator, we are all here with an equal title to the enjoyment of his bounty.'[75]

Jones concludes that the attractiveness of George's ideas rested in the fact that he was in many ways entirely consonant with the existing political prejudices and Victorian religiosity of the majority of his supporters and listeners.[76] Accepting that, it is quite clear that he dealt with his subject in a highly original and creative way, introducing a new dimension to late nineteenth century thinking about social and economic policy.

---

[74] Lawrence, *Henry George*, pp. 129-40.
[75] Cord, *Henry George*, p. 25.
[76] Jones, *Socialist*, p. 57.

PART TWO. THE CHURCHES: A CHANGING RESPONSE

Chapter 4

Evangelical Traditionalists

The urbanisation of English society in the nineteenth century did not pass evangelicals by. They were well aware of the growing centres of population which were inadequately served by the churches. The religious census of 1851 only brought to light what they already knew, that the working class were staying away from the churches in large numbers. This problem was not so marked in the countryside as it was in the large cities. Therefore, for much of the rest of the century the question of non-attendance by the urban working classes was to occupy the attention of many within the denominations. Committees were formed, conferences held and varying proposals implemented.

In attempting to meet this situation evangelicals were traditional only in the sense of the message they preached. The methods they adopted were wide ranging and at times highly original. Impelled by the apostle's injunction 'by all means to save some', a plethora of missions and philanthropic institutions were created as the following illustrations from London and Liverpool demonstrate.

The earliest attempts to reach the unchurched of the cities were by the Domestic Visitation Societies which emerged in the second quarter of the century. Rack believes that these societies were probably the most characteristic device at this time for extending religious influence to adults outside the church. Their house-to-house visitation was based on the assumption that the church must go to the masses rather than expecting the masses to come to church. Their aim to improve the pressing situation of the poor was addressed through instruction in the Bible, domestic economy, discriminating charity based on their first-hand knowledge of personal circumstances and admonitions concerning vice. In this way they sought to recreate the capacity for self-help.[1] These societies are particularly significant as they provided a model for many of the developments which were to follow later.

It was the advent of the Town and City Missions in the middle of the century that really made a success of the methods pioneered by the Domestic Visitation Societies. David Nasmith is looked upon as the founder of the movement, having been the moving force behind establishing the Glasgow Mission in 1826 and the

---

1 H.D. Rack, 'Domestic Visitation: A Chapter in Early Nineteenth Century Evangelism', in *Journal of Ecclesiastical History* 24 (1973), p. 357.

London City Mission at Hoxton in 1835. Deeply influenced by the parish ministry of Thomas Chalmers in Glasgow, Nasmith shared his conviction of linking the ideas of the growing Protestant overseas mission with work at home among 'the poor Heathen of our own city'.[2] Missionaries were engaged, given a district to serve with the expectation that every family would be visited once each month.

Independently of Nasmith a similar group - The Society for Promoting the Religious Improvement of the Poor of Liverpool - was establishing its own work along the same lines in 1829 having received inspiration from Adam Hodgson, a cotton-merchant who brought back ideas from an American trip to Boston. There he had come across a missionary who had been set apart to preach in the cellars and garrets of the poorer neighbourhoods. With James Cropper he wanted to initiate a similar work in Liverpool. It is interesting to note that Cropper had also worked hard for the abolition of slavery and that Hodgson was later to be involved with the Anti-Corn Law League and agitation for Parliamentary reform. Other supporters included Robert Gladstone (uncle to the Prime Minister), William Hartley (the Primitive Methodist jam manufacturer) and the Lever brothers from Port Sunlight.[3]

The rules for the missioners in Liverpool included visiting in all districts, not proselytising for any particular sect, not attacking the Roman Catholic Church or getting into any open dispute, but rather to openly testify against sin, including drunkenness, uncleanness, cruelty to parents, disobedience of children and Sabbath-breaking. They were to hold meetings in the homes of the 'respectable' poor, distribute tracts and keep a library for each district.[4]

Nasmith was a personal evangelist who was anxious not to create a new denomination either. His vision was to bring into being a society whose missionaries could be the servants of all evangelical churches. When Charles Booth undertook his study of London in 1886 he noted this feature as each missionary was superintended by a local clergyman or layman. He commented that the part the missionaries played was quite unique. They were not far removed from the social status of those they ministered to and were easily both friend and father confessor to local people. They were satisfied with the simple gospel they preached and were not mistrusted or pandered to. He concluded that he felt that they were in tune with the sentiments of the people.[5]

The missioners saw their task as a strictly religious one for, while they did not ignore poverty, neither did they want to compromise their evangelical and pastoral relationships with charity.[6] So deep seated was this conviction that even in the

---

[2] Ian J. Shaw, 'Thomas Chalmers, David Nasmith, and the Origins of the City Mission Movement', *Evangelical Quarterly* 76.1, (2004), pp. 34, 37.

[3] Rack, 'Domestic Visitation', p. 360; F.H. Wrintmore, *God Speaks to London* (London: London City Mission, 1954), p. 1; Gordon Read & David Jebson, *A Voice in the City* (Liverpool: Liverpool City Mission, 1979), p19.

[4] Read & Jebson, *A Voice in the City*, p. 17.

[5] Charles Booth, *Life and Labour of the People of London*, Religious Influences, vol. 7, (London: Macmillan, 1902), pp. 289-90.

[6] Rack, 'Domestic Visitation', p. 360.

1950s the Mission still maintained that social reform was not enough as the people's deepest needs were spiritual and that was where they always directed their energies.[7] In 1888 one City Missioner was pleased to declare that they were, 'battling with Socialism in its violent as well as in its more moderate and constitutional form'.[8] Their method was simple and centred on the individual. Visitation included the liberal distribution of cheap tracts and was supplemented by meetings for prayer and preaching.[9] The preaching was typically evangelical in emphasis focussing on conversion, the Bible and the Sabbath.[10] Indeed, Nasmith had set the tone of the movement believing that the Bible was 'God's unchanging word, inspired and infallible'.[11]

The Missions flourished as the century progressed and by 1850 the London City Mission alone was employing 235 lay agents.[12] Such was the success that it is claimed that both Lord Shaftesbury and General Booth gained inspiration for their work from the example of their missionaries.[13]

In the latter part of the nineteenth century the planting of mission halls became more and more popular. Established denominational churches would use these daughter congregations as a way to reach a less prosperous area as James Archer Spurgeon (brother to the famous C.H. Spurgeon) did from his West Croydon Baptist Tabernacle, establishing centres at Boston Road and Memorial Hall.[14] More frequently mission halls sprang up independently based around the work of an enthusiastic layman or missioner. Charles Booth observed, that London was, 'dotted over with buildings devoted to this work. In the poorer parts especially, in almost every street, there is a mission'.[15]

Heasman illustrates this proliferation of mission halls with reference to the Field Lane Institution (1841) and South London Mission (1861) which served the 'down-and-outs', and the George Yard (1854) and Golden Lane (1862) Missions which were run by the middle-classes. The Superintendents of the latter two, George Holland and W.J. Orsman, were both close friends of Lord Shaftesbury. Smaller concerns would not possess their own accommodation. The East Plumstead Mission (1895) met in the skittle saloon behind the Prince of Orange, and the Hammersmith Mission (1871) gathered in a small, local cottage. Heasman

---

7 Wrintmore, *God Speaks to London*, p. 15.

8 K.S. Inglis, *Churches and the Working Class in Victorian England* (London: Routledge, 1963), p. 305.

9 Rack, 'Domestic Visitation', p. 367.

10 Hugh McLeod, *Class and Religion in the Late Victorian City* (London: Croom Helm, 1974), p. 5.

11 Wrintmore, *God Speaks to London*, p. 4.

12 John Kent, *Holding the Fort: Studies in Victorian Revivalism* (London: Epworth, 1978), pp. 101-102.

13 Wrintmore, *God Speaks to London*, pp. 24 & 46-47.

14 West Croydon Baptist Church archive.

15 Booth, *Life and Labour*, p. 270.

concludes that whether large or small, 'the primary purpose was to preach the Gospel'.[16]

These developments were not restricted to London, but were the common experience of every developing urban centre. In Liverpool, for example, George Pennell established his own 'Pennell's Mission' in memory of his daughter in 1854. In the early 1860s this was being run in conjunction with the Town Mission with three further halls on Beau, Benledi and Kilshaw Streets. These were areas of acute poverty and extensive Irish penetration, yet the results were so successful that a large building on Richmond Street, a low dance hall and the Hengler's Circus had to be marshalled into use by the six full-time evangelists. W.P. Lockhart, who was much younger than Pennell, took over the work at Hengler's Circus which in 1870 became the well-known Toxteth Tabernacle.[17] Reginald Ratcliffe was active in Kensington and Bootle, building a Sun Hall in each. At Kensington the 6,000-seater hall attracted over 4,000 on a Sunday evening in 1912, predominantly from the working-class.[18]

A different kind of evangelistic work commenced in 1903 when George Wise began to attract some of the roughest to his fiercely anti-Catholic, Protestant Reformers Memorial Church on Netherfield Road. While disliked for his violent anti-Catholicism and his incitement of riots, he built a 1,400-strong midweek Bible Class and in 1909 attendance was regularly 20,000 for his 'Protestant' meetings at St Domingo's Pit. Archdeacon Madden called 'Wiseitism' a 'Bastard Protestantism which disgraces our city', and Wise himself was regularly in and out of prison. From 1908 he gave up outdoor work, preferring to lecture against biblical criticism, atheism and socialism.[19] Local supporters would parody the Sankey hymn by singing,

> Dare to be a Wiseite!
> Dare to stand alone,
> Dare to be a protestant,
> And to hell with the Pope of Rome![20]

While Wise could only have really prospered in Liverpool, the independent evangelistic mission halls seemed to thrive everywhere, often accompanied by extensive philanthropic work. Heasman follows the analysis of William James in explaining why a close-knit group of evangelicals were responsible for a very large part of the social work that was performed in the second half of the nineteenth century. James had noted that the essentially introspective personal experience of

---

[16] Kathleen Heasman, *Evangelicals in Action* (London: Geoffrey Bles, 1962), pp. 30-32.

[17] Ian Sellers, *Liverpool Nonconformity (1786-1914)* (Keele, 1969, unpublished. Ph.D Thesis), pp. 20-23.

[18] Sellers, *Liverpool*, pp. 36-37.

[19] P.J. Waller, *Democracy and Sectarianism: A Political and Social History of Liverpool, 1868-1939* (Liverpool: Liverpool University Press, 1981), pp. 207-09, 230 & 240-41.

[20] Waller, *Democracy and Sectarianism*, p. 208.

conversion had as an important result, an outpouring of brotherly love.[21] She noted the work of the mission halls as including temperance work and the provision for nursery care, health care, food, fuel and finally education through the Ragged School Movement.[22]

Heasman does take care to point out how the work of those like Dr Barnardo also originated in independent, evangelistic missions. Barnardo himself had acquired 'The Edinburgh Castle', a thriving gin palace with a music hall to the rear, in the East End. This he transformed into a church of the people. It was his subsequent exposure to the needs of orphans in the area through his East End Juvenile Mission (1867) which led to his famous work with children.[23] In fact, Heasman believes that the work George Muller began in Bristol in 1836 both legitimised and provided a model for this type of evangelistic social work. Spurgeon, Stephenson, Garrett and Archibald Brown amongst others were to make children's homes an integral feature of their ministries.

Another aspect of the churches' evangelistic response to non-attendance was revivalism. While the Evangelical Revival of the eighteenth century was in many ways a spontaneous break out of spiritual intensity and religious conversion, the mid to late nineteenth century revivalism tended to be far more planned and under the control and guidance of a professional revivalist.

The best known of these itinerant evangelists was D.L. Moody, who made a profound impact upon Britain when he toured the country in 1874-75. He held a succession of citywide events in large halls that often ran for weeks. His greatest success was amongst the middle and lower middle classes, who, having been brought up in the church had only a nominal commitment to Christ.

Moody's consuming passion was to bring 'souls to Christ', and despite a desire to reach the masses who never frequented the church, he very rarely did. Shaftesbury originally dissociated himself from Moody's London Mission because the poorer people were not attending and because Moody would not tackle social issues.[24] For the latter of these objections Moody's hands were tied because to finance his large-scale operation he had to be sensitive to the convictions of his sponsors. Indeed, at times he endorsed them, telling businessmen that if the working-class were not evangelised by the Christians they would be by the atheists and communists.[25] Moody's desire to reach the masses meant that he did draw to himself churchmen with a similar concern. To these men Moody became an enabler, using his personal influence to get projects started. He persuaded Hay Aitken, a high church Anglican, to leave his Liverpool living and become a full-time Anglican Missioner, and he was also instrumental in starting the Church Parochial Mission Society.[26] The YMCAs of London, Manchester, Glasgow,

---

21 Heasman, *Evangelicals in Action*, pp. 18-19 & 22-23.

22 Heasman, *Evangelicals in Action*, pp. 32-33.

23 Heasman, *Evangelicals in Action*, pp. 35 & 92-93.

24 Kent, *Holding the Fort*, pp. 156-57.

25 Kent, *Holding the Fort*, pp. 133-34.

26 John Pollock, *Moody without Sankey* (London: Hodder & Stoughton, 1963), p. 151.

Dundee and Liverpool were all, at least in part, made possible by his appeals.[27] Moody was also instrumental in the setting up of the British Workman Public House Movement in Liverpool and in lobbying for Charles Garrett to be released from his Wesleyan circuit appointment to superintend a new Riverside Mission in the same city.[28] Thus, despite the shortcomings of his method, Moody reinforced church-goers in their commitment, inspiring and enabling a number of able people to work among the masses along the way.

It is also significant that Moody was sympathetic to the American holiness movement, even if he never fully endorsed the explicit teaching of entire sanctification in its popular 'second blessing' form. In 1871, challenged by two women who regularly prayed for him to preach in 'the power of the Spirit', and conscious of his own sense of inadequacy, he sought to be filled with the Spirit.

> I was crying all the time that God would fill me with His Spirit. Well, one day, in the city of New York - oh, what a day! - I cannot describe it, I seldom refer to it; it is almost too sacred an experience to name . . . I can only say that God revealed Himself to me, and I had such an experience of His love that I had to ask Him to stay His hand.[29]

Subsequently he spoke of the importance of the 'enduement' with power, and while in Britain published a study called, *Power From On High.*[30] That a man of Moody's stature and influence among British evangelicals was talking in this manner is quite significant.

---

[27] James F. Findlay, Jr., *Dwight L. Moody: American Evangelist, 1837-99* (Chicago: University of Chicago Press, 1969), p. 189.

[28] London Journalist, *A Visit to the Wesleyan Mission in 1896* (London: Wesleyan Methodist Book-Room, 1896), pp. 15-16; Sellers, *Liverpool*, p. 178.

[29] W.R. Moody, *The Life of D.L. Moody* (London: Morgan & Scott, c.1900), pp. 133-35.

[30] David W. Bebbington, *Evangelicalism in Modern Britain* (London: Routledge, 1989), p. 163.

Chapter 5

Wesleyan Activists

Wesleyanism changed during the nineteenth century, not so much by rejecting its historic evangelical emphases, as by broadening the scope of its concern and work. Evangelism was supplemented with social concern and engagement in political debate. Their aim was to 'Christianise' society by preaching the gospel, relieving need and working to apply Christian principles to both public policy and the political process.

The pressure for change gathered momentum as the century progressed. Initially the denomination was stubbornly resistant on almost all issues. However, a new generation with a burning zeal to apply their faith to every facet of life began to exercise organisational as well as moral and spiritual leadership from 1875 onwards.

Three distinct periods are discernible during the century. The first fifty years were marked by the rule of the 'Conference Party', which exercised an influence that was conservative in most senses of the word. Jabez Bunting had the highest profile and exercised the greatest power of all the leaders within this group. Often called the 'Buntingites', they were extremely antagonistic to the new liberalism that was beginning to creep into their church. Their attitude led to a number of secessions, culminating in the schism that followed the Fly Sheet Controversy of 1849.

Between 1849 and 1885 there was a period of peace which some have suggested may have been 'peace at any price' after the divisions of 1849.[1] During this period Bunting died and the strength of the conservatives gradually diminished in the wake of younger leaders. These were men whose experience had been fashioned by the nineteenth, rather than the eighteenth, century.

The third period began in 1885 with the arrival of the *Methodist Times*. This weekly newspaper was launched by Hugh Price Hughes expressly to support the work of the 'Forward Party'. With such a mouthpiece, the voice of what was to become known as the Forward Movement became strong enough to be heard. The last fifteen years of the century marked the coming of age of this movement and the increasing acceptance of the platform of policies it advocated.

---

[1] Ross Peart, *Hugh Price Hughes and the Origins of the Forward Movement* (Unpublished Paper), p. 2.

Jabez Bunting and the resistance to change

To understand the position of the 'Conference Party' at this time it is necessary to go back to Wesley himself. He was a staunch Tory and disagreed with thinkers like Locke and Rousseau who wanted to transform institutions. He believed that the main impediment to progress lay not in institutions but in human nature. Believing in the ability of divine power to transform human nature he consequently concentrated on that, holding that social reform was merely external and extraneous. Neither could Wesley agree with the extension of the franchise because he held an idea of the ordering of society that bordered on the 'divine right of kings'. Thus, except on matters of slander, politics was a subject on which it 'behoves us to be silent'.[2] He was able to maintain this position by idealising society, stressing the freedom of speech, worship and ownership of property 'so that it is impossible to conceive a fuller liberty than we enjoy'.[3] Such an idealisation justified his conception of the divine right of authority in the face of scant wages, press gangs and the inhumanities of the age. The normally realistic Wesley appears to have confused the ideal with the actual and identified what ought to be with what actually was.[4]

Jabez Bunting was the central figure of Wesleyanism during the first half of the nineteenth century, and he closely followed Wesley's expressed opinions, yet did not share Wesley's tolerance and understanding. In fact, he was bitter and uncompromising in his opposition to anything with which he disagreed, particularly anything that hinted at radical politics. He was a man of great influence within the denomination, being appointed Secretary to the Conference in 1814 and elected President four times (1820; 1828; 1836 and 1844). For thirty years the greater part of the legislation passed by Conference was of his initiation and moulding, and his supremacy was largely unchecked until near to the close of his ministry. Closer inspection reveals him not to be the reactionary ogre that many portray him to be, Greet affirms that there was much to admire in his ministry, not least that amid a hail of criticism a study of his correspondence shows him always to be measured and courteous, unlike many of his supporters and detractors alike. Goodwin also highlights his achievements in marshalling the complexity and scale of the hugely expanded Wesleyan connexion.[5] Still, however, there was a growing resistance to both the autocratic style and the undemocratic content of his leadership. Even a

---

2 C.E. Gwyther, *The Methodist Social and Political Theory and Practice, 1848-1914; with special reference to The Forward Movement* (Liverpool, 1961: unpublished M.A. thesis), p36.

3 Gwyther, *The Methodist Social and Political Theory and Practice*, p. 38.

4 Gwyther, *The Methodist Social and Political Theory and Practice*, p. 39.

5 Kenneth G. Greet, *Jabez Bunting* (Peterborough: Foundery, 1995), pp. 32-33; Charles H. Goodwin, 'An evangelical pastorate: the unresolved dilemma in Wesleyan concepts of ministry and church growth', *Wesleyan Theological Journal*, 34.2 (1999), p. 238.

sympathetic biographer like Kenneth Greet concedes that it is 'difficult to resist the conclusion that he revelled in the exercise of power'.[6]

To get a clearer insight into this growing problem it is enlightening to look at denominational attitudes to various contemporary movements. Bunting is reported to have said, 'We hate democracy as we hate sin.'[7] That being the case it comes as no surprise that under his leadership Methodism had stood opposed to Chartism. While the Chartist churches that were formed adopted a pseudo-Methodist organisation with class meetings, any Wesleyan who joined or showed sympathy with the Chartist cause in general had to contend with his class leader who would not let the matter be lightly disregarded.[8] Similarly, Wesleyan leaders regarded Christian Socialism with suspicion. *The Watchman* declared, 'Mr. Kingsley's false doctrines degrade our Lord into a Socialist model man.'[9] It is therefore clear why there were so few Christian Socialists amongst the Wesleyans. On the Cornish secession over the temperance question in 1841 Bunting remarked that it was one of, 'the annoyances arising from teetotalism'.[10] On this same question there was also a prolonged controversy in Bristol during 1841-42 and South Lincolnshire and Cambridgeshire were also in open revolt against the hierarchy.

Under the dominant influence of Bunting, the Committee of Privileges urged Methodists to abstain from delusive political theories in 1819. They were threatened with expulsion if they showed any practical sympathy with the radicals.[11] The Liverpool Minutes of 1820 reinforced this and made it plain that Methodism's task was to save souls.[12] By 1833, besides being the Secretary of the Conference he was also exercising overall responsibility for the overseas work alongside also having taken up the office of President for the Theological Institution.[13] When added to his time as President, the concentration of power in his hands makes it hardly surprising that his opponents called him 'the pope of Methodism'.

The perceived rigidity and restrictive nature of the denomination led to a series of splits in the decades that followed Wesley's death. The Methodist New Connexion was formed in 1795, the Primitive Methodists broke away in 1811 and the Protestant Methodists left after the Leeds Organ Controversy of 1827. Bunting was personally involved in the dispute that led Dr Warren to form the Wesleyan Methodist Association in 1835. Each of these splinter groups took up explicitly liberal positions having gained their freedom.

---

[6] W.J. Townsend, H.B. Workman & G. Eayrs, *A New History of Methodism*, vol.1 (London: Hodder & Stoughton, 1909), pp. 406-407 & Plate xxv (opposite p. 480); Greet, *Jabez Bunting*, p. 20.

[7] Gwyther, *The Methodist Social and Political Theory and Practice*, p. 45.

[8] Cyril J. Davey, *The Methodist Story* (London: Epworth, 1955), p. 49.

[9] Davey, *Methodist Story*, p. 142.

[10] Robert Currie, *Methodism Divided* (London: Faber, 1968), pp. 67-68.

[11] Maldwyn Edwards, *Methodism and England* (London: Epworth, 1944), p. 33.

[12] Gwyther, *The Methodist Social and Political Theory and Practice*, p. 76.

[13] Greet, *Jabez Bunting*, p. 25.

A further controversy in the 1840s was hardly unforeseen, but it was the most serious by far. Ultimately 100,000 members left the Wesleyan Church as a result.[14] The attack was ostensibly about the concentration of power in the hands of ministers, but specifically the target was Bunting and his associates, 'autocracy strengthened by oligarchy'. In practice, Bunting's power was unmatched; indeed, at one Conference, while he was temporarily absent, the session was postponed. In 1846 the two notorious Fly Sheets were produced to call attention to the despotism. Unfortunately, they were intemperate in language and anonymous. A reply was issued in equally unrestrained tones, but only succeeded in provoking a further paper vindicating the original Fly Sheets. To ascertain who was responsible Bunting made every minister sign a declaration that they had not participated in the affair. Everett, Dunn and Griffith were all expelled as a result, but following a popular campaign on their behalf, with the support of the press, many members left too.

A period of peace and stability ensued that led to a sense of smugness on the part of some. Respectability had come and with it the attitude which Wesley had feared most, a religion of success.

Charles Garrett and the antecedents of the Forward Movement[15]

In February 1875 the American evangelist D.L. Moody and his companion Ira Sankey arrived in Liverpool to conduct a much-anticipated revival that had been in various stages of planning for almost two years. A temporary wooden hall measuring one hundred and seventy-four feet long and one hundred and twenty-four feet wide had been erected over a period of forty days and was described by the *Liverpool Daily Post* as, 'a simple vast pavilion of rough wood, filled with benches, and unrelieved except by some red cloth round the front of its gallery, inscribed with texts in white letters'. 'Believe on the Lord Jesus Christ', 'Be ye reconciled to God' and 'Ye must be born again.' At the platform end of the building was also exhibited in still larger letters the words 'God is Love.'[16]

For a month this 8,000-seater hall, often packed with an additional two to three thousand in attendance, witnessed Moody's remarkable ministry. A local journalist with the *Post* dismissed accusations of emotionalism with the observation that more excitement could be found in a Primitive Methodist Chapel on almost any Sunday morning.[17] A second charge levelled at the revival

---

[14] Gwyther, *The Methodist Social and Political Theory and Practice*, p. 86; Townsend, Workman & Eayrs, *A New History of Methodism*, 1. p. 438.

[15] The content of pp. 53-75 was first published as 'Charles Garrett and the birth of the Wesleyan Central Mission Movement', *Wesley and Methodist Studies* 6 (2014), pp. 89-123.

[16] W.R. Moody, *The Life of Dwight L. Moody* (London: Morgan & Scott, c1900), pp. 198-200. http://www.liverpoolrevival.org.uk/moody1.htm [accessed 26.04.2012].

[17] *Liverpool Daily Post*, 20 March 1875, p. 6.

was more difficult to dismiss, namely that it was only reaching the middle classes and those who already attended church.[18]

Recognising the need to address this Moody organised a special all-day convention. Strategically, as one account records, 'The wealth, the education, the religion and the philanthropy of Liverpool were present on the platform and in the hall.'[19] Part way through the day Moody turned to Charles Garrett, who had helped to organise the revival, and asked him to speak to the question, 'How to reach the masses – corner-men and labourers.'

The irreligion of the growing Victorian cities of Britain had long been a concern among the churches. The situation in Liverpool exemplified the situation. Church attendance in the non-Catholic churches of the city fell from 105,723 to 101,694 from 1851-81, while at the same time the general population increased from 376,056 to 552,508: a decline in real terms in the number of Protestant worshippers from 28% to 18%.[20]

Garrett's response to Moody's invitation is significant because it proves to be the catalyst in a chain of events that would ultimately transform the lives of thousands in Liverpool for the good, establish the basis for an innovative engagement in urban mission among Wesleyan Methodists that was to have national, even international, impact as well as determining the course of Garrett's own ministry until his death a quarter of a century later. That being so it merits the retelling in full in Garrett's own words as he later related:

> Having no preparation, I hesitated to respond, but found there was no alternative. I said the answer to the question was a simple one, as it had been supplied by the Saviour when communing with His disciples. I pointed out that the Saviour's words were – 'Go to every creature, and that in building churches and chapels we had been saying to the people, 'come', instead of acting upon Christ's injunction to 'Go.' The Christianity of Liverpool must go to the people. If it remained enthroned and entrenched in its churches, however widely the doors might be opened, and however sincere the welcome waiting on the threshold, the people would never come. Into the wilderness like their Master, the disciples must go to seek and save the lost: was not the town groaning at that very time under its disgraceful inability to deal with the corner-men, young fellows in gangs of 20 or 30, who neither feared God or regarded man, a terror to all respectable citizens and the despair of the police.[21] I said, 'we are mourning over the immorality of Liverpool. We have been

---

[18] A London Journalist, *A Visit to the Liverpool Wesleyan Mission* (London: Wesleyan Methodist Book-Room, 1896), p. 14; *The Porcupine*, vol. 16, 20 February 1875, p. 74.

[19] London Journalist, p. 15.

[20] R.B. Walker, 'Religious Change in Liverpool in the Nineteenth Century', *Journal of Ecclesiastical History*, 19 (1968), p. 202.

[21] 'Corner-men' was a term native to Liverpool for those who loitered outside of the public houses and made their way by petty crime and a reputation for 'scrounging, intimidation and violence'. Michael Macilwee, *The Gangs of Liverpool* (Wrea Green, Lancs: Milo, 2006), p. 33. A contemporary description from 1885 relates that Corner-men typically wore a, 'blue jacket, greasy pants, and a tight cap with a large

branded as the black spot on the Mersey, and what is the cause – the giant cause - of this immorality? Without question it is the drink traffic which has been to a large extent supreme in the city. The poverty and vice and defiant criminality of Liverpool were the direct fruit of the drink-shops which swarmed on every hand. The population was soddened with drink. Working men, even if so disposed, could not escape from the drink traps.

I said that looking to the docks they would find 10,000 to 12,000 men employed there, and yet there was not a single place where a working man could enter except a public-house, or any place where his wife or daughter could wait without danger of being insulted. I suggested that if we were really in earnest, our best plan would be to form a company, with, say, £10,000 capital and open places along the docks where the wants of the men could be supplied without the dangers and risks which must always be inseparable from public-houses. If the Christian men of Liverpool were really anxious to grapple with the frightful conditions under which people were living, let them form a company which should stud the dock-side streets and thorough-fares with comfortable and attractive houses where wholesome refreshments could be purchased at a reasonable rate, and where the wives and daughters of dock-labourers could wait with their dinners without insult, and without constant temptation to drink. Make it easy for men to do right, and so help them to resist temptation.

The proposal was received with wild enthusiasm, and Mr. Moody obtained the sanction of the meeting for ten minutes additional in which I might elaborate my scheme. While I was so doing he had temporarily vacated the chair, and, as I afterwards learned, he had gone to the late Mr. Alexander Balfour, in the meeting, and said to him, 'Mr. Balfour, here is salvation for Liverpool; will you take hold of a company like this?' Mr. Balfour at once said, 'Yes, I will take a thousand shares.' Mr Samuel Smith and a host of others followed the example, and by the time I had finished Mr. Moody was able to announce, amid tremendous cheers, that the company was formed and the capital raised. People from all parts were throwing money on the platform asking to have shares in the company, and the scene inspired the late Professor Drummond to write a pamphlet entitled, 'What Five Minutes Did.'"[22]

Responses like this were typical of Moody who, as John Coffey astutely observed, epitomised an approach that was at once democratic and egalitarian, expressing a 'moral popularism' that in its wake carried great energy for social

muffler'; P.J. Waller, *Democracy and Sectarianism: A Political and Social History of Liverpool, 1868-1939* (Liverpool: Liverpool University Press, 1981), p. 108.

22 James W. Broadbent, *The People's Life of Charles Garrett* (Leeds: James Broadbent, 1900), pp. 15-16; Professor Henry Drummond, 'How Mr. Moody Organised a Great Charity in Ten Minutes', *McClure's Magazine*, vol. 4 Dec-May1894-1895, pp. 190-91; 'An Account of Opening A Lad's Home' in *The Methodist Recorder*, 28 November 1894, p. 2 and Samuel Smith, M.P., *My Life-Work* (London: Hodder and Stoughton, 1902), pp. 93-94.

entrepreneurship and liberal social change.[23] Out of the cauldron of the Victoria Hall that Saturday in Liverpool was born the British Workman Public House Company and, as a consequence, the first Wesleyan Central Mission. Separate organisations, they were united by common concerns, the person and influence of Garrett and same wider philanthropic constituency that the city provided.

By the mid-1890s the company had established eighty Cocoa Taverns throughout the city and were serving upwards of 30,000 people a day. These 'Cokes' were fairly basic in their design and furnishings with a bar at one end, bare wooden tables and benches filling the rest of the space with a few cheap prints on the walls. A large cup of tea, coffee or Cocoa was supplied for 1d or from the abundant supply of 1d tokens that were sold to the 'well-to-do' so that they could give to the poor on the streets and be sure that it would be exchanged for a wholesome drink or provisions. The largest house, built in 1884 on the corner of Derby Road and Strand Road, could accommodate a thousand and had fifty bedrooms for boarders; by contrast the first of seven 'superior cafes' was also opened under the Corn Exchange for merchants and clerks.[24]

While the idea of establishing a type of public house to provide coffee and snacks had been around for some years, the commercialisation of the provision originated with the Liverpool initiative. From their first year of operation the shares paid a dividend of 10% to investors leading to charges of 'paying philanthropy'. An open letter to Garrett in the *Liverpool Review* of November 1896 over the name 'Diogenes' captures the essence of the concern that had rumbled on since the company's inception.

> Now it is common talk, although you may never have heard it, that the Cocoa Rooms are no better than they should be. Can it be that this 10 per cent, like most big dividends, is wrongly obtained? . . . The difference might enable the Company to improve the rooms, to supply better food-stuffs, or to provide increased remunerations for the assistants.[25]

Back in the first week of March in 1875 the Cocoa House initiative remained a future aspiration as conversations began with a view to establishing the company and making Garrett's vision a reality. However, during those discussions it emerged that Garrett's three year appointment in the Liverpool Cranmer Circuit was drawing to a close and that he was about to move to Bradford the following September. Balfour – a Scottish Presbyterian shipping merchant whose philanthropy was made possible by the success of the Balfour Williamson

[23] John Coffey, 'Democracy and Popular Religion: Moody and Sankey's Mission to Britain, 1873-1875' in Eugenio F. Biagini (ed.), *Citizenship and Community: Liberals, radicals and collective identities in the British Isles 1865-1931* (Cambridge: CUP, 1996), pp. 93-119.

[24] R.G. Milne, *The History of the British Workman Public House Company Ltd.* (unpublished Liverpool University Diploma, 1982), p. 5.

[25] 'Open letter to the Rev. Charles Garrett', *The Liverpool Review*, 28 November 1896. See also *The Liverpool Review*, 13 June 1885.

shipping line that he co-founded in Liverpool[26] – was uneasy about it and went to Garrett's home to discuss the matter, ultimately threatening to withdraw his support from the venture if he were to leave the city. Garrett later recalled,

> I said, 'The laws of the Wesleyan body were like the laws of the Medes and Persians; they cannot be interfered with.' Mr Balfour replied, 'They will have to be interfered with; for if you do not remain in Liverpool I shall give up the company. You are not going to get us into a large amount of work, and then leave us to grapple with its difficulties alone.' I assured him that it was no use to make the attempt, but he and others persisted in a memorial to the Wesleyan Conference.[27]

Strengthened by what had been a growing conviction and subject of prayer among local Methodists that the church was not doing enough to adequately grapple with the increasing evils of life in the city, Moody's assistance was also solicited in petitioning the Conference. Much to everyone's surprise, the request was granted and Garrett was appointed to superintend the new 'Riverside Mission' from September of that same year, with the 'three year rule' that governed the itinerant nature of ministerial appointments being suspended. So was born Methodism's first Central Mission, a full ten years before Samuel Collier began his work in Manchester in 1885 and Peter Thompson was appointed to oversee the new East End Mission in London. Indeed, even the Sydney Central Methodist Mission in Australia, which was long claimed as the first, was only established by W.G. Taylor in 1884. Interestingly Taylor himself had been mentored as a young man by Garrett while the latter was stationed in the Hull East Circuit (1862-65).[28]

Eight chapels were placed in the new mission, stretching from the centre of the city three miles north to Bootle, with five lay agents and a junior ministerial colleague joining Garrett in undertaking the work. Soon becoming known as the Liverpool Wesleyan Mission he remained there for twenty-five years until his retirement in 1900 at the age of 77.

Charles Garrett, early influences and ministry

Garrett was born at Shaftesbury in Dorset in 1823 into a respectable, if poor, family who gave their son what educational advantages their limited means could afford. Challenged by a neighbour standing at her cottage door with, 'Don't you think it is about time you gave your heart to God?' he remembered

---

[26] Robert G. Greenhill, 'Balfour, Alexander (1824-1886)', *Oxford Dictionary of National Biography* (Oxford: OUP, 2004) online edition, May 2006 [http://www.oxforddnb.com/view/article/46586, accessed 9 Aug 2013].

[27] Broadbent, *The People's Life*, p. 10; Drummond, *Ten Minutes*, p. 191; The Annual Report of the Liverpool Wesleyan Mission 1876, p. 6 and *The Methodist Recorder*, 30 November 1905, p. 13.

[28] William George Taylor, *Taylor of Down Under* (London: Epworth, 1921), pp. 53-55 and Don Wright, *Mantle of Christ: a history of the Sydney Central Methodist Mission* (Brisbane: University of Queensland Press, 1984), p. 44.

how her words followed him and that same day he responded to them. While he taught Sunday School from the age of 14 he was to make his first public speech at a political meeting. As a youth he was employed as a corresponding secretary by the Anti-Corn Law League, a role that brought him under the influence of its founders, Richard Cobden and John Bright, as they sought the repeal of the protectionist laws that kept cereal prices high from cheaper foreign imports. This radical side to his sympathies was further reinforced by his involvement with some of the Chartist leaders who he supported in his own time as they worked for universal male suffrage and a fairer and more inclusive electoral system.

It was also at roughly this point in his life that Garrett was converted to teetotalism having heard the publisher John Cassell speak at an Independent Chapel in the town.[29] It is no surprise therefore to find his class leader warning against the tricks of the Manchester radicals to disturb the throne, in good Wesleyan fashion. The class leader was obviously worried about the dangerous leanings he saw in the young Garrett. He was not the only one. Garrett's advocacy of temperance and commitment to teetotalism was not popular among Methodists at the time. When he went to the annual Conference for his ordination no-one could be found to provide him with hospitality because of the perceived radical nature of his convictions.[30] Wesley himself, while speaking against distilled drinks, was known to have drunk ale and wine. On one occasion he entered a lively correspondence with *the Bristol Gazette* regarding the use of hops in the brewing of Ale.[31] Indeed, only a few years before Garrett began preparing for the ordained ministry it was common practice for students in the ministerial training colleges to be daily drinking ale.[32]

The first half of Garrett's ministry took him all over the country with ministries in East Anglia, Yorkshire and finally in Lancashire. His ideas about the nature of ministry were evolving and having been stationed at Preston during the Cotton Famine of the early 1860s, he became convinced that the 'three year rule' that required all Wesleyan ministers to move circuits every third year made it almost impossible for effective ministry to be established among the poorest and most deprived communities. Itinerancy had been a key defining principle of the received Methodist tradition that stretched back to Wesley himself, and was deeply embedded in denominational culture.

---

[29] Probably 1839, cf Garrett's comment, 'working now for thirty-three years in the movement'; "Great Wesleyan Temperance Meeting at the Conference, Manchester", *Methodist Temperance Magazine*, September 1871, p. 211.

[30] Broadbent, *The People's Life*, p. 1; *Minutes, 1900*, pp. 131-33; Stanley Sowton, *Pathfinders For Modern Methodism* (London: Epworth, 1933), pp. 46-52 and B. Guinness Orchard, *Liverpool's Legion of Honour* (Birkenhead: B. Guinness Orchard, 1893), pp. 316-20.

[31] John Telford (ed), *The Letters of John Wesley*, vol. VIII (London: Epworth, 1960), pp. 164-68.

[32] W. Bardsley Brash, *The Story of our Colleges, 1835-1935* (London: Epworth, 1935), p. 77.

It was while he was at Preston that he struck up an abiding friendship with Joseph Livesey. Livesey was a local businessman, politician and advocate of teetotalism and with whom he laboured side-by-side during the Cotton Famine. In a funeral address for Livesey in 1884 he says of his friend:

> He sought the material good of those around him. He fed the hungry, clothed the naked, improved their dwellings, and sought in every way to promote their health and happiness. . . . I cannot leave this part of my subject without saying how completely Joseph Livesey's life refutes the absurd statement that teetotallers are 'men of one idea.'[33]

Ministries in Hull and Manchester followed. In 1868, along with George Maunder and T. Bowman Stephenson he founded and co-edited the *Wesleyan Temperance Magazine.* A popular monthly compendium of advocacy in the form of articles, stories, news features, and the transcripts of sermons and lectures. The editorial policy is clearly illustrative of this dimension of Garrett's ministry: in its inaugural edition it declared that total abstinence 'is a primary article in our social creed', and while it was acknowledged that there were many causes of distress, drink was considered to be the 'chief one'.[34] A later edition expanded upon this theme, 'Pauperism, education, sanitary improvements, the regulation of mines, workmen's cottages, Sabbath observance, all demand prompt and decided attention', but they were all overshadowed by the question of the drink traffic.[35] Experience ministering in the slums, prisons and workhouses had impressed on them the evidence of the critical causal and contributory nature of alcohol to the problems they encountered. Committed as the magazine was to the cause of temperance, it did so with the declared intent to be generous rather than censorious, respecting those who held different convictions to their own and resisting the temptation to conceit, dogmatism and intolerance.[36]

While in the Manchester Cheetham Hill Circuit he also actively worked towards the establishment of the Manchester and Salford Lay Mission, which came to fruition in 1872. The stated aim of the mission was, 'to seek those who were beyond the reach of existing church organisations. For this purpose halls and rooms were taken in their very midst, and a number of laymen engaged who should visit the homes of the people.'[37]

In advocating this new initiative Garrett took forward a movement within Wesleyanism that began twenty years earlier following the Religious Census of 1851. It had highlighted the relative strengths and weaknesses of the denominations across the country, where church attendance was weakest and those communities that were least well provided with churches and Christian ministry. While

---

[33] Garrett, Charles Garrett, *Loving Counsels* (London: Charles H. Kelly, 1887), pp. 176-205.

[34] *Wesleyan Temperance Magazine*, January 1868, pp. 3-5.

[35] *Wesleyan Temperance Magazine*, March 1872, p. 50.

[36] *Wesleyan Temperance Magazine,* December 1868, pp. 221-25.

[37] John Colwell, *Progress and Promise* (London: T. Woolmer, 1887), pp. 7-8.

attendance was strongest in towns of under 25,000 population at 63.3%, in London it dropped to 37% overall and was lower in the working class areas like the East End, and lowest in Shoreditch with 18.5%.[38]

Under the guidance of Charles Prest, the Wesleyan Home Mission Department was set up in 1856 and a fund started for the support of Home Mission. Ministers were expected to preach out of doors, visit and minister to the sick and dying. By the 1870s there were seventy Home Mission stations and 250 chapels had been built and integrated into the Circuits. Unfortunately, the cities were hardly touched by this development with the Oxford District in 1880 receiving the same level of financial help as Liverpool, Manchester and Bolton together.[39] Fascinatingly in an early account of this work, W. Fiddian Moulton heralds that, 'undoubtedly this forms the first chapter in the history of the Forward Movement'.[40] The 'Forward Movement' was an unconstituted grass-roots movement in the late nineteenth century that was rooted in the experiential theology of Wesleyanism. It combined a dual emphasis on evangelism and social concern which engaged with contemporary thought and worked for social and political change.[41] Often viewed as an expression of Forward Movement sentiments, the Central Mission Movement was a recognition by Methodism of the need to do something different in the centre of large cities if it was to engage with and reach a largely indifferent population. With theatre and music hall providing a model to follow, Central Halls came to embody this approach and were a common sight around the country and were, in George Sails' assessment, 'surprisingly successful'.[42]

A second issue that Garrett's work highlights is the developing place of lay people in the denomination. Methodism had always affirmed the role of local preachers; however, Garrett's use of Lay Agents potentially went to the heart of the Wesleyan understanding of the pastoral office. Such views regarding lay ministry and participation in the life of the denomination placed him among the advance guard of a developing ecclesiology which also included the introduction of lay representatives to the annual conference from 1877. Unfortunately, although the Lay Mission had distinct similarities with nondenominational City Missions, it was not as successful in achieving sufficient popular and financial support.

When Garrett left Manchester a public meeting was held to honour him at the Free Trade Hall with five thousand in attendance. The meeting combined the goodwill of the city and that of the national temperance movement, presenting him

---

[38] Bruce Coleman, 'Religion in the Victorian City', *History Today* 30.8, (1980), pp. 26-27.

[39] George Sails, *At The Centre* (London: Methodist Church Home Mission Dept., 1970), p. 7 and Davey, *Methodist Story*, p. 144.

[40] W. Fiddian Moulton, *The Story of the Manchester Mission* (London: nd), p. 7.

[41] Roger Standing, 'Hughes, Hugh Price (1847-1902)', *Oxford Dictionary of National Biography* (Oxford: OUP, 2004) online edition, May 2006 [http://www.oxforddnb.com/view/article/34043, accessed 11 Aug 2013].

[42] Sails, *At The Centre*, p. 51.

with a parting gift of 1000 guineas.[43]

Three years later the opportunity that was offered by the newly created mission in Liverpool gave Garrett the chance to bring together all the insights and concerns that he had acquired over twenty-five years of ministry. Freedom from the 'three year rule' itself enabled him to see these ideas and practices mature within the Mission itself.

The Liverpool Wesleyan Mission, anticipation of the Movement

The Liverpool Mission during Garrett's ministry was based on a dispersed model, operating from eight local centres, with a lay agent responsible for each rather than from a large central location. His conviction was that the agents should build up a 'personal influence' within the community in which they were placed and it was to this that much of the Mission's success was attributed.

> Our special form of organisation has this great advantage, that each Missionary is enabled to gain a personal knowledge of the members of his congregation, to give a welcome to strangers, and make the acquaintance of their families, finding by these means an opening to kinds of work that can never be done by public ministrations alone. It is to the exertion of this *personal* influence that the Mission owes much of its steady success.[44]

From the outset Garrett was convinced that the only way they were to reach the thousands in the poorest districts was to go them. 'The principle work of the Mission is house to house visitation.'[45] In many ways the agents were a type of community worker, helping those who did not have enough money to feed or clothe themselves or by working with those who had contracted smallpox or typhus fever when no one else would. It was said of James Dobson, who worked in the Toxteth branch of the Mission for twenty years, that, 'In times of riot or public need of him that the police and the guardians of the poor looked for his help. As for the people, they love him too much to hurt one hair of his head.'[46]

The conditions of the urban poor were shocking and the squalor appalling. Liverpool was a large, developing city with a cosmopolitan population. Its standards of housing were notoriously the worst in the country and it was alternately nicknamed the 'blackspot on the Mersey', 'the Marseilles of England' or 'squalid Liverpool'. One agent wrote of his reaction in 1878: 'the destitution and degradation of many of the people is terrible and the scenes witnessed are often horrible beyond description.'[47]

While Andrew Mearns was later to make these atrocious conditions more widely known with his landmark expose, 'The Bitter Cry of Outcast London' in 1883,

---

[43] *Wesleyan Temperance Magazine*, December 1872, pp. 267-74.

[44] *Annual Report 1894*, p. 5.

[45] *Annual Report 1879*, pp. 3-4. See also, *Annual Report 1878*, p. 4 and *Annual Report 1880*, p. 3.

[46] London Journalist, p. 63.

[47] *Annual Report 1878*, p. 4.

Liverpool's Medical Officer for health had already charted how among the tenements and multiple occupancy housing, some of the worst conditions were in cellar living where some 20,000 Liverpool residents occupied 6,000 cellars.[48]

By 1871 the census returns reveal that the population of the city had burgeoned during the century from 77,708 (1801) to 493,405 (1871),[49] while the landmark research of Parkes and Burdon-Sanderson's in their 1871 *Report on the Sanitary Conditions of Liverpool*, revealed that at 38.59 per 1000 the average mortality rate for the 1860s was also the highest in the country and significantly worse than London (24.3) and Manchester (30.2).[50] It is hardly surprising that epidemics were regular visitors to the city as with the typhus (1865), cholera (1866), relapsing fever (1870) and smallpox (1870-71, 1876-77).[51] In 1880 it was estimated that some 70,000 people lived in some 14,472 houses in 2,531 courts which were unfit for habitation.[52] As the key strategy of the Mission was house-to-house visitation, they were confronted by these stark realities again and again. One agent wrote:

> Visited today in the midst of misery and sin. I found in one house seven families, numbering forty-two persons; six were down in fever, two women had been recently confined, and three of the men were thoroughly drunk. It was a hell upon earth. I came away heart-sick, and was not surprised the next week to hear that three in the house were dead. Surely the time will come when an intelligent Christian nation will not permit such hell-holes to exist.[53]

Or again,

> Today I found a family in great distress; the man was evidently dying, and the woman had only been confined a few days; they had four little children who were evidently pining. I got them some cocoa, and bread, with some tokens, and have thus been able to keep them from starving. Shortly after, the poor fellow died, trusting in Jesus, and the widow is now a member of our church, and is trying to train her little ones for heaven.[54]

Dobson, one of the first lay agents to join Garrett at the outset of the mission, was sent to the south end of the city to the Toxteth Park district, where over the following twenty years he was responsible for the establishment and building of two thousand-strong congregations. The story is worthy of retelling as it embodies both the values and the approach that Garrett advocated. It was reputed to be one of

---

48 Gordon Read & David Jebson, *A Voice in the City* (Liverpool: Liverpool City Mission, 1979), p. 20.

49 http://liverpolitan.im/main/population.htm[accessed 10 Aug 2013].

50 http://www.yoliverpool.com/forum/showthread.php?95115-REPORT-ON-THE-SANITARY-CONDITION-OF-LIVERPOOL-1871&s=2a0ea170f40242d15be118c571311339 [accessed 10 Aug 2013].

51 Waller, *Democracy and Sectarianism*, p. 84.

52 Waller, *Democracy and Sectarianism*, p. 83.

53 *Annual Report 1879*, p. 5.

54 *Annual Report 1879*, p. 6.

the best known missionary successes of the nineteenth century and 'one of the most remarkable missions Methodism has ever undertaken'.[55]

He arrived in Toxteth and set about his work by going to preach in a courtyard of houses in the heart of the district. After two weeks 28 were signed up to a weekly class meeting and the work continued in the open air for two years before premises were acquired for the congregation that had grown to number 180. However, rather than taking over a disused chapel or building their own church, on Sundays and two nights a week the Templar Hall was rented, the former Cambridge Music Hall. Every week the members would work late on a Saturday night after the evening's entertainment to get the hall ready for Sunday morning. By 1881 a regular attendance of 700-800 had been achieved. The hall became so full that most weeks many of the members would hold a prayer meeting downstairs to allow more of their neighbours to attend upstairs. In 1888 the hall, badly in need of repair, came up for sale. The Mission bought it, renovated it and increased the capacity to 1000 at the same time.[56]

A group of the younger members from Templar Hall then began a new work ¾ mile away on Park Hill Road. Beginning in the open air the results were soon sufficient to warrant hiring a separate hall. The congregation quickly grew to the point where they built and opened their own new suite of premises including a 550 seater auditorium and gymnasium, the Hutchinson Hall. It was opened in 1893 with the services of Mr & Mrs Gypsy Evens to work as lay agents. Within twelve months it too was full and by 1895 a gallery was added and, including the children's service, a thousand were in attendance on a Sunday evening.[57]

The community base of the different centres of the Mission was important for both evangelism and community work. As regards evangelism, the chapel was seen to belong to the neighbourhood, as did the agent and members. In 1885 the comment was made that one of the most pleasing features of the work was the way converts would influence those around them by the witness of their lives, leading, in turn, to more conversions.[58] The community continued to be important after conversion too, as those people a convert lived and worked among were the same ones who joined them at the class meeting. Garrett considered this emphasis was essential to the Mission's success in terms of the mutual support, encouragement and accountability it offered. For example, it was a regular practice for classes to hold love-feasts on public holidays so that they might help each other not to drift back into old habits.[59]

Being community-based, each chapel could respond to the needs of its neighbourhood. During a severe period in the winter of 1891, the Mission provided 700 children with a free breakfast for a week, and 180 gallons of soup a day was

---

[55] London Journalist, p. 56.

[56] *Annual Report 1881*, p. 8 and London Journalist, p. 58-63.

[57] *Annual Report 1889*, p. 8; *Annual Report 1893*, p. 22 and *Annual Report 1895*, p. 6.

[58] *Annual Report 1885*, p. 6 and *Annual Report 1886*, p. 10.

[59] *Annual Report 1880*, p. 8.

also distributed for a for nine day period.[60] At Cranmer, during the cotton and coal strike of 1892 the strikers were going without food and fuel. The Chapel pitched in to help and provided more than 1,500 meals in their lecture hall.[61] Or again when, in 1895, two railwaymen were killed in an accident, one class at Cranmer Chapel collected £21 for their widows.[62]

Open-air preaching was important for the Mission and they were proud of the fact that they used no gimmicks, such as brass bands, to attract a crowd. The message that was proclaimed was a simple exposition of evangelical belief that, 'Sin was sin [and] there could be no paltering with it. And yet the sternest truths were spoken with infinite tenderness and gentleness.'[63] However, these were not necessarily incident free events as one Lay Agent recalled:

> Today has been one of the most blessed days I ever lived. I have visited a large number of houses, distributing tracts, and inviting them to my open air meeting. I have been in three fights, but have given out my tracts . . . no-one has molested me, though I seemed to be in Pandemonium. Men, and women were fighting, hissing, screaming and swearing fearfully . . . At the appointed time I began a service in their midst . . . there was a crowd of 600 surging around me. No-one interrupted me, and, before the service ended, scores of them were in tears. Many gathered round me at the end of the service to ask what they must do to be saved.[64]

Worship in the Mission's chapels was boisterously informal. If a congregation enjoyed a sermon, prolonged cheering could accompany its close! Speaking at the first World Methodist Ecumenical Conference in 1881, Garrett relayed his conviction that:

> Many congregations literally freeze the minister to death. You have no 'Amen', you have no, 'bless the Lord', you have no, 'hallelujah'; and yet the infusion of that into many of our churches would fill any of them. Men will draw to the fire when it is cold . . . and if they find in a church a hearty, earnest, genial – not extravagant – manifestation of feeling, they will find there a home.[65]

However, a visit to one of these boisterously informal services in one of the more needy parts of the city was not always easy for those not accustomed to it. Samuel

---

60 Sails, *At The Centre*, p. 29.

61 *Annual Report 1893*, p. 21.

62 London Journalist, p. 34.

63 London Journalist, p. 52. Garrett does seem to have carried some concerns about the Salvation Army and the impact of their approach that engenders a familiarity with 'religion without reverence' that will ultimately make evangelism much harder. See the letter to an anonymous correspondent, dated 17 January (no year), Methodist Archives and Research Centre, John Rylands Library, University of Manchester, ref. PLP 43.29.55.

64 *Annual Report 1880*, p. 11.

65 *The Proceedings of the First Ecumenical World Methodist Conference 1881* (London: Wesleyan Conference Office, 1881), p. 434.

Smith – one of Moody's investors who was a cotton merchant in the 1870s, a Liberal councillor (1879-83) and then Liberal MP from the city (1882-85) – was to record:

> The filth and stench of the audience were indescribable. One could hardly walk through to the platform without feeling sick. Those were the days when public baths for the poor were almost unknown, or at least unused, and when a large part of the poor population lived in enclosed 'courts' or 'closes' with no ventilation and no lighting at night.[66]

While the Mission's social work sought to address the stark needs that confronted them, their analysis of the situation was neither a spiritualised understanding of the consequence of personal sin, nor a one dimensional attribution to the drink-trade. In the annual report of 1888 Garrett maintained that the state should protect the poor against the capitalists who made fortunes upon disease and misery, as well as against publicans and poisonous literature.

> While the state deals with the CAUSES of national crime and depravity, let the church deal with the RESULTS. [Through] . . . a good hall in each degraded neighbourhood; a good agent at each hall to seek and care for those around; a good Sunday School to welcome the poorest children; a good mother's meeting for isolated and miserable women to taste Christianity; a good temperance organisation to aid those battling against drink; a sewing class to elevate, purify and train young girls; a good readable library and a comfortable room to read in.[67]

Temperance was integral to Garrett and the Mission as they witnessed first-hand the positive impact it had on the poorest and most deprived neighbourhoods. In 1881 the Mission reported, 'The importance of temperance is kept fully before the people . . . It would be impossible for them to hold their ground, even for a day, if they were not abstainers.'[68] Yet there were no illusions: in the Mission's Annual Report for 1894, while they were encouraged by the increasing fidelity Christians were showing to both their social and political duty and rejoiced that their people were alive to their responsibility for the social and moral condition of the community, still they acknowledged, 'How powerful a factor in the formation of character is environment.' The convictions of the Mission and its workers were clear, 'the sin and misery of our poorer brethren are due to bad surroundings.'[69]

The results of the Mission in its first twenty years are impressive. By 1895 the Mission had 1,000 members 2000 Sunday School scholars, and Sunday evening congregations in excess of 6000. Working in the Mission were 15 full-time workers (including 4 ministers and 11 lay agents, of whom 3 were women).[70] Through its

---

66 Smith, *My Life-Work*, p. 107.
67 *Annual Report 1888*, pp. 13-14.
68 *Annual Report 1881*, p. 9.
69 *Annual Report 1894*, p. 6.
70 *Annual Report 1895*.

annual reports the Mission communicated to its supporters the range and scope of their work, illustrated by journal extracts from those working in their various centres and a patchwork of statistical information that highlighted the focus of their work.[71] Systematic visitation, open-air meetings, tract distribution and cottage meetings were obviously central to their strategy. Consistently over this period 20,000 home visits were made, upwards of 60,000 tracts distributed, several hundred cottage meetings undertaken and 200-300 open-air meetings conducted. Yet the Mission was quite clear that the overall atmosphere of the communities in which they worked was one of 'religious indifference . . . moral obtuseness . . . [and] blank insensibility of heart'.[72]

In the face of widespread indifference to religion by the local population, the projects and initiatives the Mission undertook were both creative and wide ranging. In January 1883 the *Liverpool Review* reported how, being faced with the escalating problem of local gangs, Garrett had invited the notorious Logwood Gang for tea. Eighty-seven turned up and found more than they bargained for with not a few of them ultimately joining the church at Wesley Hall.[73] Indeed, Wesley Hall was an ex-Baptist Chapel on Soho Street that had been sold to the Mission because death and removal to better parts of the city had left it without a viable congregation. Under the Mission it became a vibrant and growing community which, in only five years, had already outgrown a hired hall and a second home of their own construction which they had also extended. Wesley Hall also opened their own penny savings bank with 230 of their own members.[74]

Bible Studies were initiated in the docks with dock-gatemen and flatmen with 80 attending a Monday night meeting at Duke's Dock. A Sunday afternoon open-air service was so successful that no place could be found to accommodate all who attended until the Bridgewater Company came to their rescue and provided a venue.[75] A parallel story relates to a service the Mission began in the Saleroom at the Exchange Station of the Lancashire and Yorkshire Railway on two nights each week in 1887. This congregation grew and was moved to the Waiting Room and expanded to include a Sunday afternoon service and a class meeting.[76] Indeed, these are not the only examples of the Mission's attempt to reach the working men who never frequented the chapels and halls of the Mission. Open-air services were held in workshop and railway sheds and, with a large number of men living in lodging houses, these too were utilised to host meetings conducted by the

---

71 Unfortunately, the statistical information is presented in a manner that makes it impossible to seriously or systematically analyse.

72 *Annual Report 1893*, p. 5.

73 *The Liverpool Review*, 30 November 1889, p. 10. The Logwood Gang was originally a group of self-appointed vigilantes ostensibly to protect their neighbourhood from the Corner-men, but ultimately proving to be as equally lawless with their 'logwood' cudgels as the Corner-man themselves. Macilwee, *The Gangs*, p. 172.

74 *Annual Report 1892*, p. 9.

75 *Annual Report 1879*, pp. 11-12.

76 *Annual Report 1887*, p. 9 and *Annual Report 1889*, p. 11.

missionaries.[77]

The 1880s also saw Liverpool emerge as a major port of embarkation for those seeking to start a new life by emigrating to the United States. The city was hit with a constant flow of people during these years and the Mission attempted to do what they could for the poorest and also made lodgings available in one of their properties.[78]

In the 1880s and 1890s the Mission was also successful in setting up children's homes, having three for boys and young men and two for girls, with an additional overnight shelter. While the girls who were old enough to work were encouraged to have positions outside in factories, shops or private homes,[79] the Mission provided initiatives for the men and boys to get them into work. The men benefitted from a Labour Bureau and the lads joined the Charles Garrett brigade which ran a shoe-black, wood chopping and messenger service. Garrett was clear with regard to their underlying rationale:

> I have gone on this principle – that the lads must help themselves . . . I don't want to raise up a generation of paupers, but a generation of men. . . . Speaking generally, the lads will do well when they get the chance. Love is a great power, and the boys are surrounded by ennobling influences. Kindness puts a lad on his pluck.[80]

Charles Garrett, the 'Father' of the Movement

If these are illustrative highlights of the life of the Mission that Garrett led for a quarter of a century, what of the man himself? An activist rather than a writer or publicist, with only one volume of published sermons to his name, the material to complete the picture of this key leader among the Wesleyans is not vast. However, what evidence there is does paint a consistent picture.

The evidence shows that outside of the Mission Garrett contributed significantly to the wider life of the denomination. With G.T. Perks and W.M. Punshon, he was one of six ministers who were responsible for the publication of the 'mildly liberal' newspaper the *Methodist Recorder* in 1861 and who formed the original 'editorial council'. Alienated by the conservatism of *The Watchman* that reflected the views of 'elderly ministers and well-to-do laymen', this rising generation of Wesleyan leaders decided to do something about it. *The Methodist Recorder* became so popular that *The Watchman* itself went out of business in 1883.[81]

Garrett's role in the formation of the *Methodist Temperance Magazine* has already been noted, but in 1883 he was to be involved in the birth of a third publication. His evangelistic passion led him to suggest to Thomas Champness the

---

[77] *Annual Report 1889*, p. 5; *Annual Report 1890*, pp. 3 & 5.

[78] *Annual Report 1888*, p. 6.

[79] London Journalist, pp. 79-80.

[80] 'Side Lights on City Life', reprinted from the *Liverpool Courier*, 1 August 1896, pp. 4-6.

[81] Ian Sellers, 'Nonconformist Attitudes in Later Nineteenth Century Liverpool' *Transactions of the Historical Society of Lancashire and Cheshire* 114 (1962), pp. 131-32.

establishment of another newspaper. Following protracted conversations, on 22 February 1883 Champness' *Joyful News* launched as an evangelistic tool. Garrett featured on the front cover of the first edition with a block print and transcript of his sermon at the closing service of the Oldham Street Chapel in Manchester.[82] Fascinatingly this sermon was in part responsible for the Oldham Street site not being sold for commercial development but retained, ultimately to provide the home of the first Central Hall. The paper itself was an early precursor of Champness' work with evangelists that began in his home in Bolton in 1883 before moving to Castleton Hall at Rochdale, ultimately migrating to Cliff College in Derbyshire in 1904.

For many years Garrett combined his work in the Mission with that of being Chairman of the Liverpool District. Then, in 1882 he was elected President of the Conference. This position of high regard within the fellowship of ministers was indicative of how the controversial views he embodied had become much more widely embraced. Indeed, Garrett himself had played a significant role in leading the denomination to embrace temperance at the annual conferences, between 1875-77.[83] Balfour made the assessment that the 'crowning work of his presidential year' was the establishment of two rest homes for ministers in Colwyn Bay and Grange over Sands. Garrett had become convinced of the need of such provision during the first year of the Mission's life when he suffered from 'a severe and long continued affliction'. It was Balfour who had provided him with a retreat at which to recuperate.[84]

Both before and after his presidential year Garrett was in much demand as a guest speaker, and it was in being one of Mr Wesley's preachers that he found his core identity. However, he was not a platform orator or an erudite speaker, rather contemporaneous reports dwell more on the homeliness and simplicity of his language. It was described variously as honest, practical, fluent, and infused with great energy, a style that clearly connected with ordinary people but lacked the sophisticated philosophical or literary allusions and rhetorical flourishes that many saw as the hallmarks of 'great preaching'.

A journalist reporting for the *Liverpool Review* on a visit to hear him preach in January 1883 observed that, while genial, he was not a very dynamic preacher and that his voice was not always audible. He also commented on a peculiar eccentricity of gesture he described as 'giving a rapid illustration of enlarged shorthand upon an imaginary blackboard'. However, the following week another contributor was keen to affirm that his preaching was, 'so practical and so inspiring. People that I know can tell today of sermons preached by Mr Garrett years ago – 10, 15, 20 years since remembering the text and part of the sermon.'[85] A review of his volume of

---

[82] *Joyful News*, No 1, 22 February 1883, p. 1.

[83] *Minutes 1901*, pp. 131-33.

[84] *Annual Report 1876*, p12; Broadbent, *The People's Life*, p. 10 and *Liverpool Daily Post*, p22 October 1900.

[85] *Liverpool Review*, 20 January 1883, p. 7.

sermons, 'Loving Counsels', in the *Wesleyan Magazine* of 1887 highlights the parallels between his preaching style and his character, articulated as 'simple, strong, pure, practical, with a manly directness and exquisitely touching tenderness; ever and again reminding one of Spurgeon'.[86] His preaching ministry is best summed up in his obituary in the Minutes of the Methodist Conference.

> As a preacher on special occasions his services were in great demand throughout the connexion. All types of hearers were charmed and profited by his discourses. The matter was richly evangelical, well arranged, and enlivened by apt illustrations, his style simple and colloquial, his voice and manner tender and eloquent, and his spirit aglow with earnestness suffused with sympathy. He was a man of . . . remarkable common sense and shrewdness, but the chief characteristic of his preaching was its power over the hearts of his hearers.[87]

Indeed, the personal qualities of generosity, good natured humour, geniality, kindness and sympathy are regular observations from those who had contact with him. One reporter who interviewed him commented on the 'intensely human, wonderfully sympathetic way which makes all who hear him linger on the tender vibrations of his voice'.[88]

Another feature of Garrett's ministry was his generosity of spirit towards Christians of other denominations and traditions. The Bishop of Manchester, at the October 1872 public meeting in the Free Trade Hall that marked his departure for Liverpool commented on 'his kindly feeling towards religious bodies other than his own', while the formal address lauded that his, 'catholicity of spirit is wide as the world.' Garrett himself responded by sharing that he felt that he belonged to the whole church and that he longed for everything which interfered with the churches standing fast and striving together to spread the gospel to be swept away.[89]

Moody's visit was, of course, non-denominational and drew many with evangelical convictions together. Further to this, working for the cause of temperance also made a significant contribution to his ecumenical outlook as shared convictions regarding alcohol abuse and drunkenness helped to bridge doctrinal and ecclesiological differences. However, this emphasis runs more deeply in Garrett than the mere pragmatics of cross-denominational collaboration, although this is clearly a vital outcome of it in his understanding.

> I am a catholic by my convictions; I am a catholic by my spiritual nature . . . so that, so far as I am concerned, . . . if other members of the church would not shake hands with me, it was their fault and not mine. . . . Why I hate bigotry more than I hate drink, and that is a strong figure.[90]

---

[86] *Wesleyan Methodist Magazine*, 1887, p. 717.

[87] *Minutes, 1901*, pp. 132-33.

[88] *Liverpool Courier*, 1 August 1896, p. 3.

[89] *Wesleyan Temperance Magazine, December 1872*, pp. 267-74.

[90] Charles J. Hall, *The Phrenological Characteristics of the Rev. Charles Garrett* (Maidstone: G.H. Graham, 1873), pp. 22-23.

In 1882 the renowned Baptist preacher C.H. Spurgeon invited him to supply the pulpit of his Metropolitan Tabernacle in London while he was away in Mentone, France. While Garrett declined because of his responsibilities as President of the Wesleyan Conference that year, his warm and affectionate response is in itself revealing.

> I have long been about the most devoted admirer that you have. I have thanked God for giving you to the Church, over and over again; and I always say that the whole Church ought to pray that God may preserve and help you . . . I would do anything in my power to relieve you from either work or anxiety.[91]

The testimony of J.C. Ryle, the first Anglican Bishop of Liverpool, is also illustrative of Garrett's generosity of spirit.

> I think my good friend Mr. Garrett, who I have known as a friend ever since I came to Liverpool, 14 years ago, will tell you that I never said 'no' to him if he asked me to do anything. ... When I came here to Liverpool, I remember the hearty welcome I had most unexpectedly received from Mr. Garrett.[92]

Indeed, each New Year's Day Garrett would visit Ryle and together they would kneel and pray for God's blessing on the city and their work for the coming year.[93] The story is also told of how the bishop's third wife, Henrietta, reputedly drew great strength from Garrett's book of sermons as she struggled with terminal illness, with Ryle regularly reading to her from it.[94]

It is perhaps even more surprising, especially for Liverpool at that time, that the Roman Catholic social reformer, Monsignor James Nugent considered Garrett, 'among his particular friends'.[95] While he continued to carry those concerns that were common to Nonconformists with regard to 'popery',[96] in speaking on Psalm 27:8 at a Baptist Chapel in Accrington Garrett makes his deeper convictions abundantly clear,

> I care not whether you are a Methodist, a Baptist, a Churchman, a Protestant, or a Catholic; if you are a child of God, my text is your spiritual history. God's family is one, though we are called by many names, and when it comes to matters of experience our unity is at once made manifest.[97]

---

91 C.H. Spurgeon, *Autobiography; compiled from his diary, letters, and records by his wife and his private secretary* (London: Passmore and Alabaster, 1900), 6. p. 153.

92 *Report of the Opening of a Lads' Home* (Liverpool, Liverpool Wesleyan Mission, 1894), p. 8.

93 *Methodist Recorder*, 6 October 1904, p. 5.

94 Broadbent, *The People's Life*, p. 5.

95 Canon Bennett, *Father Nugent of Liverpool* (Liverpool: Catholic Children's Protection Society, 1949), p. 136.

96 Letter to Dr. Osborn, dated 20 December (no year), Methodist Archives and Research Centre, John Rylands Library, University of Manchester, ref. PLP 43.29.27.

97 Garrett, *Loving Counsels*, p. 82.

On his death in 1900, the *Liverpool Daily Post* identified this catholicity as

> one of the most striking features of his career. . . . Mr. Garrett was in constant touch with ministers of all religious denominations when opportunities were afforded for working in unison for the extension of God's Kingdom and His righteousness.[98]

How do we assess the Liverpool Mission and the role of Charles Garrett? In 1891 *The Crusader* magazine observed how 'The Liverpool Mission has served as a model to London, Manchester and Birmingham and will yet, we hope, form a model of energetic prosecution of rescue work in all our large towns.'[99] Indeed, the Mission itself was clear that it was 'the oldest of its class'.[100] While there are clear parallels to the work of the non-denominational City Mission movement, the Liverpool Wesleyan Mission gives this a denominational expression with all of the advantages that brings in terms of resources, support and the ability to begin to reproduce the approach elsewhere. However, the innovative nature of the mission within Wesleyanism should not be minimised. With the exception of the failed attempts at 'Lay Missions' which had begun three years before, there was no real precedent for what Garrett initiated following the Moody campaign,[101] and the suspension of the 'three-year rule', the active leadership of Lay Agents with immediate pastoral responsibility for each hall and the strategic emphasis on temperance were all ground-breaking practices for Circuit ministry. Indeed, without the suspension of the 'three year rule' it would have been impossible to develop such a ministry or for the work of the mission to flourish. Along with these factors and the momentum created by Moody's visit, it is highly likely that it was Garrett's personal presence and oversight in Liverpool that accounted for its success over against the failure of the Manchester and Salford Lay Mission.

Throughout Garrett's ministry the Liverpool Mission remained committed to the dispersed model that he had established at the outset. Increasingly the trend was for the establishment of a large Central Hall, with over 100 ultimately following the example of Manchester. In Liverpool the old Mount Pleasant Chapel was refurbished and housed the administration of the Mission and was renamed the Central Hall even though the old model continued. Indeed, it was not until five years after Garrett's death that a state-of-the-art Central Hall was opened on Renshaw Street in 1905, but even with the opening of what some hailed as 'The best Central Hall so far erected', still the *Wesleyan Methodist Magazine* had to report that there was 'no great and general enthusiasm for this scheme'.[102]

---

[98] *Liverpool Daily Post*, 22 October 1900.

[99] *The Crusader*, August 1891, quoted in *Exploits of a Hundred Years: a brief history of the Liverpool Methodist Mission* (Liverpool: Liverpool Methodist Mission, 1975), p. 9.

[100] *Annual Report, 1894*, p. 5.

[101] The Metropolitan Lay Mission and the Manchester & Salford Lay Mission, both of which were founded in 1872 are as close to a precedent as there was, but neither of these flourished or gained widespread denominational support.

[102] *Wesleyan Methodist Magazine* (London, 1906), pp. 775-76.

As regards Garrett, in his obituary in the Minutes of the Wesleyan Conference it is stated that he

> may be regarded as one of the pioneers of the home missionary enterprises of modern Methodism in large cities. Mission halls and old chapels in destitute localities were used as centres in which humanitarian agencies were associated with directly spiritual work. . . . He became a power in the civic life of Liverpool. He waged war against insanitary areas, demoralising amusements, and especially the drink traffic.[103]

A pioneer is probably the best word to describe him, not only in terms of the mission work he engaged in, but also with regard to the influence he had on Wesleyanism as a whole. While he was not alone, he was a conspicuous leader with a national profile and held in high regard. Indeed, it is his character that is variously described as generous, genial, winsome, sympathetic, gentle, and full of brotherly kindness that helped to smooth the transitions to a more missionary orientated, socially engaged and less clerically dominated denomination. The fact that his preaching was more devotional in content and that his understanding of the gospel was warm-heartedly evangelical also inspired confidence.

Garrett himself was not as advanced in his thinking as the rising generation of leaders such as Hugh Price Hughes who would become the voice and archetypal embodiment of the Forward Movement, but Garrett was of the preceding generation. However, the projects with which he was involved illustrate the progressive nature of his thought. While some suggested that his temperance principles blinded him to the need for other social reform, he was keen to refute this. An editorial in the *Wesleyan Temperance Magazine* illustrates the balance of his convictions.

> Now we are not so foolish, – we are not such monomaniacs, – as to contend that here we have *the* great question of the day . . . we are rational enough to suppose that there may be questions occupying the public attention equal in importance even to . . . temperance.[104]

Garrett's ideas had been formed in his youth where he observed the wide platform of the Chartists running into the ground, while concentration on a single issue campaign like that of the Anti-Corn Law League bore fruit. He outlined the logic of his position in an article in the *Wesleyan Temperance Magazine* entitled, 'Our National Drink Bill for 1869'. In it he charted the cost of the national addiction to alcohol: the wasted food as grain was used for drink and not for bread, the wasted money, the injured health, the impact on the national economy, the hindrance of education as families could not afford to send their children to school, the increase of pauperism and the causation of crime.[105]

For all of his emphasis on temperance and teetotalism, his broader convictions

---

[103] *Minutes, 1901*, pp. 131-32.
[104] *Wesleyan Temperance Magazine*, January 1870, p. 2.
[105] *Wesleyan Temperance Magazine*, March 1870, pp. 62-66.

remained with him. He spoke of the courage that was required to stand alongside the poor and oppressed when everyone forsakes them; and the different form that courage needs to take when standing with the rich and not pandering to them or tolerating their vices.[106] He maintained:

> England is also 'ours' because it is not the property of monarchs, peers, or legislators, but of all the people. . . . It follows from what I have said that all of us should know something of what is called political economy, and should endeavour to ascertain the sources of our national strength, and the causes of our national weakness. . . . Nothing can be more foolish than to say, 'I'll mind my own business, and leave the affairs of the nation to those who choose to attend to them.' . . . If the price of food be artificially raised, you will have to pay a higher price for your loaf; there will be no exception made in your favour, because you didn't choose to do your duty. If trade be injured, your earnings will be materially diminished; and if our national wealth be improperly expended, and increased taxation results, we shall all feel the effect. We are a great family, we have a common interest, and we are bound to seek the common good.[107]

He concentrated upon the vice of the drink traffic he said, speaking at the Metropolitan Tabernacle in London, as his experience in the poorest and most destitute areas led him to conclude that it was 'the parent of all others'.[108]

Garrett is significant in that he represents the dawn of a new era, as the 'pioneer' epithet acknowledged by his contemporaries suggests. However, W.G. Taylor, the founder of the Sydney Central Methodist Mission, goes further and sees him as the father of the emerging Forward Movement that was to more widely transform Wesleyanism.[109] The advance guard of change is the best way to conceive of Garrett's place, perhaps more so than any other. Certainly Garrett and Hughes knew each other. As early as 1872 they shared a platform at the 'The Great Wesleyan Temperance Meeting in the Metropolitan Tabernacle' during that year's Conference. However, while both addressed the meeting Hughes was still in his first circuit appointment at Dover, while Garrett was about to begin his tenth after twenty-two years of ministry and was the main speaker.[110] Years later Garrett was happy to cede to Hugh Price Hughes as he grew older. This is evidenced in a letter at the height of the 'Indian missionary controversy' in 1890 in which he seeks to encourage his colleague who was twenty years his junior. Fearful of the toll being exacted from Hughes, and in the light of his own debilitating experience, he writes:

> My heart has been with you in your great trial, and I can't forbear writing to assure you of my love. . . . You have the faculty of winning the hearts of all who are associated with you, and that is a priceless gift. . . . You must not break down, for the hopes of

[106] Garrett, *Loving Counsels*, pp. 214-15.
[107] Garrett, *Loving Counsels*, pp. 46-47.
[108] Garrett, *Loving Counsels*, p. 143.
[109] James Colwell, *A Century in the Pacific* (Sydney: William H. Beale, 1914), p. 692.
[110] *Wesleyan Temperance Magazine*, September 1872, pp. 195-212.

hundreds of us is in you.[111]

As a minister of the gospel whose primary focus was to see people come to faith in Christ, Garrett is clearly within the mainstream of the Wesleyan tradition. Yet he is open to proactively explore new patterns of ministry when faced with the overwhelming challenges presented by the succession of northern industrialised English cities in which he exercised his calling.[112]

Engaging the services of laymen as full-time evangelistic and pastoral workers in the Mission, utilizing the methods of the city mission movement and abandoning the 'three year rule' for appointments all demonstrate the innovative and pioneering nature of his work. Establishing the British Workman Public House Company alongside using the Mission as the provider of a wide range of supportive social initiatives from residential homes, to savings banks and employment programmes would today indicate a social entrepreneurship of the highest order.

Garrett's response to the social issues of his day has to be read in the light of his evangelical convictions and his experience with the Anti-Corn Law League and the Chartists. This means he has to be read very carefully so as not to misrepresent his ideas and understanding. From a spiritual perspective the only hope for humanity was faith in Christ. Evangelism was therefore of first importance. However, when visiting among the sick and dying in the middle of an epidemic, or, when faced by the direst poverty, with people living in overcrowded accommodation that was not fit for human habitation a different and more immediate response was called for. The Mission was not in a position to provide general welfare to all, so, while they frequently extended their support into the wider community, and especially to those situations of acute need that presented themselves, at other times their focus had to be limited to their own members and the more immediate networks surrounding their chapels. The recounting of this is not the inconsistency that Sellers discerns, merely the exigencies of the intolerable context within which they worked.

Garrett's experience and analysis led him to conclude that 'the vice of drunkenness' was an unequalled evil because of the pernicious way it affected every part of a person's life and those around them.[113] However, as has been illustrated above, this neither blinded him to a wider understanding of his context nor led him to abandon the generosity of manner to those with whom he disagreed that, by many and varied testimony, epitomised his whole demeanour. Garrett was far more nuanced in his understanding and expression than the stereotype of a Victorian teetotaller. '[T]he affairs of the nation are yours as much as anybody's, and you cannot neglect them without danger,' he wrote.[114] However, he was primarily a pastor/evangelist rather than a politician/social reformer like

[111] D.P. Hughes, *The Life of Hugh Price Hughes* (London: Hodder & Stoughton, 1903), p. 316.

[112] Rochdale (1857-60), Preston (1860-63), Hull (1863-66), Manchester (1866-72), Liverpool (1872-1900).

[113] Garrett, *Loving Counsels*, p. 281.

[114] Sellers, 'Nonconformist Attitudes', p. 232.

Shaftesbury. It is possible to discern a broadening in his expression of social concerns in the late 1880s and 1890s, reflecting the developing consensus within Wesleyanism that was the fruit of the Forward Movement, and Hughes' influence in particular. His sympathies had always been broader, if the expression of them had remained largely latent over the years because of his concentration of teetotalism/temperance; yet he was regularly in the company of those with politically liberal sentiments like Samuel Smith who increasingly became aligned with Nonconformity.

At his funeral the *Liverpool Review* reported that 1000s crowded around the graveside. The best epitaph, the reporter said, was that 'His city loved him!'[115] Writing in the *Liverpool Daily Post* Bishop Royston spoke for the whole Church community of the city: 'He belongs to the whole church of Christ. He was a true man of God, a warm hearted and successful evangelist, a remarkable philanthropist, a leader of his fellow men, who set an example.'[116] The *Methodist Recorder* was also quite clear about how he should be remembered, he was, 'the best loved man in Methodism!'[117]

Hugh Price Hughes and the Forward Movement

The mid-1880s were important years for Hugh Price Hughes and the Forward Movement. Hughes began to publish and edit *The Methodist Times* in 1885. Modelled in form and substance on W.T. Stead's *Pall Mall Gazette* and his campaigning style of journalism the weekly paper quickly established itself as one of the most widely read Christian journals. By 1900 its circulation had topped 150,000 per week.[118] A year later he was appointed to superintend the newly established West London Mission. Both of these developments gave Hughes a high visibility among the new generation of Wesleyans who were coming into leadership within the denomination. Many people actually believed Hughes to be both the originator and the leader of the Forward Movement, and although this never ceased to amaze him, in many ways he was the embodiment of the movement from the mid-eighties.

The Forward Movement itself is difficult to define. It was never organised and never had a constitution or an elected leader. It was rather a broad, general stirring for a 'movement forward' within the denomination. Christianity had to address itself to the modern world, present circumstances and contemporary insights. Building on a call for renewed spiritual devotion and depth, the movement concentrated on the application of the gospel evangelistically, socially and politically. To further these aims the reform of denominational structures and unity with other evangelical Christians became important thrusts. The movement was

---

[115] *Liverpool Review*, 27 October 1900.

[116] *Liverpool Daily Post*, 25 October 1900.

[117] Orchard, *Liverpool's Legion of Honour*, p. 317.

[118] Christopher Oldstone-Moore, *Hugh Price Hughes* (Cardiff: University of Wales Press, 1999), pp. 5-6, 121.

animated by a rediscovery of the enthusiastic activism inherent within the Wesleyan tradition.

The title, 'Forward Movement' was coined by Mrs Alexander McArthur at a dinner party in her Brixton Hill home. Someone made disparaging remarks about Hughes' aspirations, and she replied, 'Oh, Mr. ----, you must not say that here. We all belong to the "Forward" party.' Her aside was spontaneously adopted and it stuck.[119]

The columns of *The Methodist Times* became the vehicle of expression for the movement and Hughes was a passionate advocate of its breadth. 'The Forward Movement is not narrow or obscurantist . . . [its] glory . . . is its many sidedness, its true catholicity, its hearty appreciation of every kind and degree of service, its readiness to welcome everything that is wise everything that is beautiful as well as everything that is good.'[120] He was convinced that science, art and literature, as well as politics, all had a place in the Kingdom of God. Any form of Christianity which neglected them was defective.[121] But political and social reform, without religious reform, was merely the cleansing of the outside of the cup. Following Bushnell's dictum, 'The soul of all improvement is the improvement of the soul', Hughes maintained,

> It is quite evident . . . that political and social reforms, unless accompanied and confirmed by spiritual reforms, will only prove a melancholy disappointment. This does not in the least degree imply that these reforms themselves are undesirable.[122]

The starting point of the Forward Movement was the realisation that the majority of the people of England were unreached with the gospel,[123] and that the pattern for all Christian work was the ministry of Jesus himself.

> That He was our human model as well as our Divine Saviour is the keynote of the Forward Movement. . . . The older evangelicalism was too self-centred, and tended to become self-absorbed. It relied too much on fear and too little upon love.[124]

Christianity ran the risk of being irrelevant if it did not address the conditions, thoughts and insights of contemporary life. Advocating a form of Social Darwinism for the church, the issue was clear, adapt or die![125]

Such a movement was bound to encounter opposition. They were accused of spiritual elitism, but they disclaimed anything so unworthy and responded that a desire to follow the example of Jesus Christ should be every Christian's passion. Others suggested that they were merely a new breed of shallow revivalists, yet they

---

119 D.P. Hughes, *Life of Hugh Price Hughes*, p. 167n; Oldstone-Moore, *Hugh Price Hughes*, p. 135.
120 MT, 27.02.1890.
121 MT, 01.01.1891.
122 MT, 02.04.1891.
123 MT, 26.04.1900.
124 MT, 19.12.1889.
125 MT, 05.03.1885.

pointed out that they maintained that Christianity should satisfy the intellect as well as the emotions and pointed to Dr Moulton, Dr Fairbairn and others who explored the rational aspect of the movement. A further charge of political radicalism was rebutted by showing that leading Methodist Tories like Sir George Chubb and Sir Henry Mitchell identified themselves with the movement. Yet there was a sensitive recognition that a certain amount of friction was bound to be the inevitable outcome of contemporary issues meeting traditional notions and customs.[126]

Aware as they were of the suspicion that attached to the movement they were eager to express their devotion to the Wesleyan spirit.

> The leaders of the Forward Movement are the most loyal, orthodox, and old-fashioned Methodists in the kingdom. Their whole influence arises from the fact that they preach the old-fashioned Gospel with the old-fashioned results.[127]

Furthermore, they rejoiced that the most eager reformers were also the most conspicuously successful men in pulpit and prayer meeting. 'Our leading progressivists do not preach to half-empty chapels, and do not report a decrease in Church members.'[128]

When Dr Moulton used his position as President to eulogise the Forward Movement from the platform of the Conference in 1890, *The Methodist Times* believed that the first stage of the movement was complete.[129] By 1893 great success was attending those who adopted the approach of the movement, 'The former days were not better than these. They were not as good.'[130] At the beginning of 1895 the initiatives of Dr Stephenson with children's provision, Charles Garrett in city mission work and Drs Jenkins, Moulton and Dallinger in intellectual life were praised. The work of the Congregationalists Andrew Mearns and Guinness Rogers, the Baptists Drs Maclaren and Clifford, and the Presbyterians Prof. Dods and Dr White were all cited to show that there was nothing sectarian or limited about the Forward Movement. Rather, it commanded the sympathy of the best Christians of all denominations and was a common heritage.[131] In 1901 they rejoiced that, 'The principles of the Forward Movement have so absolutely prevailed in the hearts and consciences of our people that no one publicly challenges them.'[132]

It became obvious that a movement with such broad sympathies, and so committed to action, ran the risk of superficiality by 'attempting too much in too many directions' and therefore dissipating its spiritual force. So many fascinating spheres and openings led them to a bewildering variety of spiritual and social

[126] MT, 30.10.1890 & 24.04.1890.
[127] MT, 11.10.1888.
[128] MT, 20.08.1891.
[129] MT, 14.08.1890.
[130] MT, 05.10.1893.
[131] MT, 03.01.1895.
[132] MT, 21.02.1901.

opportunities. They needed to beware of an Athenian craze for novelty and its consequences.[133]

On looking back to the origins of the movement, Hughes was happy to acknowledge that it 'originated with the Congregationalists and the epoch-making pamphlet of Rev. A. Mearns'.[134] It is significant too that Hughes also saw William Arthur's *Tongue of Fire* and the Brighton holiness conference of the Pearsall Smiths in 1875 as important tributaries which flowed into the movement.[135]

Yet for Hughes, it was the West London Mission itself that he continually gave himself to. It was,

> the chief and most conspicuous embodiment of those principles of aggressive and intense Christianity which this journal was established to advocate . . . the incarnation of the Forward Movement.[136]

Hugh Price Hughes, the 'Prophet' of the Movement

Hugh Price Hughes' ministry was exercised over the last quarter of the nineteenth century. For many at the time of his death in 1902 he was one of the foremost Nonconformists of the age. Those who have subsequently sought to understand and analyse his legacy have, almost without exception, failed to grasp how he synthesised fidelity to the Wesleyan tradition in which he stood, an entrepreneurial engagement in urban mission, an openness to the insights of late nineteenth century liberal scholarship and a progressivist approach to the social and political issues of the day. Most often this is the consequence of concentrating upon those things which made Hughes different to traditional Wesleyan ministers in the social and political dimensions of his work. As Christopher Oldstone-Moore perceptively points out, this defines Hughes by what he reacted against rather than what he stood for.[137]

This approach has led to a serial misreading of Hughes that fails to do justice to him and the Forward Movement of which he was a part. Variously it has been concluded that his aim was to spread his own elemental brand of 'radical-liberal-socialism' inside Wesleyanism;[138] that this was a smoke-screen that hid personal ambitions of a political and ecclesiastical nature with the lust for power corrupting his moral sense;[139] that he was merely another Victorian motivated by a sense of personal morality,[140] or that he was actually rather vague[141] and while a

[133] MT, 04.11.1897.

[134] MT, 24.10.1901.

[135] MT, 26.05.1895.

[136] MT, 19.04.1894.

[137] Oldstone-Moore, *Hugh Price Hughes*, p. 137.

[138] Jones, *Socialist*, p. 406.

[139] John Kent, 'Hugh Price Hughes and the Nonconformist Conscience' in G.V. Bennett & J.D. Walsh (eds), *Essays in Modern Church History* (New York: OUP, 1966), p. 204; Currie, *Divided Methodism*, p. 178.

[140] Robert Pope, 'Congregations and Community' in Lesley Husselbee & Paul Ballard (eds), *Free Churches and Society: The Nonconformist Contribution to Social Welfare*

decent and dedicated man, he was an unoriginal and hesitant reformer who reflected contemporary issues in the form of the archetypal Nonconformist crusader.[142]

With greater insight it has been suggested that his contribution to late Victorian religious life is best seen from 'the broad perspective of cultural change'[143] during which the churches were beginning to rethink their understanding of themselves and their mission in order to counteract the possibility of cultural isolation. This was certainly true and Hughes was committed to keeping Christianity credible, but attempting to study him as the subject of his nineteenth-century Victorian context also potentially falls into the same trap in understanding the relationship of his traditional evangelical emphases to his more contemporary social, intellectual and political outlook. This juxtaposition of the old and the new in Hughes is therefore adjudged to be a paradox in his thought, albeit a useful one as it gave him a unique position to popularise the new ideas in a framework that was more likely to be acceptable to those within his denomination.[144] Unfortunately this too fails to identify the very real connections that Hughes was making, and the coherent whole that emerges.

Hughes was a passionate evangelist and an ardent follower of John Wesley as well as being a committed social reformer who embraced and campaigned on a progressive raft of political issues. The key question is how these elements fitted together and were synthesised into a whole in his thinking. Oldstone-Moore is right to identify that Hughes' understanding arises from Methodist conversion theology,[145] but it is more than that, it is of a piece, it is a coherent and integrated whole. What emerges from a detailed study of Hughes' life is an experiential theology that is both rooted in and develops the received Wesleyan teaching on conversion and holiness. Key moments, friendships and encounters were formative in his understanding as they inspired, modified and developed his growing comprehension of the missionary challenges that were confronting late Victorian society. In many ways the Forward Movement anticipated many of the developments in mission thinking and practice that a century later would not be considered out of the ordinary. As the pre-eminent and formative voice of the movement Hughes articulated this integration of evangelism, social service and political responsibility alongside embodying it in the West London Mission. The experiential theology he advocated was the fruit of his own experience and was deeply embedded in his own ministry.

1800-2010 (London: Continuum, 2012), p. 35.

141 K.S. Inglis, *Churches and the Working Class in Victorian England* (London: Routledge, 1963), p. 70; Rupert Davies, A. Raymond George & Gordon Rupp (eds), *A History of the Methodist Church in Great Britain*, vol. 3 (London: Epworth, 1983), p. 139.

142 E.R. Norman, *Victorian Christian Socialists* (Cambridge: CUP, 1987), pp. 144-61.

143 William McGuire King, 'Hugh Price Hughes and the British "Social Gospel"', *Journal of Religious History* (June, 1984), pp. 66-67.

144 King, 'Hugh Price Hughes', p. 68.

145 Oldstone-Moore, *Hugh Price Hughes*, p. 336.

Hugh Price Hughes had an unusual ancestry being Welsh on his father's side and Jewish on his mother's. However, his home was devoutly Wesleyan, his grandfather, Hugh Hughes, being the first Welsh Wesleyan minister to be elected to the legal hundred.[146]

It was at the age of thirteen years that Hughes committed himself fully to Christianity. The claim of the faith had obviously been before him from birth, but the visit of some Cornish fishermen to the Chapel he attended at Mumbles Bay left a profound impression that was instrumental in his conversion.[147] A year later he had become a Local Preacher 'on trial', and wrote home from boarding school to his father, 'I believe it is the will of God that I should be a Methodist Preacher.'[148]

On entering Richmond College it seems that Hughes' evangelical fervour had waned. William Taylor, a contemporary of Hughes at Richmond and later to become a renowned evangelist in Australia, - himself founding the Sydney Central Methodist Mission in 1884 - relates how a group of the more devout students at the college formed a small group for prayer and fellowship. Hughes merely poured scorn on their endeavours, using it as an opportunity to exercise his crushing satire.[149] His preference was for the college cricket team, of which he was captain, and assuring the provision of a barrel of beer on the field for the refreshment of the players.[150]

He left Richmond in 1869, at the age of twenty-two and was sent for his first appointment to Dover where three experiences were to prove significant and formative for the young minister. First, on his opening Sunday he preached on the text, 'What think ye of Christ?' Much to Hughes' surprise some eighteen people were converted after hearing him preach.[151] This appears to have been a turning point for him in moving away from his previous evangelistic scepticism. Taylor remembers that when Hughes returned to college after a year in Dover, the first thing he did was to organise a prayer meeting.[152] Second, from his study window in the house adjoining Buckland Chapel he could see three public houses, and he was not slow in recognising the evils of excessive drinking. Again he moved from the position he had held in college, though many were frustrated that he would not go the way of the extreme party.[153] Third, and perhaps most significant for Hughes' later pioneering stance on social issues, was his association with Alderman Rees, a Welsh radical. Rees took him to hear Josephine Butler, the wife of an Anglican clergyman from Liverpool who was campaigning for the abolition of the

---

[146] Arthur Walters, *Hugh Price Hughes: Pioneer and Reformer* (London: Robert Culley, 1907), p. 24.

[147] D.P. Hughes, *Life of Hugh Price Hughes*, pp. 20-21; Walters, *Hugh Price Hughes*, p. 29.

[148] Walters, *Hugh Price Hughes*, p. 34.

[149] Taylor, Taylor, *Taylor of Down Under*, p. 63.

[150] Walters, *Hugh Price Hughes*, p. 45.

[151] Walters, *Hugh Price Hughes*, pp. 46-47.

[152] Taylor, *Taylor of Down Under*, p. 64.

[153] Walters, *Hugh Price Hughes*, pp. 47-50.

Contagious Diseases Acts. It is reported that the meeting reduced Hughes to tears and as a result he became actively involved in the agitation for repeal.[154] Butler said later that she could always depend upon Hughes' support, and for that she was very thankful. Oldstone-Moore reflects that as Hughes analysed the interconnection between the personal, social and religious dimension of his experience in evangelism, temperance and the Contagious Diseases Act repeal movement the shape of his future ministry begins to take shape.[155]

From Dover Hughes moved to Brighton and it was just prior to his departure from there that another significant and formative experience occurred in the summer of 1875. A combination of exhaustion from his circuit ministry combined with his educational, political and temperance work alongside disillusionment at little progress and success left Hughes wrestling with depression.[156] At this low point he attended a Holiness Convention being held in the town under the leadership of the Americans Robert and Hannah Pearsall Smith. They preached on the theme that sin was not a necessary condition of existence, but that a special outpouring of God's Spirit could lead to holiness of thought and act. Rooted in the American holiness doctrine preached by the evangelist Phoebe Palmer the message delivered by the Quaker Pearsall Smiths was an intensely hopeful one.[157] This was exactly what Hughes needed and he immediately recognised it as a restatement of part of Wesley's understanding of 'entire sanctification' which had largely been neglected by the late nineteenth century. During their meetings Hughes himself had a significant spiritual experience as he felt God dealing with certain ambitions that lurked in his own heart and mind. His daughter explained that Brighton was a time of spiritual crisis in his life, a crisis where the need was met through the ministry of the Pearsall Smiths, giving him a new spiritual depth that was to be the central beam in his own work as the Methodist Conference was later to acknowledge.[158] Certainly Hughes' daughter saw this experience as very significant to his later understanding. In fact it became more and more important to him that 'God's will concerning a man must be altogether for his ultimate and deepest self-expression and happiness.'[159]

Renewed by this experience and having moved to London to the Tottenham Circuit, he accepted the secretaryship of a new city-wide initiative, the Wesleyan

---

[154] David Bebbington, *The Nonconformist Conscience* (London: George Allen & Unwin, 1982), p. 41; Gwyther, *The Methodist Social and Political Theory and Practice*, pp. 119-20; Oldstone-Moore, *High Price Hughes*, pp. 37-39.

[155] Oldstone-Moore, *Hugh Price Hughes*, pp. 39, 46.

[156] Oldstone-Moore, *Hugh Price Hughes*, pp. 60-61.

[157] Nancy Hardesty, 'Hannah Whitehall Smith found the secret', *Daughters of Sarah*, 10.5 (1984), pp. 20-22; M.E. Dieter, 'From Vineland and Manheim to Brighton and Berlin: the holiness revival in nineteenth-century Europe', *Wesleyan Theological Journal* 9 (March 1, 1974), p. 21; Carole Dale Spencer, 'Hannah Whitall Smith and the Evolution of Quakerism: An Orthodox Heretic in an Age of Controversy', *Quaker Studies*, 18.1 (2013), pp. 7-22.

[158] D.P. Hughes, *Life of Hugh Price Hughes*, p. 105.

[159] D.P. Hughes, *Life of Hugh Price Hughes*, p. 105.

London Mission which was to be modelled on Moody's mission to the capitol the previous year. With a thousand commitments made over the eight days of meetings the mission was pronounced a success. Two months later Hughes had redesigned the strategy for his own chapel in Tottenham, mobilised as a large number of lay people from the congregation in its running and held his first 'Revival Mission'. For the next decade in Tottenham, Dulwich and Oxford this became an integral part of his evangelistic work and in 1883 the Conference appointed him as one of the Connexional Revivalists. Conducting seven Revival Missions during the year Hughes saw more than 2,500 recorded conversions under his ministry.[160]

Walters maintains that while he was in college Hughes' real passion was the desire to face the intellectual difficulties of the day.[161] His later writing was peppered with references to Carlyle, Ruskin, Browning, Spencer and others including his favourite writer, Mazzini, whose 'rights presuppose duties' doctrine Hughes found particularly attractive. It is not surprising then that in the appointments that followed Brighton Hughes undertook and completed an M.A. at London University and set himself the task of learning German so as to be able to read German philosophy. All of this he achieved without his Superintendent Minister or congregation being aware of it.[162] This desire for knowledge never left him and in its turn was to be stimulated and enlarged by his appointment to Oxford. It was there that he met and became a student and friend of the Idealist philosopher, T.H. Green with whom he made a meaningful connection.[163]

This friendship with Green and his attendance at a course of his lectures at the university had a profound and lasting effect upon him.[164] Green's teaching built on Hughes' already developing 'social emphasis', and gave him the intellectual equipment with which to state his case in the way he had desired since his college days. His emphasis on altruism, self-sacrifice and the abandonment of self-sufficiency in favour of the fulfilment of social and political obligations caught Hughes' imagination and it is easy to trace this influence on his social and philosophical understanding.[165] Furthermore, as Green's ethic of altruism was grounded in the belief that the spring of all ethical action is the human need for religious self-realisation, Hughes found what he believed to be a philosophical vehicle for expressing Wesley's understanding of Christian perfection. He later commented, 'The ethics it vehemently enforced were precisely . . . what we Methodists call Entire Sanctification, or Christian Holiness or Perfect Love.'[166]

In what may well have been Green's last public address before his premature death Hughes invited him to speak to his Chapel Literary Society. Yet however far

---

[160] Oldstone-Moore, *Hugh Price Hughes*, pp. 69-72, 102-03.
[161] Walters, *Hugh Price Hughes*, p. 43.
[162] Walters, *Hugh Price Hughes*, p. 58.
[163] Denys P. Leighton, *The Greenian moment: T.H. Green, Religion and Political Argument in Victorian Britain* (Exeter: Imprint Academic, 2004), p. 250.
[164] D.P. Hughes, *Life of Hugh Price Hughes*, p. 134.
[165] Leighton, *The greenian moment*, p. 272.
[166] Hugh Price Hughes, *Social Christianity* (London: Hodder & Stoughton, 1889), p. 97.

Hughes went with Green, he parted company with him where his theology became reductionist, albeit allowing that Green was an 'unconscious Christian'.[167]

In 1884 Hughes returned to London as the minister at Brixton Hill, and while there he launched *The Methodist Times* in 1885. The following year saw him appointed to the West London Mission, and the stage was set for his increasingly influential ministry.

In any analysis of Hughes' thought it must be remembered that of first importance to him was his own personal experience of Christ that had begun at Mumbles Bay, was re-awakened at Dover and deepened significantly at Brighton. 'Nothing was as near his heart as this - bringing individual men to Christ - for this was the end of all that he did and wished.' Yet his developing ideas regarding Social Christianity where thoroughly integrated in his understanding, as his daughter recollected: 'he knew Christ first as his own personal Saviour, and it was this aspect that he dealt with in the pulpit, though the two overlapped each other. They were so merged in him, that they became more and more merged in his teaching.'[168]

Dorothea also recalled that in the earlier part of his ministry Hughes was much in demand as a revivalist for special meetings and campaigns because of his powerful evangelistic preaching. The Wesleyan Conference also noted this in his obituary: 'His powerful preaching led to the conversions of multitudes; . . . all the gifts which he thus displayed were combined in his work as an evangelist, and consecrated by an intense passion for the salvation of men.'[169]

Hughes was disturbed by what he saw as Wesleyanism's wandering from its evangelistic origins.

> Methodism came into existence as an effort to attain a higher level of spirituality. Methodism proposed to seek a more intense, self-sacrificing and enthusiastic form of Christianity than was required by ordinary conditions of religious profession in this country. If we have lost that special desire, our raison d'être is gone.[170]

His appeal was to the experience of his hearers. He asked one of his congregations,

> Let us talk about Jesus Christ. Do you know HIM? He has been my most intimate friend for nearly 30 years. Have you any personal acquaintance with HIM? . . . Is there someone in this vast audience to whom, by my voice, God sends this last appeal? Do YOU not know that every hour you delay to accept Christ, you are changing your heart, you are forming your final character, you are making your soul proof against the love of God? The hour of final choice draws nearer, nearer, nearer. You may have entered upon it now. Repent. Escape for your life. Flee to Christ, and all will yet be well.[171]

---

[167] Hughes, *Social Christianity*, p. 98.
[168] D.P. Hughes, *Life of Hugh Price Hughes*, pp. 80 & 226.
[169] Minutes 1903, pp. 132-33.
[170] MT, 20.05.1886.
[171] Hughes, *Social Christianity*, pp. 200 & 281.

Hughes' evangelism was also alive to the ethical dimension of proselytising. He dismissed as 'a fearful perversion' that form of preaching which sought a response to the gospel from a self-interest to get to heaven. Indeed, because of his reluctance to manipulate people by fear, and his vocal condemnation of overemphasis on hell and judgement, Robert Currie charges him with being only half-hearted in his pursuit of sinners.[172] Nothing could have been further from the truth. Hughes unashamedly preached for conversions and many occurred. A personal recollection of Arthur Walters sheds eloquent light on this part of Hughes' work.

> His passion for souls was remarkable. The evangelical doctrine of conversion was an essential article of his faith . . . I have seen him weep when there has been but little visible result to his ministry, and his delight was intense when under his teaching sinners sought salvation.[173]

With many other Wesleyans, Hughes felt able to endorse the visit of the American revivalist D.L. Moody. He took his daughters to hear him speak at Oxford, and told them that they would be proud in the future to have heard him.[174] Moody was an inspiration to him as he seemed to demonstrate how ready the masses still were to respond to the gospel.[175]

His theological understanding of evangelism was evangelically orthodox, and is best summed up in his own words from the last article he wrote for *The Methodist Times*.

> It is by proclaiming the sinfulness of sin, and the love of God as revealed in the cross, and the power of the cross to deliver us from the power of sin, that we shall melt the hearts of men. . . . Real Christianity consists of a real and living union between Jesus Christ and a converted man.[176]

In this revived emphasis on evangelism Hughes believed that young Methodists were returning to their roots. He took courage from the fact that Wesley was always abreast of the times and unhesitatingly introduced startling novelties of both organisation and method. They were the heirs of Wesley and should therefore act in the same way: 'he attacked all the greatest social evils in plain, brave language, and, did his utmost for the bodies and minds, as well as the souls of men.'[177]

It was this infant social holiness that Hughes perceived in Wesley that he felt he was developing in harmony with the Methodist tradition. Rack notes his condemnation of the Anglican 'holiness' conventions of the 1880s because they lacked an ethical and social application. Yet he still spoke at the Southport

---

[172] Robert Currie, 'Were the Central Halls a Failure?' *New Directions* (Spring 1967), p. 22.
[173] Walters, *Hugh Price Hughes*, p. 15.
[174] D.P. Hughes, *Life of Hugh Price Hughes*, pp. 158-59.
[175] Oldstone-Moore, *Hugh Price Hughes*, pp. 111-12.
[176] Walters, *Hugh Price Hughes*, p. 80.
[177] MT, 01.04.1886 & 06.01.1887.

Methodist Holiness Convention that fortunately did not suffer from the weakness of the evangelical Anglicans.[178]

Hughes' position was clear. *The Wesleyan Magazine* reported that he attributed the secret of his success to 'absolute, unconditional, self-surrender to Jesus Christ and as an inevitable consequence a determination . . . that the will of God shall be done by men and women on the pavements of West London.'[179]

In the first report of the West London Mission Hughes maintains that the ethical teaching of Christ was applicable to every sphere of life, business, pleasure and politics as well as prayer meetings and the sacraments. For one address he took the text, 'The righteous taketh knowledge of the cause of the poor: the wicked hath not understanding to know it' (Proverbs 24:7). This, he felt, was the test of Scriptural goodness.[180] His view of the Kingdom of God was important for his social teaching too. He rejected Augustine's identification of the Christian church with the Kingdom preferring to see the church in relation to the Kingdom in much the same way that the British army stood in relation to the Empire.[181] His view of social holiness was positive as God's will ultimately led to man's deepest self-expression and happiness.

Traditional evangelicalism saw poverty as the result of sin or as the judgement of divinely instituted economic laws. Whether one or the other it was not prudent to question the way things were.[182] The answer was always conversion and the experience of 'redemption and lift' as the reconstructed sinner found that hard work, honesty and trustworthiness paid their own dividend. Hughes and those who thought like him challenged this: 'The Christian citizen whose imagination is inspired of God, dreams of social changes which would make it as easy for his fellow citizens to do right as it is now for them to do wrong.'[183]

In the introduction to a book of his sermons on the subject of *Social Christianity*, Hughes maintained, 'Christ came to save the nation as well as the individual . . . it is an essential feature of His mission to reconstruct human society on the basis of justice and love.'[184] Through the columns of *The Methodist Times* and the agencies of the West London Mission Hughes relentlessly pursued this policy.

He fought for improvements in recreation, sanitation, housing and medical services and advocated prison reform, child welfare legislation, the emancipation of women and the municipalisation of utilities.[185] Much of Hughes' social teaching first saw the light of day in his Sunday Afternoon Conferences at St James' Hall

---

[178] Henry Rack, *The Future of John Wesley's Methodism* (London: Lutterworth, 1965), p. 34.

[179] WMM 1892, p. 75.

[180] Hughes, *Social Christianity*, p. 167.

[181] King, 'Hugh Price Hughes', p. 80.

[182] Inglis, *Churches and the Working Class*, pp. 180-81.

[183] Norman, *Victorian Christian Socialists*, pp. 150-51.

[184] Hughes, *Social Christianity*, viii.

[185] King, 'Hugh Price Hughes', p. 77; Gwyther, *The Methodist Social and Political Theory and Practice*, pp. 235-36.

where Gwyther considers to be a land mark in the development of social witness within Methodism.[186]

It was often at these Conferences that Hughes spoke out on the issues that were also concerns of the 'Nonconformist Conscience', the conviction was that politics should have a moral foundation and that these moral principles should be applied to concrete situations. They did not believe that legislation could make people moral, but they did believe that it had an educative effect for good or ill. Most of their campaigns were turned into moral crusades against some evil or injustice. They were therefore of necessity negative, calling for immediate action for which compromise was impossible. Hughes shared these values and summed them up in a phrase he used during the Parnell affair that arose following the politician's adultery while pursuing Irish home rule. Hughes was clear, 'What is morally wrong can never be politically right.'[187]

Politically the 'Nonconformist Conscience' most often seemed to side with the Liberals, although Hughes did try to keep himself above party politics. In *The Methodist Times* of 15 January 1885 he encouraged all Christians, whether Conservative or Liberal, to get involved in the coming election for the good influence they could exert. Also in his presidential address to the Conference he maintained that every church should be broad enough to provide a home for people of all political opinions.[188]

Through it all, the desire of the movement of which Hughes was the widely acknowledged spokesman and representative was to re-awaken their elders to duties which they felt they had forgotten, especially that of working out Christianity afresh in the light of secular knowledge and opinion. This involved engaging and grappling with a changing society. Hughes wanted to make Christianity credible again for his own age. He even advocated that ministers should be relieved of administration to tackle the underlying difficulty of applying the gospel to contemporary life.[189] *The New History of Methodism* puts it very well by affirming that he wanted to clothe the old truths in present dress, while retaining an unsurpassed loyalty to the old truths themselves.[190]

The Methodist Times, the 'Voice' of the Movement

It was through the columns of *The Methodist Times* that Hughes sought to give voice to this new movement within Methodism. He had begun the paper after seeking advice from Dr Moulton at Cambridge having previously been encouraged to consider the project.[191] W.M. Crook, who met with Hughes weekly during his six years as the sub-editor at the paper only remembered three leading articles that

---

[186] Gwyther, *The Methodist Social and Political Theory and Practice*, p. 147.
[187] Gwyther, *The Methodist Social and Political Theory and Practice*, p. 155.
[188] Edwards, *Methodism*, p. 149.
[189] MT, 19.02.1885.
[190] Townsend, Workman & Eayrs, *A New History of Methodism*, 1. p. 460.
[191] MT, 10.02.1898.

were not written by his proprietor in the whole eighteen years of his editorship.[192] Hughes was no editor in name only. He took a lively interest in all aspects of the paper. A letter to Crook in 1894 took his junior to task on matters of content, presentation, vetting of articles and style.[193]

From the very outset on 1 January 1885 the direction of the paper was clearly defined by its prominent subtitle, 'A Journal of Religious and Social Movement'. Hughes later wrote, '*The Methodist Times* did not come into existence as a commercial speculation, but was started avowedly for the purpose of creating and supporting a Forward Movement in the Christian Churches at home and abroad.'[194] Convinced that this work was 'a sacred cause', he continued, 'We believe that Science, Art, and Literature, as well as Politics, must all be included in the Kingdom of GOD, and that any form of Christianity which ignores them is so far defective and destined to suffer, both in authority and in attractiveness.'[195]

In the first edition of the paper Hughes outlined its four central aims.[196] First there was to be an openness to the best modern thought, discoveries of science and the generous humanitarianism of the day. He felt this was in harmony with the broad, catholic and tender-hearted theology of early Methodism and addressed his fear that the younger generation of Methodists were in danger of being lost to the denomination, not because they were alienated from the spirit of John Wesley, but because Wesleyanism was failing to engage with the developments of the age.

The second aim was motivated by the realisation that the church had got into a lower middle-class rut. Hughes believed that they were losing touch with skilled artisans and agricultural labourers. Appropriate evangelism would be necessary, as would identification with the concerns and needs of the people.

Third, the paper was to be an organ of independent, intelligent and courteous discussion. While his own journalistic style could at times suffer from exaggerated and overblown rhetoric, this policy with regard to the content of the paper was one that was consistently followed, opening its columns to those who took alternative approaches to that taken by the editorial line of the journal. In January 1886 the Home Rule issue was debated from both sides on consecutive weeks,[197] while in June 1901 it was the turn of the anti-war party during the Boer conflict to make their argument, an issue on which Hughes had taken much criticism for supporting the policy of the Empire in prosecuting the war.[198] Commenting in an 1894 editorial Hughes wrote, 'Our Labour correspondent sometimes expresses strong opinions

---

[192] W.M. Crook, 'An Appreciation of Hugh Price Hughes' (Newpaper Cutting marked, M.L. 19.11.1902), Dover Methodist Circuit Archive material.

[193] Letter from Hugh Price Hughes to W.M. Crook, dated 26.04.1894. The papers of William Montgomery Crook, 1883-1944 (Bodleian Library, Oxford), Ref: MSS. Eng. Hist. d365-404.

[194] MT, 02.01.1890.

[195] MT, 01.01.1891.

[196] MT, 01.01.1885.

[197] MT, 14.01.1886

[198] MT, 11.07.1901.

with which we do not agree, but we do not believe that the habit of the ostrich who puts his head into the sand is a right example for Christian journalists.'[199]

The final aim was to provide information on the life of the other Christian communities and commentary on events in the world at large. The list of Members of Parliament, reformers, labour leaders and Churchmen who wrote for the paper at some point is long indeed. R.W. Dale, R.F. Horton, A.M. Fairbairn, W.T. Stead, John Clifford, F.B. Meyer and Josephine Butler were some of the prominent Christians who made contributions.[200] In its inaugural year the paper also received contributions among others from John Burnett of the Amalgamated Society of Engineers, William Crawford of the Miners' National Union, Samuel Smith, M.P., and James Howard, M.P.

Time had moved on considerably when the paper was able to report in 1898 that it was 'the most widely-quoted religious newspaper in the English speaking world'.[201] In fact, a year later as Hughes was reviewing the progress of their original aims he declared, 'That policy has now completely triumphed in the administration of modern Methodism. Every item of the programme which we announced in our first number has been realised, or is in obvious process of realisation. . . . Those who most strenuously opposed our programme in the press and on the platform are to-day among its heartiest advocates.[202]

In 1900, with the dawn of a new century, Hughes restated the paper's aims in the light of their overwhelming success. They were now committed to aggressive evangelism, the reunion of Methodism, a federation of all the Protestant Free Churches throughout the world and the application of Christian principles to every phase and aspect of human life.[203]

Hughes edited *The Methodist Times* from 1885 till his death in 1902 and the editorial columns were his own weekly opportunity to address those committed to the Forward Movement. Indeed the sub-title of the paper itself was 'A Journal of Religious and Social Movement'. These editorial leading articles provide a rich source with which to interrogate the substance of the movement. They provided the front page headline for the week, setting both the tone and the agenda of the newspaper. Beneath the stated objectives of the publication, on a week-by-week basis they are indicative of what was catching their attention, occupying their concern and mobilising their energies. Do the stated objectives stand the scrutiny of their printed copy over an extended period of time? What picture emerges from this ongoing communication and commentary from the epicentre of the Forward Movement?

An analysis of the 884 editorial leaders from 1 January 1885 to 26 December 1901 is a revealing. First and foremost it is clear that the paper is writing from a

---

[199] MT, 04.01.1894.

[200] See also the Crook papers: letter from John Clifford dated, 12.11.1892 and letter from R.W. Dale dated, 12.12.1892.

[201] MT, 06.01.1898.

[202] MT, 05.01.1899.

[203] MT, 04.01.1900.

position of evangelical commitment rooted in the Wesleyan tradition. The personal encounter with God in Christ through the experience of conversion and entire sanctification are the fountainhead from which everything else flows. Out of a vital and living faith issues a commitment not only to personal holiness and morality, but also to social holiness and the transformation of society. Informed by the best insights of contemporary thought and committed to social and political activism the movement pursued 'Applied Christianity' in the life of their communities and the life of the nation. Such an agenda threw into high relief the need for the renewal of Methodism and its democratisation, alongside the need for Christian unity to more effectively marshal their resources and through a common voice, more clearly address and influence those in power. For Hughes Christian unity had three dimensions: Methodist reunion, Free Church federation and evangelical cooperation.[204]

Experiential Theology

Hughes was an orthodox evangelical and his writing illustrated that. Yet he was also prepared to take his readers further than traditional formulations too, by criticising them, challenging them and building upon them. Illustrative of this is his treatment of evangelical individualism. In his Christmas message of 1891 he spoke in clear terms of the individual's intimate relationship with Christ:

> personal submission to the personal CHRIST, personal trust in the personal CHRIST, personal obedience to the personal CHRIST are three phases of one and the same thing . . . Christianity.[205]

On other occasions he complained that older evangelicalism had been excessively individualistic, self-centred and self-absorbed. It had depended too much upon fear and too little upon love.[206] The scope of salvation was much broader:

> The individualist Christian is quite right in his assumption that the first and fundamental necessity is to bring the individual into his right relation to CHRIST, but he is quite mistaken in supposing that this is the sole or entire work of Christianity. When the individual is truly saved, society in all its collectivist aspects must be saved also.[207]

The place of the cross was central to Hughes' evangelicalism. He held that without an adequate explanation of the atonement, Christianity was a cold and dismal failure. He considered the cross to be the full revelation of both the love of God and

---

[204] In very broad and general terms an analysis of the main subject of Hughes' leading articles sees around 35% addressing some aspect of Methodism; 30% dealing primarily with social or political issues; 10% featuring the wider life of the Christian churches outside of Methodism; 10% the consideration of contemporary secular and theological thought with the remaining 10% of a spiritual or devotional nature. Across these subjects evangelism also occurs significantly in approximately 10% of the articles.

[205] MT, 24.12.1891.

[206] MT, 19.12.1889.

[207] MT, 26.03.1896.

the sinfulness of sin[208] and was concerned at those who preached Christ, but not 'Christ crucified'. The centre of apostolic theology 'was not the cradle but the cross'.[209] To the divine side of the atonement men are strangers, but to the human side we can see that Christ 'died literally of a broken heart, and his heart was broken . . . by the wickedness of His brother-men.'[210]

It was, however, Hughes' understanding of holiness that enabled him to develop a theological basis for his social and political activities. He stood within the Wesleyan tradition with its emphasis on entire sanctification, but he took seriously the challenge of R.W. Dale to the Birmingham Conference of 1879:

> [T]he doctrine of perfect sanctification . . . ought to have led to a great and original ethical development; but the doctrine has not grown, it seems to remain just where John Wesley left it. There has been a want of the genius or the courage to attempt the solution of the immense practical questions which the doctrine suggests.[211]

Hughes wrote that he believed the launch of the Southport Methodist Holiness Convention in July 1886 would be, 'the birth of a new era . . . the Pentecost of modern Methodism'.[212] For Wesleyan minds in the late nineteenth century holiness and the baptism in the Holy Spirit went together. Holiness was the fruit of the Spirit's enabling activity following the believer's absolute surrender of their life to Christ. As Hughes rose to Dale's challenge it was inevitable that he would further explore the role of the Holy Spirit as he discovered new dimensions of 'social holiness'. By 1894 he felt that the Church had begun to address these issues.

> During the fifteen years which have elapsed since those words were uttered there has been a great change, and Methodism has done much to redeem herself from the reproach of ethical sterility. We no longer shrink . . . from the discharge of our political duties. We are beginning to apply our ethical conceptions to business, to literature, and to art.[213]

Four particular sources fed Hughes' understanding on this subject. His experiences at Brighton under the ministry of Robert and Hannah Pearsall Smith and his discernment of T.H. Green's philosophy as being of a kind with entire sanctification have already been noted. Added to these was the abiding influence of William Arthur's work on the Holy Spirit, *The Tongue of Fire*, which had been published in 1856. By this time Arthur was an elder statesman, and while his book had been widely read it had not given rise to any abiding change. Arthur's work was a wide ranging discussion of the ministry of the third person of the Trinity which in many ways anticipated much of what Hughes was to emphasise. Arthur, for example,

---

[208] MT, 30.03.1893.
[209] MT, 28.11.1895.
[210] MT, 02.04.1896.
[211] MT, 04.02.1886; A.W.W. Dale, *The Life of R.W. Dale of Birmingham* (London: Hodder & Stoughton, 1898), pp. 348-49.
[212] MT, 08.07.1886.
[213] MT, 20.12.1894.

while being concerned about entire sanctification was concerned that evangelicals had too often neglected studying the application of holiness to social evils.[214] Hughes regularly refers to Arthur – only refuting the need to 'tarry'[215] – and often quotes him with no reference at all.

The fourth source from which Hughes drew came relatively late to his experience, and he first reveals it in an article entitled, 'The "sine qua non" of the Forward Movement' in 1895. In it he traces the genesis of the movement through William Arthur and D.L. Moody. After being sanctified by Pearsall Smith the Forward Movement emerged in the 1880s receiving a fresh challenge at the appearance of Reader Harris and the Pentecostal League.

> Harris's work is the absolutely necessary complement to our own Forward Movement. We cannot carry out our programme successfully without that 'fullness of the Spirit' which he incessantly preaches; and, . . . his teaching on that subject would become dangerously subjective and sentimental unless the emotion which it awakened was incessantly expended upon the practical and social features of the Forward Movement.[216]

It was not that Harris taught Hughes anything new as his emphasis on the need for a new 'outpouring of the Holy Spirit' had been constant from the beginning. Harris did, however, stimulate a renewed concern in seeking the baptism in the Spirit and the consequential fruit of holiness. The editorials in *The Methodist Times* majored on the subject no fewer than seven times in 1895.[217] Hughes was happy to have his name associated with the Pentecostal League, and in an address to the Conference said, 'I am one of the most cautious of men in joining anything new, but I see no danger in uniting with others in praying every day that we may all be continually filled with the Holy Spirit.'[218]

The supreme and divine condition for prosperity in the Church was the sanctifying, vivifying, and strengthening influence of a Pentecostal outpouring of the Holy Spirit.[219] As President of the Conference in 1898 he called for 'fresh baptisms of the Holy Spirit' upon Methodism, and a return to first principles and the work of spreading Scriptural holiness throughout the world. To this end he then convened district gatherings for ministers and lay leaders for 'mutual encouragement and for the deepening of the spiritual life'.[220] Such a baptism was

---

[214] William Arthur, *The Tongue of Fire: Or, The True Power of Christianity* (London: Hamilton Adams, 1856), pp. 86-87; Norman W. Taggart, *William Arthur: First Among Methodists* (London: Epworth, 1993), pp. 57-58.

[215] MT, 21.01.1897.

[216] MT, 20.06.1895.

[217] MT, 14.03.1895; 02.05.1895; 23.05.1895; 30.05.1895; 20.06.1895; 04.07.1895; 11.07.1895.

[218] Mary R. Hooker, *Adventures of an Agnostic, the Life and Letters of Reader Harris, Q.C.* (London: Marshall, Morgan & Scott, 1959), p. 115.

[219] MT, 05.03.1885; 02.05.1895; 11.07.1895; 15.09.1892.

[220] MT, 11.08.1898; Oldstone-Moore, *Hugh Price Hughes*, pp. 306-07.

not an exceptional experience bestowed occasionally upon eminent saints, but an ordinary and constant experience of filling for every believer.[221] Such Pentecostal blessing was not the result of growth but was a gift bestowed by the Father in heaven.[222]

It was only 'by the direct personal action of the Spirit of God upon the spirit of man that man is saved'. Catholic ritual and Protestant rationalism could not provide the miracle,[223] neither could man change society by the ingenuity of his intellect or the hard work of his brow. But a Church that was 'founded by the Holy Spirit', released from the 'chronic spiritual dyspepsia' of lazy, over-fed Christians,[224] and 'deliberately, whole-heartedly, unreservedly, and unconditionally at the disposal of the LORD JESUS CHRIST' (which implied entire sanctification),[225] could, as Charles Garrett had said, 'do good to all men'. Such a living, unselfish Church, 'full of moral courage, invincible heroism and Divine authority',[226] would bring a Pentecostal blessing on all men, and could be called, 'if we may invent a term, Pentecostalism'. Hughes quoted Arthur, 'I expect to see cities swept from end to end, their manners elevated, their commerce purified, their politics Christianised, their criminal population reformed, their poor made to feel that they dwell amongst brethren. . . . because I believe in the Holy Ghost.'[227]

Hughes was careful in all his talk about spiritual experience, abandonment to God and dependence upon the Holy Spirit to guard his position. It did not mean idleness and carelessness; neither did an outpouring of the Spirit imply not using one's brains or wits. Such a view to Hughes was puerile and mischievous.[228] The Bible was always the check and safeguard for personal experience, and kept the believer from subjective delusion.[229]

Concentration on the work of the Holy Spirit brought new and exciting discoveries. The first Pentecostal blessing came when the early Church were 'in one place of one accord'. It was not a private blessing but a corporate one that depended upon Christian unity. In addition they recognised that, 'The Pentecostal blessing was bestowed upon every . . . man, woman and child in the primitive church of Jerusalem.' The implications for participation, involvement and democracy in church life were obvious.[230]

Hughes was convinced that he was building firmly on Wesley's foundation, not only on his development of the doctrine of the entire sanctification and the work of the Holy Spirit, but also in every dimension of his teaching as 'The Forward Party

---

[221] MT, 30.05.1895.
[222] MT, 31.05.1900.
[223] MT, 25.04.1889.
[224] MT, 31.05.1888.
[225] MT, 20.09.1900.
[226] MT, 18.05.1899.
[227] MT, 14.03.1895.
[228] MT, 08.09.1892; 11.06.1896 (+17.08.1893).
[229] MT, 24.09.1896.
[230] MT, 07.04.1898; 28.12.1893.

desires nothing that cannot be justified and illustrated from Wesley's journal.'[231] Everything Hughes did linked into this experiential theology. It was orthodox, yet interactive with the contemporary world and thus developing to meet the challenges of a new age. He was traditional in his call for more prominence to be given to the spiritual side of Trustees' Meetings and Synods,[232] and yet prophetic as he suggested that the Kingship of Christ and the Kingdom of God would become the distinctive notes of twentieth-century Christianity.[233]

Such was the evangelical experiential theology from within which Hughes sought to apply the Christian faith to contemporary issues and the situations that confronted him. This was the hallmark of the Forward Movement which, at its heart, desired a simple and yet profound devotion to Jesus Christ in everything: what Dr. Maclaren had called an 'evangelical mysticism'.[234]

Engagement with Contemporary Thought

The editorial leaders of a popular weekly newspaper are hardly the forum for learned analysis of contemporary thought and, while in other sections of the paper they occupied greater space, even in the prime front page headline of the editorial Hughes attempted to enlighten his readers to some of the talking points of the day where they had some particular relevance to Christianity. He was concerned that new ideas were often masked by prejudice and bigotry on both sides.

> Both sides must be purged of this tendency to misrepresent . . . scientists . . . must practice more of the accuracy and candour they preach; evangelicals must learn . . . from their own highest source of inspiration, to welcome and appreciate 'whatsoever things are true'.[235]

Hughes was confident that nothing in scholarship could genuinely shake the substance of faith as Christians had nothing to fear from that which was demonstrably true. Rooted in Isaiah's prophetic vision of the triumph of good, and holding Wesley to be one of the first 'scientific theologians', his optimistic postmillennial hopefulness led him to believe that the gospel was steadily transforming the world into the Kingdom of God.[236] This gave him both the willingness and the predisposition to engage with contemporary thinking and the results of scientific research. It also provided him with the tools to be a robust conversation partner as the fruit modern scholarship was subject to theological examination.

---

[231] MT, 17.03.1887.
[232] MT, 12.03.1896.
[233] MT, 12.04.1900.
[234] MT, 17.10.1901.
[235] MT, 03.09.1885.
[236] Oldstone-Moore, *Hugh Price Hughes*, p. 245; David Bebbington, 'Conscience and Politics' in Lesley Husselbee & Paul Ballard (eds), *Free Churches and Society: The Nonconformist Contribution to Social Welfare 1800-2010* (London: Continuum, 2012), p. 56.

At the close of the century he concluded that there had been three main areas of intellectual debate which had been of particular concern to evangelicals, 'Natural Science, the Higher Criticism, and Socialism'.[237] Over the years the paper had addressed each of these issues.

The main debate in science had been the continuing controversy surrounding Darwin's theory of evolution. Hughes was happy to identify the paper initially with Alfred Russell Wallace, and latterly with E. Griffith Jones. Some believed that Wallace's work on evolution antedated Darwin. This was particularly appealing to evangelicals like Hughes, as Wallace's Christian belief and rationale was a great boost to the apologetic task of encouraging believers to take seriously the insights of contemporary thought. '[T]he fact that the original discoverer of Darwinism has proved not only that there is no antagonism between Darwinism and Christianity, but that the discoveries on which Darwinism rests cannot be explained by Materialistic Atheism.' [238] Griffith Jones was a Congregationalist who demonstrated in his *Ascent Through Christ*, that he found no 'incompatibility between Evangelical Christianity and the Theory of Evolution'.[239]

The Higher Criticism of the Bible also caused trouble in many quarters, particularly among the Baptists. But again Hughes was eager to weigh the issues and accept what was good and proven. 'So far as the results of the Higher Criticism have been established they have given the Holy Scriptures new meaning, new beauty, a new power over the heart and conscience.' [240] He welcomed the disturbance that turned believers away from notions of the 'infallibility' of the Bible, towards the 'infallibility of JESUS CHRIST'.[241] However, he was also prepared to speak against those whose scepticism read more into their results than were there.[242]

The scholarship of the Revised Version of the Bible made it simply 'the best English Bible that has ever seen the light'.[243] Its accuracy meant, 'It is the only version published in the English language which gives us . . . [the] genuine teaching of the inspired men who wrote the Bible.'[244] It was this understanding of the inspiration of the Scriptures that allowed Hughes to appropriate the lessons of Higher Criticism.

Socialism had much to teach Christians if the church was really serious about reaching the working classes with the gospel and transforming society. To answer socialistic excesses it was necessary to be familiar with their thought. Ministers particularly had a duty to familiarise themselves with the thoughts and emotions which were stirring the hearts of men. Hughes wondered how many had read

---

[237] MT, 26.01.1899.
[238] MT, 11.07.1889.
[239] MT, 06.04.1899.
[240] MT, 01.12.1892.
[241] MT, 05.06.1890.
[242] MT, 31.10.1901.
[243] MT, 03.11.1887.
[244] MT, 20.05.1897.

Merrie England, a book by Nonquam – the Socialist editor of *The Clarion*, Richard Blatchford – which had sold 700,000 copies between October 1894 and January 1895.[245]

Hughes was particularly intrigued by the thought of Benjamin Kidd in his published work, *Social Darwinism*, of 1894. Kidd maintained that social improvement and democracy flowed from the ethical dimension of the Judeo-Christian tradition. Religious altruism was gradually neutralising the destructive influence of the rational selfishness of classicism. Whereas the ruling elite was schooled in Plato, Aristotle, Cicero and Horace, the masses of the people had been brought up on the teaching of Isaiah and St John. Social evolution was occurring as the emancipation of the latter was releasing their influence into the life of the nation.[246] On another occasion, having examined the Magnificat, the Old Testament law of Jubilee and the experience of slaves in the early church, Hughes exclaimed that 'Liberty, Equality, and Fraternity, is simply the social expression of the Kingdom of GOD'. With T.H. Green, and some elements gleaned from Herbert Spencer, these ideas formed part of Hughes' social understanding.[247]

Social and Political Activism

> The business of all good men is to seek first the Kingdom of GOD and His righteousness. But it a fatal error to suppose that we can effectively promote the Kingdom of GOD while we neglect the promotion of personal righteousness; or, . . . to imagine that personal righteousness can be effectively promoted while we neglect the Kingdom of GOD, which is social reconstruction of the principles of our LORD JESUS CHRIST.[248]

This was the observation of the Baptist, F.B. Meyer as he commented upon the work of the West London Mission on the occasion of their fourteenth anniversary: this was the hallmark of the Mission and *The Methodist Times*. Hughes was on record as approving of the sentiment expressed F.W. MacDonald at the 1885 Conference where MacDonald proclaimed that, 'We cannot effectively save their souls unless we also sanctify their circumstances.'[249]

Three years later, with A.M. Fairbairn and John Clifford, he maintained that the supreme necessity for Europe was '"a social gospel".[250] For CHRIST came to save society as well as the individual.' Yet Christians had developed two 'dodges'. The first was the Biblical dodge that held that religion was merely for the private life.

[245] MT, 24.01.1895.
[246] MT, 12.04.1894.
[247] For Green see: MT, 05.01.1888; 15.05.1890; for Spencer see: MT, 12.10.1886; 12.01.1893.
[248] MT, 25.04.1901.
[249] MT, 06.08.1885.
[250] MT, 18.10.1888.

The second was the chronological dodge that believed that religion was for Sunday alone.[251]

Hughes advocated a vigorous policy of political involvement, elected service on Boards of Health, School Boards and in the local Vestries held as much a part of being a Christian as saying prayers. Participation in the latter they could 'lay the axe at the root' and challenge those with a vested interest in deadly tenements. Sounding very much like Henry George, Hughes encouraged them to lobby for an equitable ground tax which would divest the landlords of their 'unearned increment' which was the legitimate property of the whole community which created it.[252]

On political issues *The Methodist Times* admitted that its sympathies more naturally inclined towards the Liberal party. They believed that the Liberal programmes were more in harmony with Christian democracy than those of their opponents, although if they ever fell they 'would have no more determined opponents than ourselves'.[253] While ministers were encouraged to support policies and not parties, laymen were strongly exhorted to get involved and influence the parties for good.[254] However, all Christians had to refrain from the 'gross moral offence' of stealing their opponents' words and making them mean what was never intended. Not to accurately represent the views of an opponent was really the sin of 'false witness'.

The most consistently covered issue was temperance, and Hughes recognised this, saying in one article, 'discussed ad nauseam, . . . we fear that not a few of our readers will be tempted by the title of this article to leave it unread'.[255] But with Richard Cobden he believed that temperance reform was at the root of every other reform. A single licensing authority; Sunday and election day closing; not serving children under 16; the direct local veto on the issue or renewal of licences; a statutory maximum number of public houses per thousand of population in cities and per six hundred in rural areas, combined with no financial compensation at the removal of a licence were the specific policies that were advocated.[256]

Following agitation in which the Nonconformists had played a central part, Hughes was jubilant when Gladstone and Harcourt received a delegation of campaigners and accepted the principle of the Direct Local Veto in December 1893. However, seven years later Hughes counselled that the frontal attack for the local veto should cease and a way round be found for the acceptance of lesser measures.[257]

Education was the other pre-eminent subject that was repeatedly addressed, with the reform of the school board system and the endowment of denominational

[251] MT, 16.02.1888.
[252] MT, 09.09.1886.
[253] MT, 11.10.1888.
[254] MT, 28.02.1889.
[255] MT, 23.06.1892.
[256] MT, 23.03.1893.
[257] MT, 14.12.1893; 15.03.1900.

schools from the rates their special concern. With other leading Nonconformists Hughes saw the danger of the 'unchecked ascendancy of Anglican Sacerdotalism'.[258] He compared the proposals of a Dr Sparrow to use taxation to fund sectarian schools with street theft. It was, 'stealing the money of Evangelical Christians and Nonconformists in order to educate children in his own ethical notions'.[259]

The Nonconformist coalition rallied around the issue to support the school boards system and resist the funding of sectarian schools through the rates. The Congregationalist Joseph Parker came in for censure for breaking ranks by advocating a purely secular education system where the others were attempting to advance the teaching of the Bible without denominational doctrines.[260] The campaign rumbled on for some years, and in 1901 *The Methodist Times* expressed its thankfulness at the withdrawal of a particularly reactionary education bill;[261] however the success was short-lived with the passing of the 1902 Education Act.

Poverty, bad housing and unfair wages were a 'gigantic and unendurable evil', but how to remove them? Hughes did not believe that a wholesale redistribution of wealth was the answer. In his view not all poverty was the consequence of exploitation as much was the result of personal sin, 'especially drunkenness and lust'. Quoting Benjamin Jones of the Co-Operative Wholesale Society, Hughes demonstrated how working-class income could be increased by up to 40%. Capitalists were criticised too. There was a need for them to see that their wealth was not their own but was entrusted to them by society and was to be administered for the good of all, especially those who worked for them.[262] In addition there was a need for society to take seriously the plight of old age poverty. There was a need for a system of universal national insurance to provide for people in their later years.[263]

Those who maintained that pauperism was a necessary condition of society were blaspheming against God. There should be no need for anyone to want for social justice and the opportunity to procure for themselves ample food for body, mind and soul. That being said, beyond the basics of human life, relative poverty was a great social advantage in terms of incentive.[264] Where the basics to sustain human life were absent and where there was social injustice, society needed to beware. Hughes believed that Peter Thompson's discoveries having penetrated the lower circles through his ministry in the East London Mission, were even more agonising than Andrew Mearns' *Bitter Cry*. Hughes concluded, 'Is it any wonder that [among] the starving poor of the EAST-END . . . Revolutionary Socialism spreads more and more?'[265]

---

[258] MT, 15.11.1894.
[259] MT, 21.03.1895.
[260] MT, 28.05.1896.
[261] MT, 04.07.1901.
[262] MT, 05.02.1885.
[263] MT, 05.11.1891; 17.05.1894; 06.06.1901.
[264] MT, 20.06.1889.
[265] MT, 06.12.1888.

The rise of the militant and violent strain of socialism on the continent filled Hughes with foreboding. 'It is about time that educated Christians should cease to use the word "socialism" as a vague term of reproach, and to learn to distinguish between the socialism of Christianity and the socialism of atheism and despair. The Christian Socialist says: "All mine is thine." The anarchic socialist says: "All thine is mine."'[266]

The increasing organisation of labour was welcomed by Hughes. The columns of *The Methodist Times* were used in support of the London Dock Strike of 1889; the dispute of North Wales slate quarrymen with Lord Penrhyn and the Engineering lock-out, both of 1897.[267] Paul had written to Timothy about the husbandman being the first to partake of his fruit. 'Translated into modern English this means clearly that the dock labourer must be well fed before the dock shareholder can claim a farthing of "profit".'

He argued that the means for resolving disputes should always be that of arbitration.[268] The excessive individualism in trade of Lord Salisbury had caused the excessive reaction in collectivism of Keir Hardie, who had favoured at the Trades Union Congress the 'nationalising of the whole means of production, distribution and exchange'. Biblically, both principles were necessary.[269] Hughes welcomed the T.U.C. and believed that it was a social revolution of which few had recognised the magnitude and far-reaching significance because it had been achieved without bloodshed.[270]

Industrial safety[271] and the problem of unemployment[272] were also picked up by Hughes. For the latter he proposed supplementing the provision of the Poor Law with work for the unemployed so that they might earn more benefit. A network of labour bureaux to disseminate information and to secure work from private employers was also advocated. Responsibility for these schemes needed to rest with the municipality or the state as the extent of the problem was too vast for voluntary agencies.

Moral issues such as gambling and social purity were also very important to late Victorian Nonconformists. The former caused Hughes difficulties with Lord Rosebery and the latter led to the downfall of Sir Charles Dilke and Charles Stewart Parnell and the ensuing Irish Home Rule crisis.

Following Herbert Spencer, Nonconformists argued that gambling was wrong because it brought gain without merit through the loss of another.[273] When Hughes agreed with the Congregational minister Ambrose Shepherd that 'the

---

266 MT, 03.03.1887; 20.12.1888.
267 London Dock Strike see: MT, 19.09.1889; Slate Quarrymen's Strike see: MT, 28.01.1897; for the Engineering lock-out see: MT, 30.09.1897.
268 MT, 04.01.1894.
269 MT, 13.09.1894.
270 MT, 11.09.1890.
271 MT, 17.09.1895.
272 MT, 03.11.1892.
273 MT, 19.06.1890.

Nonconformist Conscience will not long tolerate a racing PREMIER', there was a strong backlash from other Liberals. Later Hughes pleaded, 'Are we to be regarded as the enemies of Lord ROSEBERY because we frankly invite his attention to the deep convictions of some of his most sincere and influential supporters?'[274]

The concerns of social purity had been a part of Nonconformist political concern since the agitation of Josephine Butler for the repeal of the Contagious Diseases Acts which she began in 1870. Butler herself was a regular contributor to *The Methodist Times* and Hughes likened her to Catherine of Siena, a true prophetess of God.[275] With W.T. Stead she kept the paper abreast of the issues regarding prostitution, the campaign to raise the legal age of consent for sex and related subjects.[276] Hughes believed with many others that strenuous efforts to reclaim those who were morally fallen needed to be supplemented by legislative and administrative efforts to suppress the opportunity and temptation to immorality.[277]

The revelations of the divorce court spelt the end to Parnell's leadership in the agitation for Irish Home Rule. Hughes had declared in 1885 that unchaste behaviour demonstrated that an individual would be incapable of understanding the moral aspects of legislation.[278] This principle must have been hard to apply in Parnell's case for support of Home Rule had cost English Nonconformists dearly in misunderstanding and misrepresentation with their Irish co-religionists.[279] In 1886 Hughes had written, 'Upon our treatment of Ireland during the next few years will depend the future history of the British race in Europe.'[280]

The Golden Rule, British injustice and Cromwellian atrocities were the arguments that had been marshalled in favour of Home Rule.[281] Kent is cynical and unfair to attribute notions of punishment and manoeuvring for political power to the Nonconformists' response to the Parnell disclosure.[282] Removing their support for his leadership and setting aside the real possibility of change in Ireland for which they had fought was a painful one, especially for Hughes.[283] The call that 'Mr. Parnell must go' began with John Clifford and was echoed by Joseph Parker before Hughes added his own voice to the growing chorus. For them, personal character

---

274 MT, 21.06.1894. For fuller comment see, Bebbington, *The Nonconformist Conscience* (London: George Allen & Unwin, 1982). pp. 52-53; Oldstone-Moore, *Hugh Price Hughes*, pp. 285-88.

275 MT, 06.12.1894.

276 MT, 10.09.1885; 05.11.1896.

277 MT, 06.06.1895.

278 MT, 08.10.1885.

279 MT, 21.05.1896. Hempton, 'For God and Ulster: Evangelical Protestantism and the Home Rule Crisis of 1886' in Keith Robbins (ed.), *Studies in Church History, Subsidia 7* (Oxford: Blackwell, 1990), pp. 225-54; Oldstone-Moore, *Hugh Price Hughes*, pp. 209-18.

280 MT, 15.04.1886.

281 MT, 30.06.1892.

282 Kent, *Hughes*, pp. 192-94.

283 D.P. Hughes, *Life of Hugh Price Hughes*, pp. 347-58; particularly pp. 347-48 on Hughes' personal distress prior to speaking out on the issue.

was an essential qualification for public confidence and trusted leadership.[284] Even so, Parnell's demise came as a revelation to Hughes as he discovered 'the immense influence of British Nonconformity in our national counsels'.[285]

In 1889 Hughes wrote that the time had come to 'make war on war'. A frequent theme in his writing, he believed that an International Tribunal of Arbitration, after the pattern of the U.S. Supreme Court, should be established to mediate in disputes.[286] With Victor Hugo he favoured the development of a United States of Europe[287] and a scaling down of the military build-up that had increased European standing armies from 2,195,000 in 1869, to 21,800,500 in 1892.[288] International bankruptcy would make the present 'Armed Peace' more destructive than the long-dreaded 'Great War'.[289]

Many found Hughes' change of heart at the outset of the Boer War hard to believe. But he maintained that he was not inconsistent as he had never held the extreme Quaker position. Following the counsel of fellow Methodists on the spot he felt that Britain was justified because of the slavery practised by the Boers. He urged that the Imperial government needed to act with magnanimity towards their opponents if there was to be a lasting peace. He found the division between Clifford, Meyer, Horton and the others who were against the war and himself to be a particularly difficult one, yet he stood by them against those who called them 'traitors and imbeciles'.[290]

Hughes believed that just as the first half of the nineteenth century was known for abolishing slavery, so the second half of the century would be remembered for bringing to an end the subjection of women. The Mosaic story showed that her subjection was the consequence of the fall. In addition, the implication of the Pentecostal blessing - which was bestowed without the distinction of sex - was that a new era had dawned.[291]

> As ST.PAUL has explained, in striking and much misunderstood phraseology, the great mission of man is to elevate woman into an absolute equality with himself, to take no more advantage of superior brute force in order to dominate her, but to give every capacity and aspiration of her soul the same freedom and scope which he has always demanded for himself.[292]

---

[284] MT, 05.01.1899.
[285] MT, 11.12.1890.
[286] MT, 07.03.1889.
[287] MT, 25.12.1890.
[288] MT, 21.12.1893.
[289] MT, 22.12.1898.
[290] MT, 28.12.1899; 04.01.1900; 01.03.1900; 08.03.1900; 03.01.1901; 27.06.1901; 11.07.1901. See also Kent, *Hughes*, p. 198.
[291] MT, 09.04.1891; 28.04.1892.
[292] MT, 28.04.1892.

The paper touched on many other issues during Hughes' editorship, including police violence;[293] child abuse;[294] judicial reform;[295] agriculture[296] and local government reorganisation[297] all figured at one time or another. They were part of Hughes' commitment to further the modern democratic spirit which he believed to be an attempt to carry out Christian principles in the public life of nations.[298] For, 'True democracy is the system which gives the individual every encouragement to do his best and his highest.'[299]

The Methodist Times also had an international concern that reflected these same issues as illustrated by Hughes' comments on social purity in India;[300] German militarism;[301] the Armenian genocide at the hands of the Turks[302] and lynch-mobs in America.[303] Such was the spirit and tenor of the social and political emphases in Hughes' thought, mediated through his editorial work for *The Methodist Times*.

Passion for Saving Souls and Entrepreneurial Evangelism

While the Forward Movement may have given much time and energy to social and political issues, their evangelistic concern was not blunted, rather, it was sharpened by the sense of urgency they had to relate every facet of the Christian gospel to contemporary life. Neither did it lose its ascendancy in the increasing array of activities for which they became responsible. Hughes' evangelistic passion to see souls saved was a consistent emphasis throughout his ministry that has often been neglected or overlooked. With relish Hughes quoted John Wesley, 'We have nothing to do but to save souls', as he called for a revival of vigorous, progressive Christianity.[304] 'The first essential duty of every Christian worker is to secure the conversion of individuals . . . fail to do that, and the fabric you build may be splendid, but it is founded upon sand, and will fall.'[305]

Therefore it was quite in keeping with the ethos of *The Methodist Times* when Hughes challenged those ministers who had not seen a conversion in the previous twelve months to examine themselves carefully. For Hughes, a 'fruitless' minister could be no more condoned than an immoral or lazy minister.[306] King sees this juxtaposition of traditional evangelistic fervour alongside the developing social

---

[293] MT, 15.12.1887.
[294] MT, 28.03.1889.
[295] MT, 15.08.1889.
[296] MT, 15.02.1895.
[297] MT, 17.02.1898.
[298] MT, 23.04.1885.
[299] MT, 05.12.1895.
[300] MT, 03.05.1888.
[301] MT, 15.03.1888.
[302] MT, 01.10.1896.
[303] MT, 06.09.1894.
[304] MT, 01.07.1897.
[305] MT, 01.09.1887.
[306] MT, 02.09.1897.

gospel as a paradox.[307] Such a view totally misunderstands Hughes for he saw the two elements as very much a part of each other. Speaking in the debate about establishing the London Mission Hughes said,

> It is impossible to deal effectively with the spiritual destitution of London, unless you also deal effectively with its physical and mental destitution. . . . Christ came not to establish an ecclesiastical society of which the sole functions were worship and theological orthodoxy; but to found a kingdom of self-sacrificing love, in which the distribution of loaves and fishes, the healing of sick bodies, and pleasant social intercourse with the poor were essential features.[308]

When the Forward Movement was described by a writer in *The British Weekly* as being a purely evangelistic force Hughes welcomed the advocacy but pointed out that the scope of the movement had been seriously underestimated. 'But we have always maintained that evangelistic enterprise should be preceded, environed and supplemented by social work for the bodies and minds of the poor.'[309]

In the late 1890s many were complaining that conversions were becoming rare. Hughes believed that attention given to four crucial areas would greatly improve the situation.[310] First, there needed to be recognition that a conversion was a miraculous event, through the agency of the Holy Spirit. To see it as merely the result of education or unaided human effort was paralysing. Second, there was a need for Christians to put their wills absolutely at the disposal of Jesus Christ. Quoting Josephine Butler, he pointed out how many humble and ill-qualified evangelists in human terms were greatly used by God. The essential qualification was an absolute submission to the will of Christ.

Third, there was a need for an adequate supply of 'the raw material'. The church was required to act on 'the Great Commission' and 'Go' to the unreached majority, rather than just expecting them to come to church. Finally there was a need to both expect and arrange for the results of the evangelism. This was his severest criticism of D.L. Moody's campaigns in the 1870s. Their lack of organisation meant that many who came under religious influence fell away again 'for want of protection and nurture'.[311]

Hughes further believed that an openness to new ideas and novel approaches was necessary for evangelistic success. 'The Forward Movement has broken the snare of the devil. A new life beats in our veins. We are increasingly realising that the salvation of souls is ten thousand times more important than our ridiculous ideas of propriety. . . . We are prepared now to modify and adapt our methods and agencies so as to reach and win the crowd.'[312]

---

[307] King, 'Hugh Price Hughes', p. 68.
[308] MT, 19.03.1885.
[309] MT, 14.04.1887.
[310] MT, 15.04.1897.
[311] MT, 14.11.1895.
[312] MT, 25.06.1891.

However, there was a need to recapture open-air work from the 'vulgarity and stupidity' by which too many earnest souls had brought the practice into disrepute. Methodism, he believed, had become 'fat and respectable and lazy and luxurious, and more or less impotent'. It was time for highly-educated and saintly men to lead Christians back into the open-air and redeem such preaching from 'the mere repetition of superficial truisms and stale platitudes'.[313]

Hughes agitated for room to be made in the Conference programme during the 'Conversation on the work of God' for the facing of the great problem of the evangelisation of England. 'It seems to us that what we want, above everything else, just now, is a good old-fashioned Revival - one of those spontaneous and irresistible movements which lay hold of entire populations and spread like fire in all directions.'[314]

It is highly unlikely that such a revival actually occurred, but positive results were very encouraging. In the late 1880s and early 1890s there was tremendous optimism. As evangelistic agencies the new Central Missions were a 'conspicuous and unprecedented success . . . marked by scores of conversions every week'.[315] Indeed, on another occasion *The Methodist Times* reported that, 'No famous revivalist of the past ever witnessed so many conversions as our Connexional and other Evangelists now witness. When before have we or our fathers seen a thousand enquiries in one week?'[316]

In these optimistic days Thomas Champness was heralded by many, including Charles Garrett, as the man who would evangelise England's villages. He would lead the Forward Movement there as the Central Missions had reached out into the great cities.[317] However, as the century drew to a close previous euphoria at the numbers of conversions was being replaced by more modest gains. A distinguished Methodist claimed in 1897 that there were few sudden and miraculous conversions as in the days of Wesley. *The Methodist Times* pointed out that,

> Mr. PRICE HUGHES has often said on public platforms that never once, for more than nine years, has he preached in St. James's Hall on Sunday evenings without visible results and instantaneous conversions. Nor are these constant results superficial or evanescent.'[318]

Unfortunately the great Simultaneous Mission which was organised together with the Evangelical Free Churches to commence the new century, and much heralded by Hughes, was disappointing in its results, particularly in the capital. While there were conversions Hughes consoled his readers with the thought that special missions were not 'an end-in-themselves, but a means-to-an-end'. He hoped that one of the results would be that London evangelicals would become more

---

313 MT, 12.06.1890; MT, 29.06.1893.
314 MT, 07.08.1890.
315 MT, 02.02.1888.
316 MT, 14.11.1889.
317 MT, 10.02.1887.
318 MT, 14.01.1897.

evangelistic.[319] Later in 1901, as Methodists gathered from all over the world for their third Oecumenical Conference, Hughes asked, 'Where is our "passion for souls" which laid the foundation for our world-wide prosperity?'[320]

Methodist Reform

It was inevitable in a weekly newspaper that serviced the needs of Methodists that domestic denominational affairs would be a major concern. Among these everyday concerns the distinctive Methodist notes of instantaneous conversion and instantaneous Scriptural holiness were regularly sounded. Evangelists were needed in the connexion to reach the educated as well as the poor, but this was only a part of the full work of the gospel that led people to the place of absolute and immediate self-surrender to Christ. Without this doctrine of entire sanctification Methodist preaching was like a Samson shorn of his locks. For, according to Wesley, Scriptural holiness was the grand depositum that God had given Methodism to propagate.

The influence of Dale's comment to the Wesleyan Conference in Birmingham in 1879 was profound. Methodism had begun to wake up to the fact that they 'were called of God to purify earth as well as to people heaven'.[321] Yet Hughes felt that Wesleyanism had lost ground during the Fly Sheet controversy. While they had concentrated upon the internal turmoil surrounding the democratic aspirations of their members, modern England had been born with the growth of the northern cities. It had been estimated that 80,000 ex-Methodists had slipped into the fold of the Salvation Army alone, where they 'found among our fiery brethren . . . the enterprise, the audacity, the thoroughness which their souls craved'.[322]

1849 had left a legacy with the denomination. There was fearfulness on the part of some to undertake bold, new, aggressive measures. But, 'A new generation . . . is growing up, a robust and hopeful generation, quite disposed to laugh at the exaggerated fears of those who have no adequate faith in the future of their own Church.'[323]

For Hughes this was the ecclesiastical crux of the matter. The older leaders still held onto an achronistic view of Methodism as a private religious society, whereas the younger generation believed passionately that they were a church in their own right.[324] The former lacked the self-confidence in themselves and their calling to reform their church and take adventurous steps in mission and ministry.

---

[319] MT, 07.02.1901.
[320] MT, 29.08.1901.
[321] MT, 20.09.1900; 26.07.1894; 07.07.1887.
[322] MT, 06.08.1885.
[323] MT, 03.08.1893.
[324] MT, 19.12.1895.

> The great warfare between good and evil cannot be successfully accomplished without discussions, experiments, and innovations, all of which are harmless and commendable if they result in bringing men to CHRIST.[325]

He appealed to the memory of Wesley who met new situations without regard to his own preferences or the demands of logical consistency. Rather, he permitted God to lead him 'by a way he knew not', leading to the continual improvement of both his creed and his ecclesiastical polity.[326] Hughes believed that Wesleyanism stood at a crossroads where the decisions that they took as a denomination had serious implications for the future. 'We either go back into the obscurity . . . and the impotence of a moribund sect; or we must go forward into the blessed opportunities and far reaching beneficence of a national religion.'[327]

Believing that the future lay with the latter course, the Forward Party pressed for structural change. The three-year rule of itinerancy was their prime target. It needed to be relaxed so as to allow men the time to build relationships and develop the influence of their ministries. Garrett had begun this in Liverpool with his twenty-five years at the Mission, but it needed to be widened so that all could benefit from concentration and continuity.[328]

The paper also pressed for open and representative government in church affairs. They were pleased that their campaigning style of journalism had 'driven a coach and four' through the traditional practice of secret decisions behind closed doors.[329] They also maintained that the Pentecostal dispensation gave the laity undoubted rights of government as well as rights of service.[330] They felt that to organise the representation at the annual Conference so as to favour those with private means and thereby to exclude working men was detrimental to the vitality of the denomination.[331]

The election of Miss Dawson, a Circuit Steward from Redhill, to the Conference of 1894 gave to Hughes a further opportunity to campaign on behalf of women. Methodist polity did not exclude her, but following the Conference there was pressure to clarify the situation. Hughes exposed the fatuous nature of some of the arguments levelled against female participation. He particularly took relish in exposing a remark made by one minister that women were physiologically incapable of contributing to the legislative process. Hughes asked whether this was said of Queen Victoria.[332]

A Conference committee voted in favour of women delegates by 16 votes to 12 the following year, but Conference rejected the proposal by a slim margin of 18

---

[325] MT, 01.12.1887.
[326] MT, 14.04.1892.
[327] MT, 19.03.1885.
[328] MT, 25.10.1900.
[329] MT, 15.01.1891.
[330] MT, 06.06.1889.
[331] MT, 17.03.1887.
[332] MT, 01.08.1889.

votes. Hughes maintained that, 'The fact is that there is no serious argument against admitting women into all the assemblies of the Christian Church.' Such discrimination was a 'barbaric and prehistoric sentiment' that denied the teaching of Galatians 3:28. Just as slavery had been abolished, so, 'In a precisely analogous manner the slavery of woman and sex disability must cease.' [333] The issue was raised again in the Conference of 1909 by Samuel Keeble, and in 1910 the majority in favour was 26.

Proposals for separated Chairmen of District;[334] calls for the reorganisation of Missionary work in India;[335] and the initiation and wholehearted support of a scheme of Methodist reunion[336] - all of which embodied the principles of the Forward Party in one form or another - made the schedule for reform quite extensive. Some opponents accused him of neglecting the spiritual work, but Hughes maintained that it was a false opposition between reform and getting on with spiritual work; there was no antagonism between them.

> Our attitude must not be negative, critical, destructive, but positive, encouraging, and constructive. We must aim not at results, but at deep-seated causes. Make the tree good and the fruit will be good - that is our method.[337]

Recognising the importance and necessity of reshaping Wesleyanism for the twentieth century Hughes' commitment to denominational reform required an immersion into the structures and politics of the connexion. While the Forward Party provided support and encouragement there was significant resistance from the more conservative and traditionalist wing of the church. Indeed it is likely that the animosity created by his advocacy for change delayed his election to the office of President of the Conference by some years. By the mid-1990s it appeared as though the construction of a new Methodism was moving forward apace, and while the impetus was to set the direction for the coming century, many of the objectives would not be realised until well after Hughes' death.

As the century closed *The Methodist Times* gave its columns regularly to support the progress of the Twentieth Century Fund. The aim was to raise one million guineas to endow the future progress of the denomination, and to build a Central Hall in the heart of the empire's life in Westminster.[338] It was with pride that Hughes quoted Dr Chalmers who believed that the success of Methodism was that they were 'all at it, and always at it'.[339] This indeed summed up the denomination who were at heart, thoroughgoing activists.

---

[333] MT, 07.02.1893.

[334] MT, 19.09.1895; Gwyther, *The Methodist Social and Political Theory and Practice*, p. 143.

[335] MT, 29.01.1885; 25.02.1892; 07.12.1893; 05.04.1894.

[336] MT, 01.05.1890; 04.04.1889; 08.08.1889; 26.09.1889.

[337] MT, 18.11.1886; 25.11.1886; 16.12.1886; 15.08.1895.

[338] MT, 29.07.1897.

[339] MT, 27.01.1898; 13.06.1901.

Christian Unity

Currie considers that the Forward Movement should be understood in the light of a crisis in Methodism caused by the resurgence of Anglicanism,[340] though this runs counter to the evidence. Talk of Methodist reunion and Nonconformist collaboration was not to establish an evangelical bulwark against Anglicanism, rather, it was to facilitate a more powerful and effective force to work in establishing the Kingdom of God.

Through *The Methodist Times* Hughes maintained that the different churches were 'friendly rivals'. They were equals in principle if not in size and power, and they should divide up the field of Christian labour so that each could fulfil its work to the limits of its ability. Even in 1886 he believed that things could progress further, because 'the friendliness of equal Churches will lead to co-operation, to alliance, to federation, possibly to fusion. The way to union is through equality.'[341]

Churches needed to understand that no fragment, however big, could be the whole. As the churches fraternised together and co-operated and discovered the richness of fellowship together, a 'Visible unity will grow out of a realised spiritual unity.' Hughes had a vision that the churches would then act as living branches of the one church, even in their diversity.[342]

He was pleasantly surprised at the beginning of 1889 when Lord Nelson, an extreme high church Anglican, wrote a piece warmly advocating the ideas of J.B. Paton in *Church Bells*. Hughes responded, 'If he really means what he says, . . . the reunion of the British Churches has come within the range of practical consideration.' Similarly, when the Archdeacon of London preached at St. Paul's, appealing for sympathy and co-operation, Hughes again responded to reciprocate the good will, 'he will always find the Evangelical Nonconformists . . . ready to co-operate with them in extending the Kingdom of GOD and implementing personal righteousness.'[343]

The discussions that were the immediate catalyst of drawing the Nonconformist churches closer together were initiated by an article in *The Methodist Times* of 20 February 1890. The Congregationalist, Guinness Rogers, had been approached by the paper to address the subject, and he wrote asking the question, 'Has not the time come when the true unity which, I believe, undoubtedly exists between the different Evangelical and Nonconformist churches of this country should be made more distinctly visible?'

In the following weeks' edition the suggestion was strongly echoed by Dr Clifford, Dr Stephenson, F.B. Meyer and later by Dr A.M. Fairbairn. In the December of that year the principal of the Congregational Training Institute at Nottingham, J.B. Paton, added his voice to the growing consensus. He argued that evangelical brethren had a duty to unite together in local unions for mutual aid,

---

[340] Currie, *Methodism Divided*, pp. 177-78.

[341] MT, 18.03.1886.

[342] MT, 21.04.1887.

[343] MT, 17.01.1889; 10.03.1892.

encouragement and united counsel. Together they could co-operate to advance social Christianity, temperance, social morality and the various kinds of evangelistic and benevolent work in poor and needy districts. Paton had in fact set up a council in Nottingham in 1873 to co-ordinate the social work of churches and charities.[344]

The next significant step was taken at the Grindlewald Conferences that were master-minded by the pioneer travel agent, Henry Lunn, a former colleague of Hughes who had fallen from grace as a result of articles he wrote for *The Methodist Times* having initiated the Indian Missionary Controversy.[345] In preparation for the initial conference Hughes wrote in the first edition of *The Review of the Churches*, seeing a vision of the whole-scale reunion of British Protestantism into a National Christianity including the Anglicans, 'Personally, I have no objection to an Epsicopalian system.'[346]

Lunn managed to draw together a formidable array of Church leaders and Hughes later wrote, 'With a unanimity absolutely unprecedented since the disruptions of the sixteenth century, great ecclesiastical leaders in all the leading communities of Christians have been pondering and discussing Reunion.'[347]

The result was the founding of the Free Church Congress on 7 November 1892. Hughes was open to the movement towards unity being even broader but neither his Nonconformist colleagues nor the Anglicans present shared his vision. Indeed, Anglican hostility was not uncommon with incidents like the Vicar of Hoo repelling a communicant for having attended a dissenting chapel,[348] or the Bishop of London being accused of 'fraternising with the enemy' for having appeared on the platform of the Children's Home during the Wesleyan Conference.[349] Such incidents only served to exacerbate the deep-seated distrust between certain quarters of the churches.

For a long time Hughes felt that disestablishment was the answer so that the churches could relate together as equals,[350] but towards the end of the century, wounded by the constant rebuff of evangelical Anglicans, he lamented that he had wanted, 'the most friendly relations possible between Anglicanism and Methodism. But we have long realised that the real difficulties in the way are neither doctrine nor ecclesiastical policy, but unbridled snobbery and crass ignorance.'[351]

---

[344] MT, 20.02.1890; 17.11.1892; 18.12.1890; E.K.H. Jordan, *Free Church Unity* (London: Luterworth, 1956), pp. 20-25; Bebbington, *The Nonconformist Conscience*, pp. 61-62.

[345] For the Indian Missionary Controversy see Oldstone-Moore, *Hugh Price Hughes*, pp. 184-202; John Prichard, *Methodists and their Missionary Societies 1760-1900* (Farnham: Ashgate, 2013), pp. 113-15.

[346] *Review of the Churches*, 1.1 (October 1891), p. 14.

[347] MT, 17.10.1895.

[348] MT, 28.11.1889.

[349] MT, 07.09.1899.

[350] MT, 04.10.1894; 15.06.1899.

[351] MT, 19.10.1899.

However, he rejoiced that the National Free Church Council had achieved an elastic form that tolerated differences, and yet allowed the churches to work together on matters of common interest. Thus they displayed the visible unity for which the Lord had prayed.[352]

The power of Nonconformists working together was striking. Of the Nonconformist Conscience Hughes wrote,

> Sir CHARLES DILKE defied the Nonconformist Conscience and is a political outcast to this day. Mr. PARNELL despised the Nonconformist Conscience, and so doing destroyed himself and his party. Lord ROSEBERY ignored the Nonconformist Conscience for the sake of a racehorse, and the whole world sees the result.[353]

Yet the primary reason for unity was to advance the Kingdom of God. This was impossible unless Nonconformists depended upon the Pentecostal gift of the Holy Spirit. Such was the advice offered by Prof. Rendel Harris to the National Council in a devotional address as it planned the Simultaneous Mission for the beginning of the new century.[354] F.B. Meyer and Hughes picked up the same theme at a preparatory meeting when they shared their personal experiences of 'yielding . . . utterly to CHRIST'.[355] That the Mission was not all it was hoped to be is perhaps secondary to the milestone that was passed in evangelical co-operation in evangelism. 'We must combine everywhere to carry the war into the enemy's country,' mused Hughes following the provincial thrust of the Simultaneous Mission; 'if we fail to evangelise England it will be our own fault.'[356]

Central missions, the 'Expression' of the Movement

The progress of urbanisation and Mearns' *Bitter Cry* had led Hughes to the conviction that 'The "Church of England" in the twentieth century will be that Church which grapples most energetically and most successfully with the problem of the great cities.'[357]

The Central Missions, especially those with a Central Hall, were the Wesleyan attempt to meet this challenge. They were the most tangible fruit of the Forward Movement, epitomising much of what the movement stood for hence the popular misunderstanding that the Central Hall movement was the Forward Movement and that they were one and the same thing. Passionate evangelism and the desire to see conversions were supplemented with an intense concern for people's material welfare and it was in the missions that these two concerns found their clearest expression.

---

[352] MT, 03.03.1898.
[353] MT, 15.10.1896.
[354] MT, 22.03.1900.
[355] MT, 13.12.1900.
[356] MT, 28.02.1901.
[357] MT, 30.09.1886.

Historically the dynamic development of missionary responses to the Victorian city can be clearly mapped. Beginning with the religious problem of non-attendance it was tackled by aggressive evangelism while at the same time attempts were made to alleviate the social needs they discovered by targeting their limited sources of philanthropy. The intimate knowledge of the conditions and needs that they gained from this work was then used in municipal life and in the wider political sphere in an attempt to change the root causes of social misery. It was in this way that their synthesis of evangelistic, social and political concern became a distinguishing feature of their work.

The Central Halls, which were to become a central plank in the Wesleyan urban strategy, were designed not to be like churches at all. Actually they were more like theatres with tip-up seats and their own brass bands. They represented the recognition by men like Hughes and Henry Pope – Secretary at the Chapel Office and also a national leader in the forward party – that the church needed to bridge the gap between it and the urban working class.

The pioneering work of Charles Garrett in the Manchester and Salford Lay Mission and the Liverpool Mission laid the foundation for what was to follow. In Australia an embryonic Central Mission was inaugurated in Sydney on 13 April 1884 by the Rev. W.G. Taylor. He later considered himself to be a part of the Forward Movement and had been much influenced by Garrett. A college contemporary of Hughes, he returned to England in 1888 and spent twelve months studying the developments in England, particularly in the work of Garrett and Samuel Collier in Manchester. On returning to Australia he advocated the full adoption of their principles for Sydney to the Conference of January 1889.[358] Taylor defined the Forward Movement as 'personal, aggressive, philanthropic evangelism'.[359]

As illustrative of the growing ministry and influence of the Central Missions that followed in the wake of Garrett's work in Liverpool, the establishment of the missions in Manchester and London give insight into the founding and development of these innovative initiatives.

The Manchester Mission

The large, central Oldham Street chapel, denuded of its congregation, posed a problem to the Wesleyan Conference as early as 1875 when a scheme was suggested to erect new premises in the centre of Manchester.[360] The matter was unresolved until 1885 when Samuel Collier, having been a district missionary in Kent, was appointed to take care of the new mission until the Central Hall was completed and an older minister appointed. Under the direction of the Conference appointed committee, the Central Hall – the first of its kind – was built. When it was completed a year later everyone was surprised when the young Collier was appointed as Superintendent. Many within the Forward Movement considered it a

[358] Wright, *Mantle of Christ*, pp. 42-43; Taylor, *Taylor of Down Under*, p. 53.
[359] Taylor, *Taylor of Down Under*, p. 243.
[360] Minutes, 1875, p713.

rash and ill-considered choice.[361] In 1887 the Conference consented to the Manchester and Salford Lay Mission being placed under the care of the Manchester Mission Committee and the beginnings of the work were complete.[362] Henry Pope of the Chapel Office had been a moving force behind all of these developments.

Soon the Central Hall could not contain the crowds that came, and other meetings were held first in the St James' Theatre and then in the Free Trade Hall, before finally the Albert Hall was built and opened. By 1890 6,000 people were attending the mission's services each Sunday, of whom 75% were unaccustomed to attending a place of worship.[363] Indeed, in the preface to a booklet of testimonies from the first four years of the Mission's life Henry Pope noted that

> It is a feature of the Mission that, to a great extent, its successes have been amongst working men . . . In a comparatively short time the Mission has issued in the raising up of a large, new, and intelligent Church in the centre of a vast city; in addition to its agencies for good . . . [it is] a powerful and fervent evangelistic force.[364]

Collier was pleased that the lives of so many were being changed through conversion as this was his primary desire. Yet, his real gift was as an administrator and pioneer of new forms of social service. With the motto of 'need not creed', the Mission established a labour yard, employment bureau, maternity home and hospital amongst other agencies. In response to the 'sleeping-out problem' of 1902 the *Manchester Guardian* reported that, 'The Mission was teaching the Poor Law experts how to deal with the vagrant.'[365] Collier's work was such that it came to have a world-wide reputation as a centre of excellence for the urban application of the principles of Social Christianity.[366] Even with such a reputation Collier's biographer concludes, 'it was no predetermined theory about the relation of the church to our modern social problems which led Collier . . . these things were forced upon him in order that he might do the work of an evangelist.'[367]

The London Mission

In London, in addition to the well-worn debate of 'how to reach the masses', Mearns' *Bitter Cry of Outcast London* rocked the Metropolis. The Wesleyans responded quite quickly. In the spring of 1884 George Lester addressed the London ministers on the subject.[368] J.H. Morgan wrote a paper on *Wesleyan Methodism and Destitute London* and Forster Crozier produced his *Methodism and the Bitter Cry of*

---

[361] George Jackson, *Collier of Manchester* (London: Hodder & Stoughton, 1923), p. 44.
[362] Minutes, 1887, p. 229.
[363] Sails, *At The Centre*, p. 18.
[364] Walter Sackett, *Saving Wonders, being incidents in the Manchester Mission* (London: Charles H. Kelley, 1891), pp. 8-9.
[365] Jackson, *Collier of Manchester*, p. 131.
[366] Jackson, *Collier of Manchester*, p. 62.
[367] Jackson, *Collier of Manchester*, p. 125.
[368] The London Wesleyan Mission: *Summary of its Purpose, Policy and Work* (London, nd), p. 1; Rosalie Budgett Thompson, *Peter Thompson* (London: Charles H. Kelley, 1910), p. 33.

Outcast London. Hugh Price Hughes commented in the first annual report of the West London Mission that *The Bitter Cry* had awoken the London churches to their responsibility for the condition of the city. The climax of the Wesleyan response was the formation of the London Mission and its branches between 1885 and 1889.[369]

THE EAST LONDON MISSION was born when, in 1885, Peter Thompson was appointed to superintend the first branch of the Mission in the East End. When he arrived at St George's he found that 65 of the most active and well-to-do members had left in anticipation of the new style of ministry. He began by visiting from house to house and was appalled and distressed by what he found. Bewildered about how he might address the situation he prayed. 'Then, as with the ancient energy that came upon the old prophets, God's grand message was borne in upon our souls by the Holy Ghost, with all the light and power of deep conviction of the mind and heart.'[370] He was transformed and within a few months he had set up various agencies of social service and the Mission quickly got a name for disinterested philanthropy.[371] Still attempting to understand the situation into which he had come he reflected in his first annual report, 'We require to make an effort to explain to ourselves what we see, and so to understand the awful difficulties we have to deal with. Suppose . . . we could put the strongest spiritual man into the actual lot of these people . . . it would be almost certain ruin to him.'[372]

Thompson believed that it was a part of the shepherd's duty to catch the wolf as well as to tend the wounded sheep. So he founded a local newspaper, *The East End*, where they applied Christian ethics to local situations. For twenty years he served on the local Vestry, arguing for temperance reform, better sanitation and seeking to outlaw the sweat-shops. Good Samaritanism was fine, but there was also a need to police the highway from Jericho to Jerusalem to catch the thieves at large. '[W]e are politicians . . . for we believe that all political, social, and economic questions have a moral character; and that religion lies at the root of all real reform. . . . The Bible is our standard and guide.'[373]

The Mission took over two old drinking venues, Paddy's Goose and the Old Mahogany Bar, which became meeting places and mission centres. The former quickly gained local credibility and was used as a strike centre during the London Dock Strike of 1889. It housed union meetings and distributed food to the strikers' families. Thompson himself intervened in the strike with Cardinal Manning to help with the mediation. The latter was to become the home of the first Medical Mission in London also in 1889.[374]

---

369 East London (1885); Central London (1886); West London (1887); South London (1889).

370 Thompson, *Peter Thompson*, p. 46.

371 R.G. Burnett, *These My Brethren* (London: Epworth, 1946), p. 50.

372 Burnett, *These My Brethren*, p. 53.

373 Burnett, *These My Brethren*, p. 80.

374 Thompson, *Peter Thompson*, pp. 54-82; Burnett, *These My Brethren*, p. 82; Sowton,

A personal friendship with Joseph Livesey in his formative years profoundly influenced Thompson towards temperance and other social causes,[375] but he considered himself to be primarily an evangelist, and was much inspired by William Arthur's *Tongue of Fire*, which he read and reread.[376] Later his wife was to confirm that all his temperance work, social reforms and his books were secondary to his desire to see conversions.[377] It is not surprising therefore that he was particularly concerned with the number of converted people who fell away from the faith. A careful study revealed that roughly one in five were ultimately lost and that the first three months after a confession of faith was a particularly critical period. It was with great pleasure he reported that over the first seven years of the Mission's life 995 new members had been received by the mission and a further 216 were 'on trial'.[378] Thompson believed that, 'The Holy Ghost alone can save and keep these people . . . We must live to be filled and used of the Holy Ghost, in every service, on every visit, and in every talk.'[379]

THE WEST LONDON MISSION commenced its work in 1887, following Edward Smith's appointment to the Central London Mission in 1886.[380] Hugh Price Hughes was invited to lead the West London Mission in January 1886[381] and, after a month of prayerful reflection he accepted. In the October of 1887 the Mission began its work with C.H. Spurgeon conducting the opening service.[382] By the end of the century its vast extension into many different areas of work was staggering. Charles Booth gave a warm account of its ministry and considered it 'astonishing . . . triumphant and wonderful' as it summed up nearly everything that anyone else had tried elsewhere.[383] The Mission's numerous agencies testify to that. They ran Thrift Societies; a Labour Bureau; a Poor Man's Lawyer; a Soup Kitchen; two Dispensaries; a Rescue Home; People's Drawing Rooms for the poor; various recreational and literary clubs; a University Extension lecture series; a Guild of Brave Poor Things.

A particularly gratifying initiative for Hughes was the establishment of the Sisters of the People, inspired by Mazzini's 'Young Italy' they lived in community under the supervision of Mrs Price Hughes and offered humanitarian aid to the

---

Pathfinders, p. 32.

375 Thompson, *Peter Thompson*, p. 84.

376 Thompson, *Peter Thompson*, pp. 153-54.

377 Thompson, *Peter Thompson*, p. 148.

378 Burnett, *These My Brethren*, p. 56.

379 Burnett, *These My Brethren*, p. 53.

380 Rupert Davies, A. Raymond George & Gordon Rupp (eds), *A History of the Methodist Church in Great Britain*, vol. 3 (London: Epworth, 1983), p. 135. Joseph Hopkins established the South London Mission in 1889 (Beasley, p17).

381 MT, 18.02.1886; 27.05.1886.

382 Philip S. Bagwell, *Outcast London: A Christian Response. The West London Mission of the Methodist Church, 1887-1987* (London: Epworth, 1987), p. 15.

383 Charles Booth, *Life and Labour of the People of London*, Religious Influences, vol. 7, (London: Macmillan, 1902), p. 285.

poor.[384] They were not limited to the traditional roles of dispensing tracts and serving soup. Under Mrs Price Hughes tutelage they led outdoor services and preached, talked politics with workers, were elected to school boards and undertook social work through district visiting. Hughes believed that this particular development gave to women the opportunity to 'lead and organise . . . in every kind of Christian and philanthropic work'. It was a real step forward towards emancipation.[385] One of the innovative projects that the sisters undertook was to establish a crèche facility for the infants and children of working mothers[386] and 'a home of peace' for the terminally ill.[387] Over sixty women served as Sisters during its first fifteen years including Emmeline Pethick-Lawrence who was to later become a Suffragette leader. She credited the Mission as giving her the first opportunity for emancipation working as a free person in a community of equals.[388]

Affecting change in the life of the local community was important too, so they encouraged Christians to be elected as Vestrymen. The Rev. C. Ensor Walters served with George Bernard Shaw on the St Pancras Vestry for many years.[389]

Much of Hughes' social teaching first saw the light of day in his Sunday Afternoon Conferences at St James' Hall. Gwyther considers these to be a land-mark in the development of social witness within Methodism.[390] It was often at these Conferences that Hughes spoke out on the issues that came to be seen as the concerns of the Nonconformist Conscience. This was the conviction that politics should have a moral foundation, and that these moral principles should be applied to concrete situations. For Bebbington, the Nonconformist Conscience is summed up in the understanding that there was no boundary between religion and politics; that politicians should be of the highest character as they enabled the state to promote the moral welfare of its citizens.[391]

Three years into the work they were very encouraged and Hughes was delighted to report that,[392] 'The West London Mission has never held a Sunday evening service without actual decisions for CHRIST.' Furthermore, by 1892 the Mission had 1500 members among the 8000 who attended the services at its main centres and smaller local halls each Sunday.[393] The Mission had become 'the most pronounced and extensive and many-sided development of the Forward Movement', indeed it was its 'incarnation'.[394]

---

[384] King, 'Hugh Price Hughes', p. 75; Oldstone-Moore, *Hugh Price Hughes*, pp. 166-69
[385] MT, 29.03.1888; 06.02.1890; Bagwell, *Outcast London*, p. 25; Katherine Price Hughes, *The Story of My Life* (London: Epworth, 1945), p. 67.
[386] Bagwell, *Outcast London*, p. 37.
[387] MT, 14.05.1891.
[388] Oldstone-Moore, *Hugh Price Hughes*, pp. 168-69.
[389] Gwyther, *The Methodist Social and Political Theory and Practice*, pp. 248-49.
[390] Gwyther, *The Methodist Social and Political Theory and Practice*, p. 147.
[391] Bebbington, *The Nonconformist Conscience*, p. 11.
[392] MT, 16.10.1890.
[393] MT, 06.10.1892.
[394] MT, 31.03.1892; 19.04.1894.

With the early successes of Liverpool, Manchester and London, other Missions were established following the same pattern. F. Luke Wiseman began an important work at Birmingham in 1887 and Samuel Chadwick, who had assisted Thompson in the East End, was appointed to Leeds in 1894. By 1909 no fewer than 41 Central Missions had been inaugurated.[395]

The Central Missions have elicited some searching criticism. Currie is the most dismissive with his critique falling in four main areas.[396] First, he maintains that their philanthropy was limited in scope, paternal in nature and therefore external to the poor. When the poor did occasionally attend worship it was to 'humour the missioners'. Second, he points out that the assistance that was given to the poor was temporary and only given to a very small proportion of the needy. Third, he says that because of the failure to attract the poor, the Central Halls attracted suburban residents by expository preaching. Fourth, he points out that the combined increase of the West London and Manchester Mission between 1888 and 1902, 4664, when compared with the total Wesleyan membership of 463,225, indicates that the Connexional effect of the Missions was very limited. However, Currie's use of statistics is misleading. Sails points out that the increase in membership of five in the year 1900 (London, Manchester, Birmingham, Liverpool and Leeds) accounted for one third of the Connexional increase.[397] Moreover, McLeod, while holding that Currie may be partially correct about suburban hearers for the West London Mission, believes that it is scarcely true of the others.[398]

Were the Central Missions and Central Halls a failure or not? The popular view that they heralded a second Wesleyan awakening and brought the church back from the brink is obviously an overstatement and it is better to judge them as a qualified success, qualified in the sense that their philanthropy was indeed limited and that only a small percentage of the poorer classes benefited from it. The same can also be said regarding the reach of their gospel preaching and of the numbers of people confessing faith. They totalled only a very small proportion of the unchurched, urban poor. However, they did reach and help thousands and while they may not have achieved the results that they hoped and prayed for, in the context of the late nineteenth and early twentieth centuries this is a significant achievement in evangelistic endeavour, creative social welfare and progressive social policy. Of their failure to transform society they were only too painfully aware themselves. The Conference of 1898 admitted that despite all the efforts of the new missions, 'The mass of irreligion and indifference at our doors shows little sign of abatement.'[399]

---

[395] Sails, *At The Centre*, pp. 54 & 71; Davies, et al, *A History of the Methodist Church*, 3. p. 135.

[396] Currie, *Failure*, pp. 21-25.

[397] Sails, *At the Centre*, p. 36;

[398] Hugh McLeod, *Class and Religion in the Late Victorian City* (London: Croom Helm, 1974), p. 124.

[399] *Minutes, 1898*, p. 427.

Other Leaders: Further dimensions to the Movement

In the columns of *The Methodist Times* Hugh Price Hughes recognised other leaders within the Forward Movement who were not involved in establishing the Central Missions. They were following the ethos of the movement, but pioneering new forms of Christian service in other spheres.[400]

BOWMAN STEPHENSON had been converted in his teens at Dudley and having entered the ministry in the early 1860s soon came to the notice of his superiors. As a probationer minister in Norwich he took over a theatre for popular Sunday evening services much to the dislike of some within his congregation.[401] His next appointment in Manchester saw him undertaking a similar ministry, but this time falling under the criticism of the mill owners for during the Cotton Famine his radical politics led him to speak out in favour of 'the Yankees'.[402] In Bolton (1865-68) he engaged women workers whom he styled 'deaconesses', who were especially significant as they formed the basis of his later work in the Children's Home and the Wesley Deaconess Order which began in 1891.[403]

He was particularly influenced by the work of Immanuel Wichern in Hamburg, with his 'Raue Haus' for destitute boys.[404] Therefore, it was only natural that as his next appointment in Lambeth brought him face to face with similar destitution amongst the young, that he should attempt a similar response. His 'Children's Home' was opened in 1869 and, following a visit to view Wichern's work at Kaiserwerth in 1871, he began to explore more fully the use of women 'Sisters of the Children'. The aims of the work were clear: 'To rescue children who, through the death or vice or extreme poverty of their parents, are in danger of falling into criminal ways . . . to shelter, feed, clothe, educate, train to industrious habits, and, by God's blessing, lead to Christ.'[405]

In 1873 he was set apart from Circuit ministry to pursue the children's work. He was also an advocate of temperance as well as the reform of Methodism for which he was a leader in the agitation for the inclusion of laymen at the Conference. He was an organiser of Moody's London campaign and never lost his evangelistic concern. He was elected to be the President of the Conference for 1891.[406]

W. FIDDIAN MOULTON also served as the President of the Conference, the year before Stephenson, in 1890. He was a scholar of note and had been involved in the revision of the New Testament. Turning his back on a chair of Theology he

---

[400] MT, 03.01.1895, Stephenson and Moulton among others; MT, 10.02.1887, Champness.

[401] Cyril Davey, *A Man for all Children* (London: Epworth, 1968), p. 18.

[402] Davey, *A Man*, p. 21.

[403] Townsend, Workman & Eayrs, *A New History of Methodism*, 1. pp. 454-55; Davey, *A Man*, p. 29.

[404] Davey, *A Man*, pp. 38 & 59.

[405] Davey, *A Man*, p. 44.

[406] Davey, *A Man*, p. 93 (Methodist restructuring); p. 75 (Moody campaign); p. 99 (President of the Conference).

accepted the position of headmaster at the Leys School at Cambridge when it was opened in 1875 as a Methodist Public School.[407]

He had earned his reputation while a tutor at the ministerial training college at Richmond. It was there that he had first encountered Hugh Price Hughes and had defended him when Hughes had got into serious trouble with the authorities.[408] A friendship developed between them in which Hughes viewed his old tutor as a counsellor whose advice could be trusted. Indeed, it was to Moulton that Hughes had gone to seek out counsel as to whether to commence *The Methodist Times* or not. Indeed, Hughes rejoiced that Moulton used his occupancy of Wesley's chair to endorse the progressive stream within the denomination. 'He was the first President who ever dared to mention and bless from the Chair of the Conference the "Forward Movement" of modern Methodism. He was an enthusiastic supporter of the new missions and developments which are reviving the primitive soul-winning character of Methodism.'[409]

In many ways the Leys School epitomised the desire of the Forward Movement to be intelligent and articulate on the subjects of contemporary thought and insight. Old Leysians were also enthusiastic supporters of the movement. From the late 1880s a group of them undertook to work in Whitechapel, and in the early years of the twentieth century erected new buildings in which to house their Leysian Mission on the City Road which was a hybrid form of Central Mission and Settlement activity.[410]

THOMAS CHAMPNESS had an early exposure to radicalism in witnessing first-hand the Chartist riots in Manchester and by reading the speeches of John Bright in the *Manchester Guardian* during the 'hungry forties'.[411] He spoke out clearly for temperance and, aged 72, was imprisoned for three days at Leicester in 1904 when he refused to pay his rates as a protest against the 1902 Education Act.[412] However, his main concern was evangelism. It led him to Sierra Leone as a missionary, and, on his return to England he pioneered an Evangelists' Training College at Castleton Hall, Rochdale followed by the Joyful News Mission in 1886. At the opening of the College, Garrett raised the flag and Hughes gave the address.[413]

Hughes saw Champness as the man to take Forward Movement principles into the villages whereas he and others had taken them into the cities.[414] Like Hughes,

---

407 MT, 28.09.1899.

408 D.P. Hughes, *Life of Hugh Price Hughes*, pp. 57-60.

409 MT, 28.09.1899.

410 Townsend, Workman & Eayrs, *A New History of Methodism*, 1. pp. 473-74 & 466; D.P. Hughes, *Life of Hugh Price Hughes*, pp. 206-207.

411 Sowton, *Pathfinders*, p. 16; E.M. Champness, *The Life Story of Thomas Champness* (London: Charles H. Kelley, 1907), p. 25.

412 Champness, *Life Story of Thomas Champness* pp303 & 306.

413 Champness, *Life Story of Thomas Champness* p247; Josiah Mee, *Thomas Champness as I Knew Him* (London: Charles H. Kelley, nd), pp. 81-82; Davies, et al, *A History of the Methodist Church*, 3. p. 134.

414 MT, 16.02.1887.

Champness too looked to the agency of the Holy Spirit.[415] In fact, his emphasis on the Holy Spirit and personal holiness became characteristic of Champness' Lay Evangelists and the teaching of Cliff College, to which the work was transferred. 'The fires of Evangelism are kindled at Pentecost, and the College stands for the Pentecostal experience. We are Methodists who believe in the Methodist Doctrine of Full Salvation. . . . The Cliff spirit is the fruit of the Spirit of Pentecost.'[416]

Samuel Chadwick, whose work with Peter Thompson and at the Leeds Mission has already been noted, followed Champness as the Principal at Cliff College. His book, *The Way to Pentecost*, became the classic popular statement of traditional Wesleyan holiness theology. Chadwick had himself been profoundly changed after reading William Arthur's *Tongue of Fire*, and summed up his own ministry by saying, 'The Holy Ghost has been the key to my thinking, the defence of my faith, the inspiration of my life, and the effective power in all my work. No wonder I love Pentecost.'[417]

SAMUEL KEEBLE is a less well-known figure and yet was perhaps the most advanced social thinker in the Wesleyan Church of his day. He was well versed in Maurice and Kingsley, and had also read Ruskin and Marx when the latter was still relatively unknown. Keeble had never been to university and was entirely self-taught, believing that if a man came to Christ then his whole perspective on life should change. He argued for the redemption of the whole of human life within the framework of a transformed society.[418] He had met Hughes during his first ministerial appointment and became a hearty advocate of the Forward Movement, writing for *The Methodist Times* the 'Labour lore' column between 1889-1895, then contributing occasional pieces until he broke with Hughes in 1900.[419]

Ultimately Keeble's views were not popular. Hughes dropped his column from *The Methodist Times* because it was too radical, although they remained firm friends. His own paper, *The Methodist Weekly*, was a failure, only lasting three years. He also fell out with Peter Thompson after criticising the East End Mission for not being radical enough in its approach. He was a sincere man but much misunderstood by many people. His most important book was *Industrial Daydreams*, and in it he dwelt upon the teaching of Gore, Barnett, Scott Holland and Clifford as being forerunners of a new era. It sold only 208 of its initial print run of 475 and he had to buy back the rest from the publisher.[420] With all his forward thinking Keeble never left his evangelical roots. In 1907 he rejected the 'New

---

[415] Davies, et al, *A History of the Methodist Church*, 3. p. 228.

[416] D.W. Lambert, *The Testament of Samuel Chadwick, 1860-1932* (London: Epworth, 1957), p. 34.

[417] Lambert, *Testament of Samuel Chadwick*, pp. 76-78.

[418] Maldwyn Edwards, *S.E. Keeble: Pioneer and Prophet* (London: Epworth, 1949), p. 23; Gwyther, *The Methodist Social and Political Theory and Practice*, p. 132.

[419] Michael S. Edwards, *S.E. Keeble: The Rejected Prophet* (Chester: Wesley Historical Society, 1977), p. 19.

[420] Edwards, *Keeble*, p. 21.

Theology' of R.J. Campbell because it 'denies sin, grace, redeeming love, and the new birth'.[421] Edwards observed, 'Here was an Old Testament prophet with a New Testament message. Here was an evangelist who was also a reformer.'[422]

JOHN SCOTT LIDGETT was responsible for establishing the Methodist Settlement at Bermondsey. At each stage of his ministry he formed important friendships that were to help his practical and spiritual development. At Southport he had become acquainted with Alexander Maclaren, the forward looking Baptist from Manchester.[423] In Wolverhampton he struck up an abiding friendship with Dr. J.B. Paton,[424] and in Cambridge it was Moulton who became his confidant, advisor and sponsor.[425]

He owned that he had been profoundly inspired and influenced by the work of Maurice, Kingsley and T.H. Green[426] along with D.L. Moody's revivalism which had also left a deep impression upon him.[427] Already in sympathy with the Forward Movement, it was while ministering in Cambridge in 1889 that he vowed to be true to God's call to him to obey his convictions. He desired to establish a Methodist example of Toynbee Hall, 'to be carried out in a distinctively evangelical spirit'.[428] Where the Forward Movement had previously stood for the salvation of the body as well as the soul, Lidgett was determined to add 'the mind'. From the outset of his ministerial career theology had been his main concern and the educational work of the Settlement naturally flowed from this intellectual passion.[429]

It was Moulton to whom he went for advice, and who also introduced Lidgett's Settlement proposition to the Conference of 1889. Indeed Moulton also chaired the Conference as President when the Settlement was finally approved in 1891.[430] Mark Guy Pearse, Hughes' colleague in the West London Mission, considered the Settlement to be 'the last child of the Forward Movement'.[431] With the other settlements it aimed to place educated men in a poorer district so that their presence and contribution might help to elevate the neighbourhood. Their programme of work was structured with educational and social activities to further this aim.[432]

---

[421] Edwards, *Keeble*, p. 8.
[422] Maldwyn Edwards, *Keeble*, p. 19.
[423] J. Scott Lidgett, *My Guided Life* (London: Methuen, 1936), pp. 88-89.
[424] Lidgett, *My Guided Life*, p. 102.
[425] Lidgett, *My Guided Life*, pp. 106 & 110.
[426] Lidgett, *My Guided Life*, p. 73.
[427] Lidgett, *My Guided Life*, p. 89-90.
[428] Lidgett, *My Guided Life*, p. 63.
[429] Lidgett, *My Guided Life*, pp. 61 & 144.
[430] J. Scott Lidgett, *Reminiscences* (London: Epworth, 1928), p. 29; Lidgett, *My Guided Life*, p. 110; Rupert Davies (ed.), *John Scott Lidgett, A Symposium* (London: Epworth, 1957), p. 52.
[431] Gwyther, *The Methodist Social and Political Theory and Practice*, p. 204-05.
[432] For the *Aims of the Settlement*, see Lidgett, *Reminiscences*, pp. 30-31; for the subjects taught, see Lidgett, *My Guided Life*, pp. 118-19.

Following Hughes' death in 1902 Percy Bunting took temporary charge of *The Methodist Times*. However, in March 1906 the editorship was handed over to Scott Lidgett who continued to edit the paper until December 1918.[433] As less of an evangelist and more of an educationalist the paper, along with the Forward Movement, were led in a different direction under Lidgett. While he maintained that, above all else, the particular Methodist emphasis related to the gift of the Holy Spirit,[434] he preferred to build on the Maurician theme of the Fatherhood of God. 'The restoration of the truth of the Fatherhood of God to its primacy in Christian thought and life was the greatest Theological and Religious achievement of the nineteenth century . . . the influence of Maurice was the most important personal factor.'[435]

Under Lidgett the fundamental theological basis for social action and social reconstruction shifted. The Forward Movement had previously developed its ethical teaching on holiness and the power of the Holy Spirit as its theological and experiential imperative. This was now supplanted with the more widely accepted teaching that was popularised by Charles Gore and Henry Scott Holland. Their understanding that looked back to Maurice and drew its inspiration from the Fatherly love of God.[436]

The characteristic feature of Wesleyanism during this period was frenetic activity. That is not to imply that these men were unthinking, far from it, but under the leadership of Garrett, Stephenson, Hughes, Collier and their contemporaries the Christian faith was practical and had to relate to every dimension of life. One wonders whether Hughes' premature death at 55 years suddenly taken by an 'apoplectic seizure' following an extended period of fourteen months when he had been away from the ministry, was in fact the result of the overwork that typified him and the movement for which he was the most eloquent spokesman.[437]

---

433 Lidgett, *My Guided Life*, pp. 162-63.

434 J. Scott Lidgett, *The Fatherhood of God (Second Edition)* (London: Charles H. Kelley, 1913), p. 268.

435 Davies, *Symposium*, p. 84, see also p. 100.

436 Alan Turberfield, *John Scott Lidgett: Archbishop of British Methodism* (Peterborough: Epworth, 2003), p. 374-75.

437 D.P. Hughes, *Life of Hugh Price Hughes*, p. 660.

Chapter 6

Congregational Strategists

As with many of the denominations in this period Congregationalism contained a broad cross-section of theological and social views. Attempting to analyse how they brought together traditional evangelicalism with a developing social teaching is further complicated by the congregational nature of their churches. This resulted in a high degree of individualism and independence which makes any serious consideration of the denomination a survey of eminent individuals, an eminence marked by the creative innovation and adaptation of ideas they adopted. If their churches had exhibited more cohesion and less independence their work might have prospered significantly better. As it was, the strategic advantage that these forward thinkers provided was lost as the progressive thought and activity among them was at best inconsistent. To fully appreciate their pioneering contribution an understanding of the general milieu of Congregationalism is helpful.

In the first half of the nineteenth century Congregationalism was convinced of its mission to minister only to the middle-classes. This went out of vogue in the mid-century when there was much talk of 'How to reach the masses'. Thus in 1891, when R.W. Dale of Birmingham revived the notion that reaching the masses was not their special mission, there was shock and disdain in some quarters.[1] Yet he was only telling the denomination what they really ought to have known. *The Congregational Year-book* of 1893 spelt it out: 'Our churches . . . consist . . . for the most part of sections of the working-class, the lower middle-class, and middle-classes, and they represent very largely the comparatively well-to-do side of those classes; they consist, if I may say so, of the "haves".'[2]

This analysis was corroborated by Charles Booth's extensive survey of turn of the century London. He concluded that the Congregationalists were strong where the middle-classes were strong, and weak where the middle-classes were weak.[3] Inglis observes that they had 'become more middle-class, affluent and stylish, both in action and in church building'.[4]

---

1 K.S. Inglis, *Churches and the Working Class in Victorian England* (London: Routledge, 1963), pp. 103-04.

2 Inglis, *Churches and the Working Class*, p. 102.

3 Charles Booth, *Life and Labour of the People of London*, Religious Influences, vol. 7, (London: Macmillan, 1902), p. 112.

4 Inglis, *Churches and the Working Class*, pp. 72-73.

In some places there were real attempts made at reaching the unchurched masses. In this regard it is important to remember that the Pleasant Sunday Afternoon Movement originated under the leadership of the Congregationalist John Blackham following the visit of Moody to Birmingham in 1875.[5] In September 1903 Charles Silvester Horne began the work that was to put him at the forefront of developing the 'Institutional Church' method in Britain, at Whitefield's Tabernacle in London, albeit that he styled it Whitefield's Central Mission.[6] Neither were the Congregationalists reticent in establishing Settlements with Mansfield House in Canning Town (1890) and the Browning Settlement at Walworth (1895). Yet these were the exceptions rather than the rule. Between 1892 and 1895 the Congregational Union had discussed setting up a Church Extension Fund to meet the new century with funds for development, progress and expansion, yet by late 1901 this had only raised £35,000. As Hugh Price Hughes reflected on the Wesleyans' success in raising a million guineas compared with the Congregationalists' failure to reach their target of half a million, he concluded that it was the impediment of church government which stopped them making the kind of unified response his own denomination had achieved.[7]

At this point a significant theological change was in progress within the denomination, and there was a growing unease with the theology of the Calvinist system and the prevailing view of the inspiration of the Bible. Dale is representative of this himself. He was at the forefront of those seeking to throw off the fetters of Calvinist orthodoxy and rejoiced in the emancipation that was being won. Guinness Rogers justified this development by saying that the link to Puritanism was not through the same creed but through 'the same law of ecclesiastical and theological progress'.[8] This liberation from Calvinism ultimately led to R.J. Campbell being able in 1907 to dismiss the fall; the scriptural basis of revelation; blood atonement; salvation; punishment for sin; heaven and hell as not only misleading, but as completely unethical.[9] At the time he was minister of the prestigious City Temple in London.

Another area of development in Congregationalism during this period was in their social teaching and not surprisingly the issue of temperance was at the forefront of the thinking of many, particularly Dale and Horton. The fact that they were now prepared to engage with such issues was also a result of the slackening of the old Calvinism. Grant maintains that the emerging Social Christianity among

---

5 R. Tudor Jones, *Congregationalism in England (1662-1962)* (London: Independent Press, 1962), p. 317.

6 C. Silvester Horne, *Pulpit, Platform and Parliament* (London: Hodder & Stoughton, 1913), p. 20; W.B. Selbie, *The Life of Charles Silvester Horne* (London: Hodder & Stoughton, 1920), pp. 134-35.

7 MT, 24.10.1901.

8 J.W. Grant, *Free Churchmanship in England* (London: Independent Press, 1955), p. 92.

9 Keith Robbins, 'The Spiritual Pilgrimage of the Rev R.J. Campbell', *Journal of Ecclesiastical History* 30 (1979), p. 271.

them was based on three basic tenets. First, that the Christian ideal is not the salvation of a remnant but of the whole world, and as a result of this the churches were not arks of refuge but centres of activity. Second, the redemption of humanity is equivalent to the coming of the Kingdom of God and is to be achieved in this world. Third, this is a social ideal and therefore the church is to be a social agency.[10] While the Baptists mostly remained aloof and the Presbyterians uninterested these developments were possible in Congregationalism because of individuals like Charles Berry, A.M. Fairbairn and R.F. Horton. They were open to the thought of the new era that was dawning and were familiar with Maurice, Ruskin, Toynbee, Henry George and T.H. Green. The spirit of reform was in the air and for some there was a feeling that Nonconformity might be facing its final intellectual and social challenge and they were rising to meet it.

There were political developments too as their middle-class worshippers developed aspirations that were unknown to their forefathers. The social handicaps of marriage, burial and education which were experienced by Nonconformists were increasingly becoming issues, as was the disestablishment of the Anglican Church. Grant sees the bridge into political dissent being participation in municipal affairs, and, in this, R.W. Dale is the pre-eminent example and Andrew Mearns' *Bitter Cry of Outcast London* the spur.[11]

Having noted the various developments that were occurring with Congregationalism it is right to point out that this was only representative of the cutting edge of the denomination, rather than the whole. For most of this period Joseph Parker was the minister at City Temple and he was the embodiment of the old school. A theological and social conservative he did not approve of the move away from old-style Calvinism, for him the doctrines of verbal inspiration and inerrancy of the Scriptures were sacrosanct. He considered Horton's books on the Bible that encompassed the Higher Criticism undermined the word of God and brought upon Horton a 'wild, unreasoning, fanatical denunciation'.[12]

R.W. DALE was the minister of Carr's Lane Chapel in Birmingham between 1853-1895 and Tudor Jones considers him to be the 'most remarkable Congregationalist of the nineteenth century'.[13] There can be no argument over the extent of his influence on the denomination. What he said and did laid the foundations for many of the developments that were to follow. In many ways his role and contribution can be compared to Charles Garrett among the Wesleyans, as his thought and activity pioneered the way for the developing life of Congregationalism. Because of the popularity of his published work and the depth of his theological insight it is certain that his influence in his own denomination was far greater than Garrett's was within Wesleyanism. In fact, it could well be argued

[10] Grant, *Free Churchmanship*, p. 171.
[11] Grant, *Free Churchmanship*, pp. 174-75.
[12] Albert Peel & John Marriott, *Robert Forman Horton* (London: George Allen & Unwin, 1937), pp. 159-60.
[13] Tudor Jones, *Congregationalism*, p. 266.

that between 1875 and 1886 the Congregationalists were potentially much further forward in their thinking and action.

Dale wanted Christianity to address itself to the modern world and be relevant. He said, '[A]re we mastering the world by the power of God and making it what God wanted it to be, or is the world mastering us?'[14] He recognised that the influence of F.D. Maurice upon him and others was instrumental in starting them thinking along another line, particularly as many had come to the assumption that political activity lay beyond the province of the Christian life.[15] Many were shocked at his involvement in municipal politics and the active support he gave to John Bright's political campaigning as MP for Birmingham.[16]

He saw great shortcomings in old-style Calvinism and was glad that it was disappearing.[17] He attempted himself to restate his belief in other terms. In his classic 1875 work on the atonement he did just that using both the language and forms of his own theological tradition. He saw sin as impatience with divine control and resentment against divine authority.[18] As such sin affected the whole human race and redemption therefore needed to embrace the race as well as the individual. In the atonement therefore 'Christ is the Head and Representative of mankind'.[19] His understanding of the sovereignty of God also helped form the basis of his rationale for municipal and political involvement. For him the living Christ is the reigning Christ whose will is to be done on earth as it is in heaven[20] and his authority therefore reaches into every province of human energy. 'His authority extends over every province of human life; over the business of men and their pleasures; over science, literature, art; over the family; over the State as well as over the Church.'[21]

The supreme duty of every true Christian was to make that authority effective and to put into practice the ethics that God himself had sanctioned. For God's sovereignty in Christ was '"a redemptive sovereignty"; "His sovereignty over nations - like His sovereignty over individuals - is not a sovereignty of mere authority, but of redemption."'[22] Furthermore, by developing the Maurician emphasis on the incarnation which revealed the 'sacredness of human life', Dale argued that it was the duty of Christian citizens to carry the law and Spirit of God

---

14 R.W. Dale, *The Old Evangelicalism and the New* (London: Hodder & Stoughton, 1889), a separately published single sermon.

15 R.W. Dale, *Fellowship With Christ* (London: Hodder & Stoughton, 1891), p. 201.

16 A.W.W. Dale, *The Life of R.W. Dale of Birmingham* (London: Hodder & Stoughton, 1898), pp. 264, 320 & 436-37.

17 Dale, *Life of Dale*, p. 707.

18 MT, 28.11.1895.

19 R.W. Dale, *The Atonement* (London: Congregational Union of England & Wales, 1902), p. 404.

20 Dale, *Life of Dale*, p. 398.

21 Dale, *Fellowship*, p. 199.

22 Thompson, David, 'John Clifford's Social Gospel', *The Baptist Quarterly*, 31.5 (January 1986), p. 264.

into municipal and political life.[23] Thus he argued for laws to prevent the exploitation of farmers and labourers and the removal of obstructions in industrial relations as part of the proper redemptive work of Christ.

> All municipal laws that improve the health of a town, reduce the death-rate, promote cleanliness, give fresh air and pure water to the people, are as truly part of that redemptive work which the Church has to carry on in the name of Christ, as the preaching of the remission of sins, or the establishment of Churches.[24]

Silvester Horne observed that the application of his theology led Dale to be a leader in the educational, municipal, political and religious life of Birmingham.[25] With such a clearly articulated theology and being held in such high regard for the engagement with civic life that flowed from it, it seems strange that Dale felt one of the most significant moments in his ministry was to challenge the Methodists to apply their understanding of Christian Perfection to public life, as Wesley had applied it to private life. Indeed, he believed that nothing had been 'inspired with a graver sense of responsibility, or a deeper desire to secure a hearing' than this message to the Methodists, with the possible exception of his work on the atonement.[26] This sense of urgency in Dale's address to the 1879 Wesleyan Conference was taken up by Hugh Price Hughes who regularly referred to it in the columns of the *Methodist Times*. Some fifteen years later Hughes maintained that much had been done to act upon Dale's justified reproach.[27]

Dale's concern was his desire to root his theology in Christian experience as he saw both faith and theology being verified by personal experience.[28] More than that, experience gave the direction and vitality which sustained Christian work and witness. He drew attention to what Methodism would have been like without Wesley's revelation of Christ's loving forgiveness on 24 May 1738. 'But for THAT, there would have been no Methodist Revival.'[29] Hughes believed that his highlighting of the importance of Christian experience was one of the most significant contributions that Dale made. One of the 'great step[s] in the evolution of his best self was the ever-increasing importance which he attached to personal experience'.[30] It was therefore very much in character that his first objective was to bring individuals to an encounter with Christ, 'Seek ye first the Kingdom of God'

---

23 R.W. Dale, *Laws of Life for Common Life* (London: Hodder & Stoughton, 1903), pp. 187-88.

24 *Contemporary Review*, 1883, p. 494, quoted by Thompson, *Social Gospel*, pp. 264-65.

25 C. Silvester Horne, *A Popular History of the Free Churches* (London: James Clarke, 1903), p. 420.

26 Dale, *Life of Dale*, p. 350.

27 R.W. Dale, *The Evangelical Revival* (London: Hodder & Stoughton, 1880), p. 39; MT, 20.12.1894; 04.02.1886; 08.07,1886; 07.07.1887; 08.11.1888; 09.02.1893.

28 R.W. Dale, *The Living Christ and the Four Gospels* (London: Hodder & Stoughton, 1905), pp. 270-71.

29 Dale, *Fellowship*, p. 221.

30 MT, 29.12.1898.

was a favourite text of his.[31] In 1873-74 he wrote a series of articles for *The Congregationalist* magazine. The tenor of his writing was that Christians should be praying for and expecting a spiritual revival by the power of the Holy Spirit.[32]

When Moody and Sankey came he had great reservations about their method and message, but his reticence vanished when the meetings began and he witnessed what took place at the Bingley Hall. He received 120 converts at Carr's Lane though he continued to disagree with Moody that instantaneous conversion was necessarily the norm.[33]

An insight into Dale's own evangelistic ministry can be gained by examining a call to commitment he gave at Birmingham Town Hall while Carr's Lane was being extended. At the time the Town Hall location was bringing many unchurched people to their services. 'I have . . . urged you to repent of sin and trust in the mercy of God, as revealed through our Lord Jesus Christ, for forgiveness, for the baptism in the Holy Ghost, and for eternal life; but now once more and for the last time . . . I implore you.'[34]

The reference to the 'baptism in the Holy Ghost' alluded to Wesleyan theology and the Spirit as the agent of sanctification. For Dale the partial reformation of the sixteenth century had been completed by the Methodist reformation of the eighteenth. Melanchthon's theology of justification was corrected and complemented by Fletcher's teaching on sanctification.[35] But although the evangelical revival had led to a great reformation in morals, it had not led to a new morality.[36]

Dale already considered that personal holiness was of the utmost importance, and would actually expel members of his congregation for irregularities in their business affairs.[37] Christian conduct was as important as Christian truth and he was impressed at the way the Pearsall Smiths' had managed to put holiness and sanctification before the people, but felt they were prophets with no teachers and feared their excesses.[38]

Dale looked for an ethical revival that would complete the work of the evangelical revival: an ethical revival that went beyond personal morality and applied holiness to society,[39] providing an experiential foundation within which his theological understanding could be sustained. Thus, he exhorted Methodists to reclaim the teaching of Wesley on the Holy Spirit by affirming the confession of the creed, 'I believe in the Holy Ghost'.[40] In fact, at his death he was already making

---

[31] Dale, *Fellowship*, p. 259.
[32] Dale, *Life of Dale*, pp. 316-17.
[33] Dale, *Life of Dale*, pp. 317-21.
[34] Dale, *Life of Dale*, p. 210.
[35] MT, 08.07.1886.
[36] Dale, *Life of Dale*, pp. 348-49.
[37] Dale, *Life of Dale*, pp. 106-07.
[38] Dale, *Life of Dale*, pp. 329-31.
[39] Dale, *Life of Dale*, p. 351.
[40] Dale, *Life of Dale*, p. 347.

preparations for the book on the Holy Spirit that had been on his mind for many years.[41]

He had a high view of the Holy Spirit, for the indwelling of the Spirit was the indispensable 'centre and source of divine activity' in the life of the believer.[42] It was through the baptism in the Spirit that new heights of perfection and power were available to the Christian as he was taken into 'union with Christ'.[43] For it was not a baptism of a 'Power' so much as the in-filling with the 'Personality' of the Spirit of Jesus.[44] In this way human life was drawn into perfect union with the life of God, from which influence and grace flowed.

The activity of the Spirit therefore touched every part of Christian life and witness. The Spirit gave gifts for all forms of service.[45] Not only must preaching be in 'the power of the Holy Ghost',[46] but Dale also looked for a time in the churches' civic involvement 'when the equity, truthfulness, frankness, courage, industry, patience, temperance, self-sacrifice, public spirit, gentleness, charity of those who bear the Christian name will be a perpetual demonstration of the presence and the power of the Holy Ghost'.[47] Because 'God's great end is our perfection,' in both private and public life,[48] it was only possible through the activity of the Spirit. So Dale exhorts, 'unless you have received the gift of the Holy Spirit. Seek it - seek it reverently, persistently, in the name of Christ . . . seek it until you have it.'[49]

Yet having developed such a theology that enabled and sustained engagement with social and political forces Dale still saw a sharp dichotomy between it and purely spiritual work. He would never use the pulpit for anything other than a spiritual message, and he felt that using the Free Church Councils for social and political work would downgrade the church.[50]

Tudor Jones concludes that Dale combined 'intellectual ability, a burning moral passion, deep conviction, and a gift of powerful utterance in a unique way'.[51] Of his theology A.M. Fairbairn noted that although he existed in a milieu of Puritanism, Calvinism, Arminianism, the evangelical revival, higher criticism and F.D. Maurice, he managed to cease being a Calvinist without becoming an Arminian, and he incorporated liberal theology so as to modify, without surrendering, the old evangelical doctrines.[52] Dale's biographer concludes that the blending of his political, social and evangelistic enthusiasms is the paradox of his life.[53] In doing so

---

41 Dale, *Life of Dale*, p. 685.
42 R.W. Dale, *Christian Doctrine* (London: Hodder & Stoughton, 1894), p. 143.
43 Dale, *Doctrine*, p. 146.
44 Dale, *Doctrine*, pp. 141-42.
45 Dale, *Fellowship*, p. 84.
46 Dale, *Fellowship*, p. 58.
47 Dale, *Laws*, p. 302.
48 R.W. Dale, *The Ten Commandments* (London: Hodder & Stoughton, 1872), p. 19.
49 Dale, *Fellowship*, p. 83.
50 Dale, *Life of Dale*, p. 648.
51 Tudor Jones, *Congregationalism*, p. 301.
52 Dale, *Life of Dale*, p. 707.
53 Dale, *Life of Dale*, pp. 320-21

he completely misunderstands Dale as the outline above reveals. The threads of his thought are combined in the same experiential and theological tapestry. His pulpit dichotomy may have been a personal quirk, a concession to the inexorable pressure to conform to received-orthodoxy, but his theology was a coherent and integrated whole. However Dale is viewed it is hardly surprising that he exercised immense influence among those within his own denomination. He was a pioneer who blended the old and the new in a way that drew the positive from both in a constructive way. It is no wonder that many considered that they owed their faith to his writing, preaching and actions.

J.B. PATON was the principal of the Congregational Training Institute at Nottingham and had been a college friend of Dale. He was the editor of the *Eclectic Review* between 1857-62 and in the *Review* he gave prominence to the discussion of social questions. Later he took over the *Contemporary Review* before ultimately passing the editorship to Percy Bunting, a lay leader at the West London Mission under Hughes and son of Jabez Bunting the former Wesleyan leader.[54]

Paton had been greatly influenced by the work of J.A. Wichern's 'Inner Mission' in Germany. Wichern had sought to co-ordinate prison visiting, colportage, the alleviation of prostitution, corrupt literature and drunkenness, the relief of poverty and the care of children through a central committee of his denomination.[55] As early as 1873 Paton had organised a conference in Nottingham to discuss the ideas he had brought back from his regular trips on the continent.[56] In 1883 he was advocating the establishment of rural labour colonies to alleviate the problems of urban unemployment and while these were eventually established in the late 1890s, they were not a great success as they lacked popular support.[57]

In the early 1870s Paton had organised a local council of churches and charities in Nottingham to oversee and co-ordinate their social work. His convictions influenced Bunting and Guinness Rogers and when the latter was invited by Hughes to write an article for the *Methodist Times* advocating a Free Church Congress, Paton was only too pleased to become involved with the scheme, drawing up a letter to be circulated over the names Hughes, Lidgett, Horton, Berry, Clifford and himself.[58]

ANDREW MEARNS' contribution to the movement with the publication of *The Bitter Cry of Outcast London* in October 1883, and its subsequent serialization by W.T. Stead in the *Pall Mall Gazette* has already been noted, as has Hughes' assessment of its significant contribution to the origins of the Forward Movement.

---

[54] Thompson, *Social Gospel*, pp. 261-62.

[55] Thompson, *Social Gospel*, p. 268.

[56] Thompson, *Social Gospel*, p. 269.

[57] Bebbington, *The Nonconformist Conscience*, pp. 56-57.

[58] Bebbington, *The Nonconformist Conscience*, pp. 61-63; E.K.H. Jordan, *Free Church Unity* (London: Luterworth, 1956), p. 26; MT, 17.01.1889 & 18.12.1890; Thompson, *Social Gospel*, p. 276.

It was an environmental and missionary tract but its evangelical origin through Mearns ensured that there was a strong connection between the absence of religious feelings and prevalent living conditions. These sentiments were largely omitted by Stead in his publication of the work.

The Bitter Cry had a special message for the churches. The emphasis on the connection between non-attendance, slum-living, overcrowding and immorality came with clarity and force. But it was far from being a tract on pre-evangelism and therefore marked a new departure for the churches. 'Many pressing needs are taxing the resources of the London Congregational Union, but the Committee feel that this work amongst the poor must no longer be neglected, and that they must do all they can to arouse the churches of their order to undertake their share of responsibility.'[59]

The ripples of effect from this tract were far reaching in many directions, and again it was the Congregationalists who were at the spearhead. They gave the impetus to the other denominations whose own response enabled work to be undertaken that the Congregationalists could never have managed themselves. Indeed, Joseph Parker told the London Congregational Union in November 1890 that they were unable to organise a 'Forward Movement' of their own, and that therefore they should support the work of other denominations along this line.[60] In fact they were doing so already and *The Methodist Times* reported that Mearns had arranged for their Wardour Chapel to be placed at the West London Mission's disposal, and Westminster Chapel had twice contributed 100 guineas to the funds of the Mission.

While the Congregationalists could not organise a Forward Movement of their own, Hughes was grateful not only for their support and the impetus given by Mearns' *Bitter Cry*, but also for the influence of Dr Berry of Wolverhampton.

CHARLES BERRY was the first, according to Hugh Price Hughes, 'to formulate definitely and articulately the essential theological and ecclesiastical doctrines of the great Movement which is revolutionising the Protestant world'.[61] A pastoral experience with a dying woman at Bolton had shaken a young Berry who had slipped away from his Calvinist upbringing into latitudinarianism. While she had drawn no comfort from his witness to the Fatherhood of God and Eternal Love, in a presentation of the cross and pardon for sin she found rest and peace.[62]

Berry began his ministry in Wolverhampton in 1883 resisting a number of invitations to more prestigious congregations as the years passed. His reputation and influence were greatly enhanced when he was invited to follow Henry Ward Beecher at the Plymouth Church, Brooklyn, in 1887.[63] Resisting the call to

---

[59] Anthony S. Wohl, *The Bitter Cry of Outcast London by Andrew Mearns with other selections and an introduction by Anthony S. Wohl* (Leicester: Leicester University Press, 1970), p. 71.

[60] MT, 04.12.1890.

[61] MT, 07.12.1890.

[62] James S. Drummond, *Charles A. Berry, D.D.* (London: Cassell, 1899), p. 35.

[63] Drummond, *Charles A. Berry*, pp. 52-67.

America was particularly hard as Beecher had been a role model for him as a young minister. Through his writing Beecher had taught Berry a new method of theology that looked to Christian experience as the 'invulnerable castle of truth'.[64] Beecher had departed from the strictures of Calvinism, disbelieving in a literal hell, and embracing the approach to be a political activist and reformer.[65]

Like Dale, Berry sought to ground his theology in experience and develop it into political activism. As Dale was actively involved with Liberalism and civic politics in Birmingham, so Berry eagerly engaged himself in similar activities in Wolverhampton, as is illustrated in his support of the miners at Cannock Chase during their dispute and lock-out in 1893.[66]

In an important sermon he preached before the Congregational Union meeting at Swansea in September 1890, he addressed the subject, 'Spiritual Power and the Need of the Churches'. He believed that,

> Everything of intellectual development, of moral elevation, of political justice, of social progress, of international amity, of human enlightenment and assuagement, springs directly from Him.[67]

> But in themselves, these things were not enough. The church was not without witness to the work of the third person of the Trinity, and they needed to increasingly seek 'a fresh baptism in the Holy Ghost'.[68]

For him,

> Pentecost is, therefore, the soul and centre of our faith, its characteristic equipment, its peculiar note. Not by might, nor by the power of man, but by the Spirit of God does it stand and work.[69]

He wanted the Spirit to throb through them for the gospel offered the power of the gift of the Spirit, an omnipotent power that brought a new wealth of spiritual resource. If the claim was taken away, the gospel was no gospel.[70] Pentecost repeated itself in the experience of every soul that sought 'complete consecration', and as lives were devoted to God they demonstrated the presence and power of Christ.[71] While Berry is not as explicit in his application as Dale, he too was eager to lay an experiential foundation for his social and political involvements.

R.F. HORTON and C.S. HORNE are worth studying together given a number of similarities between them. They both spent time studying at Oxford, warmed to

---

64 Drummond, *Charles A. Berry*, pp. 161-62.
65 DCC, p. 115.
66 Drummond, *Charles A. Berry*, pp. 80 & 227-29.
67 Charles A. Berry, *Vision and Duty* (London: Sampson Low Marston, 1893), p. 123.
68 Berry, *Vision*, p. 129.
69 Berry, *Vision*, p. 126.
70 Berry, *Vision*, pp. 132 &125.
71 Berry, *Vision*, p. 195.

higher criticism, were in demand as evangelists and personally acknowledged a debt to R.W. Dale.

At the beginning of the 1890s both were also advocating the need for a Congregational Forward Movement. Horne had spoken for the adoption of forward principles at the International Congregational Council that met in London in July 1890.[72] Horton, on the other hand, had used the columns of *The British Weekly* in his advocacy of the movement, the first explicit reference being on 9 February 1893. Robertson Nicoll had founded *The British Weekly* in 1886 as 'a paper for Christian radicals'. It served the same purpose among the Congregationalists as Hughes' paper did amongst the Wesleyans[73] and, two years later, Hughes rejoiced when the Congregational Union recognised the need 'for a Forward Movement' at their annual meeting being held in Brighton.[74]

Binfield points out that the Congregationalists had been looking for a practical expression for their Forward Movement throughout the early 1890s and at one point had attempted to lure Horton to Westminster Chapel. They had to wait until 1902 when Claremont Chapel in Pentonville was revived as a Central Hall, closely followed by Whitefield's Tabernacle, which began to be turned into an Institutional Church by Horne in 1903.[75]

> The purpose of an institutional church was to reconstruct human society on the basis of brotherhood. . . . The cardinal point is institutional methods, second to a tremendous belief in the fatherhood of God and the brotherhood of Jesus Christ, upon the belief in the sacredness of man.[76]

Both Horton and Horne looked to Dale as their mentor. Horton recognised that he stood in the Congregationalist succession to him, and Horne, whose father was at college with Dale, recognised his debt to the man as inestimable.[77] As evangelists both men were accomplished, having conducted many missions, including campaigns for each other. Horton had been greatly impressed with D.L. Moody, and was thrilled to have brought 'several distressed souls to the joy and peace of believing' following Moody's meetings.[78] Prior to a mission at Huddersfield he exhorted the organisers to pray that 'our God will open the windows of Heaven and bless us',[79] so that they might 'speak boldly and in the fullness of the Holy Spirit' it was said of his own evangelistic style that 'There was nothing hysterical, nothing

---

72 Clyde Binfield, *So Down To Prayers* (London: J.M. Dent, 1977), p. 201.

73 *British Weekly*, 09.02.1893, quoted by Inglis, *Churches and the Working Class*, pp. 70-71.

74 MT, 10.10.1895.

75 Binfield, *So Down To Prayers*, pp. 203-204.

76 Robert Pope, 'Congregations and Community' in Lesley Husselbee & Paul Ballard (eds), *Free Churches and Society: The Nonconformist Contribution to Social Welfare 1800-2010* (London: Continuum, 2012), p. 37.

77 Grant, *Free Churchmanship*, p. 122; Selbie, *Horne*, p. 91.

78 R.F. Horton, *An Autobiography* (London: George Allen & Unwin, 1918), pp. 37-38.

79 Peel & Marriott, *Robert Forman Horton*, pp. 152-53.

extravagant: all was quiet, thoughtful and yet fervent.'[80] Horne's views on the importance of evangelism were straightforward. 'The ministry that is not an evangelistic ministry is not in the full sense a Christian ministry, for we cannot obey our Lord's command and leave His Divine appeal unuttered.'[81]

For the most part, both tacitly accepted Dale's teaching of the place and role of the Holy Spirit. Horne acknowledged that, 'for the soul that received by faith the power and influence of the Holy Spirit, . . . all things were possible'.[82] Horton, however, found new understanding and experience when he met Reader Harris and became involved with the activities of the Pentecostal League. He related that as a result he made a simple discovery that was, 'quite revolutionary in its effect. I found that faith in Christ means not only a deliverance from the ultimate results of sin, but also a deliverance from the actual power of sin.'[83]

The two men differed in regard to their special interests and talents. Horton was the more profound thinker being particularly influenced by biblical criticism and by the thought of his friend T.H. Green.[84] He delivered the Yale lectures on Preaching in 1893, later published as *Verbum Dei*, in which he ascribed to the Spirit the determinative role,[85] and had also previously written books on the relationship between inspiration, revelation and the Bible [86] which had allowed many Congregationalists to rediscover the Bible in the light of the higher criticism. In the process many shed their notions of verbal inspiration and inerrancy. Throughout Horton's writing and speaking those who distrusted the holiness teaching of the Keswick Convention found in Horton an alternative, 'a Keswick with brains'.[87] He was the first Nonconformist to be elected a fellow at Oxford yet was quite content to become a minister at Hampstead where the church he helped to establish grew to number 1200 members under his ministry.[88]

Henry George's *Progress and Poverty* touched his conscience but did not altogether convince his understanding[89] he was actually far more partial to the thought of his hero, John Bright.[90] Horton organised a Social Reform League among those who attended his lectures in the winter of 1889, from which they formed a Sanitary Committee that worked to apply the law in the vast areas of slum housing prior to the formation of the Hampstead Council for Social Welfare. Inglis

---

[80] Grant, *Free Churchmanship*, pp. 168 & 182; Selbie, *Horne*, pp. 91 & 96.
[81] C. Silvester Horne, *The Romance of Preaching* (London: James Clarke, 1914), p. 218.
[82] C. Silvester Horne, *The Soul's Awakening* (London: Passmore and Alabaster, 1902), p. 165.
[83] Horton, *Autobiography*, pp. 105-107.
[84] Horton, *Autobiography*, pp. 43 & 76; Peel & Marriott, *Robert Forman Horton*, pp. 99 & 109.
[85] Horton, *Autobiography*, p. 130; MT, 01.06.1893.
[86] R.F. Horton, *Inspiration and the Bible* (London: T. Fisher Unwin, 1888); R.F. Horton, *Revelation and the Bible* (London: T. Fisher Unwin, 1892).
[87] Binfield, *So Down To Prayers*, p. 222.
[88] Peel & Marriott, *Robert Forman Horton*, p. 150.
[89] Horton, *Autobiography*, p. 81.
[90] Peel & Marriott, *Robert Forman Horton*, p. 90.

concludes that he held together both an evangelical zeal and a desire to improve social conditions.[91]

Silvester Horne began to come into his own when he was appointed minister at Whitefield's Tabernacle in 1903. It was difficult at first to reconcile the needs of the shop girls and clerks that thronged around Tottenham Court Road on the one hand and the slums and brothels in close proximity on the other. Soon he had developed all the trappings of a Wesleyan Mission. Whitefield's became an Institutional Church with a clear purpose to help people develop all their faculties as provision was made for soul, mind and spirit. Everything that was felt to enrich life had a place there and these principles brought new life to the place. Horne himself became a most persuasive advocate of the idea and wrote a book on the subject.[92] Unfortunately the pioneering was not without its tensions and Horne resigned in 1914, though at least in part this was due to his election to Parliament as the representative for Ipswich in 1910, becoming the first sitting MP to be a minister in full charge since Cromwell. Silvester Horne was convinced that it was necessary to bring religion into politics and then to reconstruct both municipal and national affairs on a Christian basis.[93] 'The only thing that really matters is that we give ourselves to Christ, to live, to work, to think and dare for Him. That is everything.'[94]

A.M. FAIRBAIRN's appointment as the first principal of Mansfield College, Oxford in 1885 gave him an unrivalled position of influence as well as access to leading English thinkers like T.H. Green. A year in Germany in the mid-1860s following a crisis of faith in his first pastorate led him to rediscover the Sonship of Christ. This in turn gave a new significance to the Fatherhood of God in his developing understanding of the Kingdom of God.[95]

In no small way he was also responsible for divorcing higher criticism from rationalism and making it acceptable to Congregationalists by wedding it to evangelical theology. However, he steered clear of doctrinal theology because he did not think that modern men would be won for Christ by it.[96] His eagerness to Christianize society while maintaining the primary aims of teaching the truth and saving souls led him establish to the Mansfield House Settlement in Canning Town.[97]

When addressing the Congregational Union in 1883 he suggested that industrial and social questions could not be wisely or justly determined without reference to religion. However, in the same speech, wary of being misrepresented, he also reiterated,

---

[91] Inglis, *Churches and the Working Class*, p. 111.
[92] Binfield, *So Down To Prayers*, pp. 203-04; Grant, *Free Churchmanship*, p. 177.
[93] Binfield, *So Down To Prayers*, pp. 205-206, Selbie, *Horne*, p. 175.
[94] Selbie, *Horne*, p. 279.
[95] Thompson, *Social Gospel*, p. 265.
[96] Tudor Jones, *Congregationalism*, p. 255; Grant, *Free Churchmanship*, p. 168.
[97] Tudor Jones, *Congregationalism*, p. 345

> I wish, indeed, not to be misunderstood. To me the primary work of the religion is to save men; of the churches, to preach the gospel. This is fundamental, work that must be done before anything else is possible; that left undone disqualifies for everything else.[98]

Thompson has pointed out that *The Spectator* noted the significance of this address as indicative of the 'change in the modern religious temper', remarking that thirty years previous the address could not have been delivered at such a gathering.[99]

The Fatherhood of God, the incarnation of the Son and the theme of the Kingdom of God were the hallmarks of Fairbairn's theology. Remaining evangelically orthodox he developed an understanding that personal individuality was supplemented by societal unity, and that as man had suffered loss collectively, he could also be saved collectively. From this foundation he therefore argued for a social, as well as a personal, recovery that followed as a consequence from salvation.[100]

He was a close friend of Dale and his evangelical orthodoxy also led him to make religious experience the essential basis of his theology, yet he did not give it the prominence of his friend. Neither did he seek to develop an ethical framework of entire sanctification and baptism in the Holy Spirit to further support his social theology. His debt lay far more clearly with Maurice, and under Fairbairn's theological influence Dale's embryonic thought was gradually eclipsed.

The level of initiative in terms of strategic thought and activity within Congregationalism was staggering. Blackham's PSAs; Dale's theology and municipal involvement; Paton's German insights for mission and unity; Mearns' *Bitter Cry*; Berry's socio-religious progressivism; Horton's work towards a thoughtful evangelicalism; Horne's application of the Institutional Church principle and entry into Parliament; and Fairbairn's sojourn at Oxford and development of the Mansfield House Settlement, all ought to have stood the denomination at the forefront of the Forward Movement. However, their failure to gather widespread support is a negative testimony to the congregational form of church government. Hughes recognised this irony a matter of months before he died. 'Again, the Forward Movement originated with the Congregationalists . . . but it is the Methodists who reaped the advantage of that Congregational Movement.'[101]

While Dale enthused Hughes and others with the thought of providing an experiential basis for the social gospel, founded upon a developed understanding of Entire Sanctification and the baptism in the Holy Spirit, latterly it was largely lost sight of for two main reasons. First, among forward thinkers it became overshadowed by the emerging dominance of the doctrines of the Fatherhood of

---

98 A.M. Fairbairn, *Studies in Religion and Theology* (London: Hodder & Stoughton, 1910), pp. 99 & 97.

99 Thompson, *Social Gospel*, p. 267.

100 W.B. Selbie, *The Life of Andrew Martin Fairbairn* (London: Hodder & Stoughton, 1914), pp. 40-41.

101 MT, 24.10.1901.

God and the Incarnation of the Son, doctrines which they had themselves also embraced and preached. Second, within Congregationalism, those who did not depart from Calvinistic orthodoxy had never embraced Dale's move from dogma to experience.

The response of Congregationalists to the emergent Social Christianity of the Forward Movement was at best intermittent. There were those who were fully in sympathy with all that the progressive movement stood for: a commitment to evangelism, Christian experience and righteousness that was applied to the whole of life. As Dale commented,

> God's commandments are much broader than some good people imagine, and to fulfil them properly they must surrender their whole heart and will to Him . . . His commandments cover your municipal life, and no devoutness can be an excuse for not paying your rates, neither can it be an excuse for keeping away from the polling booth at the time of an election.'[102]

[102] Dale, *Life of Dale*, p. 400.

Chapter 7

Baptist Conversionists

If one issue stood as the pre-eminent concern of every Baptist at the end of the nineteenth century it was evangelism. In many ways it was the touchstone of orthodoxy among them. Self-confessed Calvinists committed theological gymnastics to participate in evangelism and adherents of the newly emerging social gospel did not forget that this was their primary concern either. This is hardly surprising given that the other traditional emphases of Calvinistic theology, social separation and political non-involvement, were in a state of flux.

As with the Congregationalists, Baptist ecclesiology made it difficult to develop a co-ordinated response to the needs and demands of the age with each congregation remaining very much their own master. While there were exceptions, conservatism and slowness typified the overall response of the denomination to the issues that had brought about such significant changes among the Wesleyans and Congregationalists.

As other Nonconformists were pioneering new forms of mission and ministry the two preoccupations of corporate Baptist life were theological in nature. The 'Downgrade Controversy' of 1887-88 and the merger of the Particular Baptists with the New Connexion of General Baptists in 1891 were both the fruit of the declining influence of Calvinism.

The influence of the eighteenth century Evangelical Revival combined with this looser form of Calvinism to contribute significantly to the wholehearted commitment of most Baptists to evangelism. In 1876 William Landels expressed this commitment in his presidential address to the Baptist Union, speaking of the need to evangelise the whole of the country and the importance of the growing strength of the Union to accomplish it. Indeed, the primary impact on London Baptist Association of the social distress outlined in *The Bitter Cry*, was a redoubling of their efforts in evangelism.[1]

David Bebbington sees three stages in their developing political mobilisation.[2] Up until the first Reform Act of 1832 Baptists adopted a policy of 'quietism' and non-involvement. The period that led up to the second Reform Act of 1867 saw an

---

1 A. LeBarbour, *Victorian Baptists: A Study of Denominational Development* (Maryland, 1977: unpublished Ph.D. Thesis), pp. 126 & 128.

2 D.W. Bebbington, 'The Baptist Conscience in the Nineteenth Century', *The Baptist Quarterly* 34.1 (January 1991), pp13 & 22.

increasing activity on issues where they thought that sin could be attacked. While the Chartists benefited little from Baptist support, the Anti-Corn Law League actually had their programme endorsed by the Baptist Union in 1843,[3] with a League meeting for ministers in Manchester during August 1841 attracting 182 Baptists out of a total attendance of 645.[4] It is rather ironic that at that stage the Baptist Union's own meetings had never attracted so many ministers. The last third of the century witnessed the erosion of lingering suspicions about political involvement as Baptists began joining with their Nonconformist compatriots in the debates centring around disestablishment, education, political morality and crusades designed to alleviate major social problems and injustices. Yet a relative slowness in their response remained for most of them. Issues of social purity or morality gained sympathetic support, but Baptists were noticeable by their absence when Joseph Arch appealed on behalf of the agricultural workers and when help was sought on behalf of the London Dockers in 1889. LeBarbour believes that this was because Baptist leaders generally failed to see beyond their middle-class perspective to grasp the need for social and economic changes within society.[5] By contrast temperance was an issue that gradually brought about a denominational consensus. In 1860 only a sixth of Baptist ministers were abstainers. This number had grown to 1,100 out of 1,900 in 1886, and in 1907, 211 out of 214 theological students were committed to abstain.[6]

CHARLES HADDON SPURGEON was the Nonconformist pulpit giant of the late nineteenth century. Between 1859 and 1892 thousands of worshippers flocked to his Metropolitan Tabernacle at the Elephant and Castle. However, an attendance of nearly 11,000 each Sunday at the height of his influence had fallen to a little over 3,500 some twelve years after his death.[7] His primary concern was evangelism. The question was not, 'Will the heathen be lost if they do not hear the gospel? [but] shall we be saved if we do not take it to them?'[8]

Some considered his preaching to be coarse and vulgar, but Spurgeon was unrepentant as he believed his personal mission was to the masses of poor, ignorant and unenlightened people that thronged south London. Nevertheless, his sermons were more widely read than those of his contemporaries.[9]

While he maintained that he was a Calvinist, Spurgeon resolutely refused to reconcile or even recognise the fundamental conflict between the theological demands of Calvin and the emotional demands of his evangelism. John Clifford commented of Spurgeon and those he trained at his Pastors' College,

---

3 Bebbington, *The Nonconformist Conscience*, p16.
4 Ernest Payne, *The Baptist Union* (London: Carey Kingsgate, 1959), p. 70.
5 LeBarbour, *Victorian Baptists*, p. 257.
6 Bebbington, *The Nonconformist Conscience*, p. 46.
7 R. Mudie-Smith, *The Religious Life of London* (London: Hodder & Stoughton, 1904), p. 289.
8 John Clifford, *Typical Christian Leaders* (London: Marshall, 1898), p. 93.
9 Clifford, *Typical Christian Leaders*, p. 91.

> They preach Calvinism, warm glowing and sympathetic; and leap over any five-barred gate to save a soul, and fling all metaphysical systems to the winds that stands in the way of the redemption of men. Avowedly believing in restrictions, yet they work as if there were none, and so they compel men to come in.[10]

Alongside his evangelistic endeavours Spurgeon organised a wide variety of philanthropic activities. In the Tabernacle itself were twenty rooms for classes and clubs and the adjoining alms-houses provided quarters for seventeen poor women. There was a maternity society for expectant mothers, alongside benevolent and provident societies, and the more widely supported Stockwell Orphanage.[11] These agencies were exceptional, and due in no small part to Spurgeon's popularity which placed at his disposal a pool of financial and human resources that were not available to others. It is doubtful whether it ever occurred to him that fundamental changes were needed in social structure.

The 'Downgrade Controversy' broke through the pages of Spurgeon's paper, *The Sword and the Trowel*.[12] An article by Robert Shindler, a Baptist minister from Addlestone, in March 1887 identified evangelical truth with Calvinism and spoke of the theological 'downgrade' of those Nonconformists who gave up this position. Spurgeon himself took up the issue and wrote an article on the subject almost every month until his death five years later. The Baptist Union bore the brunt of Spurgeon's criticism, but he never substantiated his claims because of an undertaking he made to the General Secretary of the Union. He also feared that if he did the issue would become one of personalities which he wanted to resist. Through the columns of the *Pall Mall Gazette* John Clifford became the Union's chief defender. He isolated the six main areas of Spurgeon's concern as relating to: the atonement; Holy Scripture; the fall; the personality of the Holy Spirit; justification by faith and mankind's eternal destiny.[13] While these points were later addressed by the Union things had gone too far. Talking of 'confederacies of evil' Spurgeon announced on 28 October 1887 that 'We retire at once and distinctly from the Baptist Union.'[14]

While stricter Calvinists held that Spurgeon was the source of his own Downgrade for offering the hospitality of an open communion table and departing from the cardinal doctrines of the Bible, the Union sought reconciliation.[15] Various attempts failed and when the matter was brought to the Union's assembly John

---

[10] LeBarbour, *Victorian Baptists*, p. 193.

[11] Kathleen Heasman, *Evangelicals in Action* (London: Geoffrey Bles, 1962), p. 52

[12] Fuller accounts of the Downgrade Controversy may be found in Payne, *The Baptist Union*, pp. 127-43; LeBarbour, *Victorian Baptists*, pp. 204-23; H. Leon McBeth, *The Baptist Heritage* (Nashville: B&H Academic, 1987), pp. 302-306; A.C. Underwood, *A History of the English Baptists* (London: Carey Kingsgate), pp. 229-32.

[13] James Marchant, *Dr. John Clifford: Life, Letters and Reminiscences* (London: Cassell, 1924), p. 163.

[14] LeBarbour, *Victorian Baptists*, p. 22; McBeth, *The Baptist Heritage*, p. 304.

[15] J.H.Y. Briggs, 'Evangelical Ecumenism: The Amalgamation of General and Particular Baptists in 1891', *The Baptist Quarterly* 34.3 (July 1991), p. 106.

Clifford's statesmanship from the Presidential chair prevailed and at least denominational harmony was restored. The Assembly hosted some five to six hundred visitors on that occasion including Guinness Rogers and Hugh Price Hughes.[16] Hughes had taken an active interest in the controversy and believed that, 'It can no longer be concealed that Mr. Spurgeon is out of touch with the new democracy and the younger generation of devout evangelicals. He is standing still, but the Church of God moves on.'[17]

Hughes' sentiments proved to be correct for while Spurgeon commanded immense personal support and sympathy, there was no widespread desertion from the Union either by the ministers or by the churches, and by 1889, while five churches had left, a further 61 had joined.[18] Some have attempted to portray the controversy as a personal struggle between Spurgeon and Clifford. Both men rejected this view, and despite their theological differences remained warm personal friends.[19] What the controversy did reveal was that even a modified Calvinism like Spurgeon's was too narrow for the majority within the Union. Effectively it made the Calvinist/Arminian debate within the denomination inconsequential in the face of larger issues.

In many ways the merger of the Particular Baptists and the New Connexion of General Baptists in 1891 is indicative of this same issue. Briggs sees the merger as the mature fruit of the Evangelical Revival, for the revival had given birth to the New Connexion and occasioned the need for theological revisionism amongst the Particulars.[20] From the very beginning, New Connexion pastors had participated in the Union, and in 1842 one of their number, J.G. Pike, was President. Jabez Burns was the next in 1850, followed by John Clifford in the year of the Downgrade Controversy, 1888.[21] In 1873 the assembly heard a call for 'a complete amalgamation of the two sections of the Baptist body' and it might have taken place almost at once had it not been for the reticence of the northern churches of the New Connexion and the injudicious remarks of some Particular Baptists in welcoming their brethren to 'the Calvinist faith'.[22] However, the substance of their differences had disappeared and ever-increasing collaboration was inevitable. In 1868 the *General Baptist Magazine* argued that, 'There is no need now that we should be distinct from the other section of the Baptist body. The extravagant Calvinism of years gone by in Particular Baptist churches has been discarded or moderated and rendered agreeable. . . . Our greater brother has become wiser; we need not now protest but may walk and prosper with him.'[23]

---

16 Payne, *The Baptist Union*, p. 139.
17 MT, 17.11.1887.
18 Payne, *The Baptist Union*, p. 144.
19 McBeth, *The Baptist Heritage*, p. 305
20 Briggs, 'Evangelical Ecumenism', p. 99.
21 Briggs, 'Evangelical Ecumenism', p. 105.
22 McBeth, *The Baptist Heritage*, p. 306.
23 *General Baptist Magazine*, May 1868, p. 101, cited by Briggs, 'Evangelical Ecumenism', p. 109.

On 25 June 1891 the General Baptist Association met for the last time. After a four-hour session they voted by 155 to 39 in favour of dissolving their Association and uniting with the Baptist Union.[24]

JOHN CLIFFORD was only two years younger than Spurgeon, but they really belonged to different generations. At ten years of age he had begun work as a 'jacker-off' in a lace factory at Beeston[25] and when taunted by some working men at a Fabian meeting in the 1880s about what he knew of hard work, George Bernard Shaw recalled how Clifford related to them his experiences of child labour before the Factory Acts.[26]

Under the influence of his father who was an active member of the Leicester Chartist Association Clifford embraced the Chartist cause.[27] Thomas Cooper, the leader at Leicester, was a particular hero while the fiery orations of Feargus O'Connor were detested. Clifford remembered,

> The factory was full of it. Lads talked about the fall of kings as though they were ninepins. . . . The Chartist activities were all directed toward securing opportunity for the development of the individual and specially of the weakest and the most wronged individual. They aim at securing a fine and free life for each one. And that I wanted.[28]

Clifford's was an instantaneous conversion just prior to his fourteenth birthday in November 1850. After months of battling with guilt and the sense of evil in his heart, the 'spiritual emancipation' and sense of peace were life transforming.[29] He was never to forget the importance and power of that experience in his later ministry. Neither did he lose his sympathy for the struggles of the working man. His youthful experiences combined together to make him the pioneer that he was to become.

His life echoed his mother's advice to discover the teaching of Jesus and stick to it, advice which he regularly affirmed for he believed that, 'Our first business is to make men see Christ.'[30] Making Christ known was thus the unifying centre of his evangelistic, social and political ministry. Clifford wrote,

> Men do not believe in Christ Jesus enough to use Him and His gospel always, everywhere, and out and out . . . We keep Him out of our politics, and go on in wrong; out of our trade, and make bad paper, bad clothes, bad buildings; out of our social life, and grind the poor and stop our ears with cottonwool so that the cries and agony and

---

24 Payne, *The Baptist Union*, pp. 146-47.

25 Charles T. Bateman, *John Clifford* (London: Partridge, 1902), pp. 10-11.

26 David Thompson, 'John Clifford's Social Gospel', *The Baptist Quarterly* 31.5 (January 1986), p. 205.

27 G.W. Byrt, *John Clifford, A Fighting Free Churchman* (London: Kingsgate, 1947), p. 19.

28 Marchant, *Dr. John Clifford*, pp. 4-6.

29 Byrt, *John Clifford*, p. 25; Bateman, *John Clifford*, p. 16; Marchant, *Dr. John Clifford*, p. 14.

30 Underwood, *A History*, p. 228.

> misery may not disturb us, . . . out of our churches, and so perish because of our conventionalisms and respectabilities. The incarnation of the Christ of the Cross is the one thing needful[31]

He began his ministry at Praed Street, Paddington in October 1858 and in his first annual report he made explicit the spiritual manifesto that he was working to:

> We exist as a church and congregation, not only for our own spiritual improvement, but also and specially for saving the souls and bodies of the people in the neighbourhood in which we are located. We have a private object - the consolidation and help of each other in the endeavour after spiritual manhood. We have a public object, the decrease of the evils of society, and the increase of individual and social good by the dissemination of the Gospel of Christ.[32]

To this end, in 1861 they formed a Mutual Economic Benefit Society to which the payment of 4d a week secured for the members both medical aid and 12s a week in times of sickness.[33]

In 1877 a new suite of premises was opened at Westbourne Park to accommodate the burgeoning life of the church. Clifford's work continued to develop and from 1885 became one of the first attempts in London at emulating the Institutional Church experiments of Thomas Beecher at Elmira, and William S. Rainsford at St George's East Side, New York.[34] Clifford's vision was for a spiritual, intellectual and cultural centre which was pervaded by the spirit of intimate fellowship that only a church could provide. Seventy classes were held every week including on the curriculum: literature; science; geology; archaeology; modern languages; mathematics; shorthand; building construction and sport. A gymnasium was added in 1888 and cricket, rambling and cycling clubs were also established.[35] In the Institute Clifford often encouraged the discussion of important questions:

> Can the excesses of competition be adequately restrained by government interference, or by any authority external to the industrial organisation itself? . . . Must there always be a large class of society dependent for maintenance on the more common forms of physical labour, and constituting what we know as a 'labouring class'?[36]

In 1902 the Institute had a membership of 1300, of which around a half were on the educational programmes and the others availing themselves of the other facilities.[37] Always open to new ideas Clifford began a temperance house like Garrett's British

---

[31] Byrt, *John Clifford*, pp. 128-29.
[32] Marchant, *Dr. John Clifford*, p. 40.
[33] Byrt, *John Clifford*, p. 55
[34] Marchant, *Dr. John Clifford*, p. 62; DCC, pp. 512-13.
[35] Byrt, *John Clifford*, pp. 62-63.
[36] Marchant, *Dr. John Clifford*, pp. 62-63.
[37] Bateman, *John Clifford*, p. 61.

Workman Public House Company, funded by 5,000 £1 shares, and nicknamed 'Clifford's Inn'.[38]

Bebbington is correct in maintaining that Clifford always remained an evangelical.[39] From first to last his primary concern was always evangelism. At his ordination at Praed Street he declared that they were to expect,

> that sinners shall be brought to repentance, . . . I know it is for all men, and therefore I am anxious to turn men from darkness to light, and from the power of Satan unto God, so that they may receive forgiveness of sins . . . Therefore I gladly bear my testimony to the reality of conversion. I am conscious of an internal change and a change of such a nature as to prove that a Divine agent has produced it.[40]

While he was the President of the National Council of the Evangelical Free Churches in 1898, he argued for closer unity to quicken the evangelistic fervour and activity of the churches.[41] This theme was also behind a campaign he launched amongst the Free Churches in the early 1920s and only his health stopped him giving an address on 'The Aims of Personal Evangelism' to the Council in March 1922. The exhortation to 'get men to Jesus Himself' was read to the assembled leaders.[42] He was present at a Baptist Union Council meeting on 20 November 1923 simply because the subject of personal evangelism was to be discussed and he wanted to show his support. Poignantly, he died at the meeting as he continued to pursue that which had been the primary focus of his ministry.[43]

Clifford had reservations about 'mass' evangelism, and though he conceded that it served a purpose, in his opinion it left much to be desired. He was concerned that the churches lost depth and spiritual temperature when they neglected personal evangelism and, for himself, such was the intensity of his concern for those outside the faith that in praying for them or preaching for conversions would often reduce him to tears.[44]

While he owned that evangelism was his primary concern, it was only a part of his understanding of the application of the gospel. In his 1888 address to the Baptist Union Clifford maintained that all social problems were spiritual at heart. Social salvation was as necessary as individual salvation for it gave society what it lacked in 'heart forces'. Thus, the message of 'Christ crucified' was for social as well as personal crises.[45] Thompson believes that Clifford's use of the term 'Social Gospel' in the title of this address is one of its earliest usages in Britain.[46]

---

[38] Marchant, *Dr. John Clifford*, p. 71.
[39] Bebbington, 'The Baptist Conscience', p. 21.
[40] Bateman, *John Clifford*, pp. 37-38.
[41] Bateman, *John Clifford*, pp. 133-34.
[42] Byrt, *John Clifford*, p. 119.
[43] Marchant, *Dr. John Clifford*, p. 284.
[44] Marchant, *Dr. John Clifford*, pp. 212-16.
[45] Thompson, *Clifford*, p. 208.
[46] Thompson, *Social Gospel*, p. 260.

On another occasion, expressing sentiments that strongly echoed those of T.H. Green, Clifford held that a village or a city is one of the organs by which individuals realise themselves. The greatness of any community had to do with its capacity as a whole for unselfish effort, justice, liberty, progress and devotion to the public good.[47] In a study on the early life of Moses Clifford posed a scenario that must have troubled many of his thinking listeners. His sympathies were with his oppressed fellow Hebrews, while his place was in the Court of the oppressor to whom he owed all his dignity and advantages.[48]

Clifford believed that advocacy and work for the social gospel was inevitable when a Christian realised and accepted the worth of individuals in the eyes of Christ. Speaking to the Baptist World Alliance in Philadelphia in 1911 he maintained that, 'deliverance of the poor out of the hand of the evildoers becomes a primary duty . . . Charity must not be accepted as a substitute for justice.'[49]

Politics was therefore one of the organs and instruments by which to hasten the coming of the Kingdom of God. He hated the selfishness that left the world to the domain of the devil,[50] yet his involvement with politics evoked conflicting responses within him. In 1903, such was his standing within Liberalism that he was elected to the National Liberal Federation Executive with the highest number of votes. On a number of occasions he was also approached by Liberal friends seeking to encourage him to stand for Parliament in North Paddington.[51] However, he also expressed an intense dislike of having to be involved in political matters, with its attendant deflection from his pastoral work. 'I hate politics, with a perfect hatred, and if I could have got rid of my conscience I should never have touched them, and if I could escape them now and be at peace with the pursuits of my own choice, nothing would delight me more. But it cannot be. A conscience is a most inconvenient commodity.'[52]

His reputation and personal integrity were beyond reproach. Lloyd George is reported to have said, 'There is no man in England upon whose conscience I would sooner ring a coin than John Clifford's', and with Ramsey MacDonald, Herbert Asquith and William Gladstone, Lloyd George is known to have sought out his counsel.[53]

Clifford joined the Fabian Society when it was founded and later wrote two tracts for the movement.[54] In them he explored the theme of socialism in relation to

---

47 Thompson, *Social Gospel*, p. 277.

48 John Clifford, *Is Life Worth Living?* (London: E. Marlborough, 1884), pp. 18-19.

49 Thompson, *Clifford*, p. 215.

50 Marchant, *Dr. John Clifford*, pp. xi-xii.

51 Bebbington, *The Nonconformist Conscience*, p. 146; Bateman, *John Clifford*, p. 144; Marchant, *Dr. John Clifford*, p. 92.

52 Marchant, *Dr. John Clifford*, p. 91.

53 Philip R. Hart, 'John Clifford: An English Social Reformer in the Pastorate', *Perspectives in Religious Studies* 16.3 (1989), p. 227.

54 John Clifford, *Socialism and the Teaching of Christ* (London: The Fabian Society, 1897); John Clifford, *Socialism and the Churches* (London: The Fabian Society,

the teaching of Christ, defining socialism as 'the collective ownership of the means of production by the community'. In the tracts he was anxious to avoid being misinterpreted as advocating the excesses of other 'socialists' who wanted to suppress the family and achieve their ends by violence. Using the homely and familiar picture of the Postal Service he explained how it is 'the socialistic idea in operation'.[55]

Along with other Nonconformist leaders Clifford made a contribution to the agitations of the Nonconformist Conscience which was as significant as that of Hugh Price Hughes. He drew particular strength from a group of Baptists and Congregationalists who called themselves 'X', which included both Guinness Rogers and Silvester Horne.[56] In 1893 he was elected Honorary Secretary of a group interested in a progressive education policy and he threw himself into campaigning through letter writing and articles which were submitted to the Christian press.[57] In his opposition to the Boer War he confessed to 'boiling over with indignation against the iniquity of the concentration camps'[58] and his stance brought rioting crowds outside his Paddington church at Westbourne Park for three nights running in 1900.[59] His own proposals reported by Hughes in the *Methodist Times* were, however, eminently thoughtful and reasonable.[60] The London dock strike, slum housing, the Armenian massacres, temperance and gambling were all issues that attracted his attention and activity, as did the Parnell divorce case. With another member of 'X', Joseph Parker, he fired the initial salvo of 'Parnell must go'.[61] He was Chairman of the National Passive Resistance Committee, set up to oppose the 1902 Education Act, and prior to the outbreak of World War I he was taken to court no fewer than forty-one times.[62]

His reading of Emerson taught him the value of ideas and he was careful to apply this knowledge to theological and biblical matters as well as social and political issues. Yet he always differentiated between the permanent element in Christianity and its temporary theological expression.[63] He believed that ninety per cent of believers' difficulties with the Bible had to do with theories about its inspiration, theology or interpretation rather than the Bible itself. He taught that the Scriptures were written as men were moved by the Holy Spirit, 'but they were men, and their

1908).

55 Thompson, *Clifford*, pp. 211-12.

56 Bateman, *John Clifford*, p. 136.

57 Bateman, *John Clifford*, pp. 138-39.

58 Byrt, *John Clifford*, p. 140.

59 Marchant, *Dr. John Clifford*, pp. 146-47.

60 MT, 11.07.1901.

61 Marchant, *Dr. John Clifford*, pp. 144-50; on Irish Home Rule see Kent, *Hughes*, p. 190.

62 Bebbington, *The Nonconformist Conscience*, p. 144.

63 Bateman, *John Clifford*, p. 12; Underwood, *A History*, p. 232.

words can only be accurately explained and fully understood as the ordinary, literary, textual and critical methods of study are faithfully applied'.[64]

Having looked extensively at Clifford's background and the connections that he made with his particular emphases, the question remains as to whether there are any other links that held together the evangelistic and social expressions of the gospel of Christ.

It is perhaps not insignificant that Clifford regards R.W. Dale as 'The ideal chief of our modern Nonconformity', and he draws attention to the centrality of Christian experience in Dale's preaching.[65] While Clifford's exploration of the relationship between the Holy Spirit and social holiness is neither as explicit nor as thorough-going as Dale's, it is clear that he followed the same line to a certain extent. His understanding of the Sonship and Fatherhood of God built upon his passion for Jesus.

In his ordination address at Praed Street Clifford betrayed the Wesleyan influence of his paternal grandmother when he spoke of the need to 'grow in grace . . . and go on to perfection'.[66] She had taught him the three great universalities of God's love, Christ's sacrifice and the work of the Holy Spirit in convicting of sin and righteousness, which he happily remembered and repeated in an address sent by letter to the Baptist World Alliance meeting at Stockholm in 1923.[67] Bateman maintained that the Methodist influence was strong having heard him speak for Hughes at the St. James' Hall. He was a Baptist speaker with 'Methodist fire'.[68]

Clifford believed that the Evangelical Revival under the Wesley's brought forth a new experience of the love of God in the forgiveness of sins and the gift of the Spirit.[69] He looked for a similar revival for he believed that it would bring with it a self-surrender to the Spirit of God and a new Pentecost. Considering the Fatherly love of God he quotes Luke 11:13: 'If ye then, being evil, know how to give good things to your children, how much more shall your Heavenly Father give the Holy Spirit to them that ask Him?'[70]

He was frustrated with those who were saying that the next revival would be an 'ethical revival', for he maintained that all revivals were ethical, pointing to the personal transformation of the converts of Wesley and Jonathan Edwards.[71] He also believed that revivals ought to inspire Christians to join the battle-front in the attack against those things that opposed Christ's desire for the well-being of

---

[64] John Clifford, *The Inspiration and the Authority of the Bible* (London: James Clarke, 1892), p. 3.

[65] Clifford, *Typical Christian Leaders*, pp. 131 & 137.

[66] Bateman, *John Clifford*, p. 40.

[67] Byrt, *John Clifford*, pp. 11 &15.

[68] Bateman, *John Clifford*, pp. 154-55.

[69] John Clifford, *The Ultimate Problems of Christianity* (London: Kingsgate, 1906), pp. 264-65.

[70] John Clifford, *The Gospel of Gladness* (Edinburgh: T&T Clarke, 1912), pp. 110-11.

[71] Clifford, *The Gospel of Gladness*, pp. 93-94.

mankind. He recognised that such ideals would 'drive us to despair had we not the promise of His all-sufficing power and the actual indwelling of His Spirit'.[72]

He maintained that the one distinctive mark of the new Christian society was the presence and power of the Spirit of God. Believers who were filled with the Spirit spoke and acted with heroism and abandon.[73] It was in the Spirit that Christians found the 'complete sufficiency and abiding efficiency of the ever-present Spirit for securing the redemption and the renewal of mankind'.[74]

He follows Paul, whom he was convinced saw the doctrine of the Holy Spirit as the soul of his theology and ethics.[75] The Wesleyan influence on Clifford is clear as he declares that it is only with the aid of the gift of the Spirit that the redeemed life can be lived. The believer is to be filled with the all-capacious Spirit of Christ, which enables him to live a life animated by the example of Christ, and in which the character of the Son of God is formed.

Using the example of Barnabas, Clifford wanted to show how an individual when wholly surrendered to the leadership of the Spirit would be open to daring new moves beyond the confines of accepted practice, thus, keeping in step with the advancing grace of God, not suspicious of every new voice and not captive to the traditions of the past. 'The Spirit of God is the spirit of progress, the force which impels humanity on the upward path . . . Where the Spirit of God is there is progress.'[76]

Barnabas was 'a man full of the Holy Ghost', and Clifford longed for the incalculable value of such men in educational, ecclesiastical, municipal and State affairs.[77] The personal experience of the witness of the Spirit attesting to the divine relationship is the spring of heroism, patience, hope and the assurance of his all-sufficient help.[78] Thus, with Dale, Clifford looked for the doctrine of entire sanctification to be the experiential bulwark of the emerging social gospel. Christ's miracles, preaching and teaching were of no avail by themselves. Christian religion only began to ascend to its new path at the cross and tellingly he adds, 'Pentecost follows Calvary.'[79]

Like Dale he also came to believe that there was a need for a 'fresh investigation' of the doctrine of the Spirit, but this was not accomplished during his over-full life.[80] Following his death the Baptist Union drew attention to his many activities and involvements, but remembered especially that his face would light up when he

---

72 Clifford, *The Gospel of Gladness*, pp. 108-09.
73 Clifford, *The Gospel of Gladness*, p. 173.
74 Clifford, *The Gospel of Gladness*, p.206.
75 Clifford, *The Gospel of Gladness*, p. 207.
76 Byrt, *John Clifford*, p. 98; Clifford, *Worth Living*, p. 129.
77 Clifford, *The Gospel of Gladness*, pp. 182-84
78 Clifford, *The Ultimate Problems*, pp. 252-53
79 Clifford, *The Gospel of Gladness*, p. 102.
80 Byrt, *John Clifford*, p. 91.

spoke of the salvation through Christ, as it was from his own experience that his passion for evangelism sprang.[81]

F.B. MEYER began his ministerial career as assistant to C.M. Birrell at Pembroke Chapel in Liverpool in 1870.[82] Birrell was a close supporter of the locally based reformer Josephine Butler. It was while in York that he became one of the first people to welcome D.L. Moody to Britain, establishing in the process a relationship that would last over the years.[83] From York he moved to Leicester, but the application of what were seen as 'mission' methods at the Victoria Road Church led to his resignation after four years in 1878. Friends and supporters persuaded him to stay in Leicester and a new forward-looking church was born that subsequently grew into the new Melbourne Hall in July 1880. The hall's raison d'être was to evangelise those outside the reach of ordinary Christian agencies, and they determined that as far as possible to that end, every member would be a worker.[84] It is interesting to note that Dr Henry Pope of the Methodist Chapel Department who was to be instrumental in the building of the first Central Hall for the Wesleyan's Manchester Mission admitted that it was Meyer's Melbourne Hall that had given him the idea.[85]

At the Hall Meyer developed a prison-gate work; boys' home; wood-chopping yard and a window cleaning brigade. Temperance and Sunday School work prospered, the latter catering for 2,500 children in three public schools that were hired for the purpose. Such was the work that Melbourne Hall and F.B. Meyer began to establish a national reputation.[86] A *Methodist Times* article of 1888 drew attention to many of the novel aspects of their ministry, particularly the fact that all members were expected to be workers and that the church took no weekly collection.[87]

It was while he was at Melbourne Hall that Meyer had an experience of 'entire sanctification' and 'absolute surrender' under the ministry of C.T. Studd and Stanley Smith. He had also attended the Holiness Conventions with the Pearsall Smiths' at Oxford and Brighton in 1875. Later, in 1887 whilst at the Keswick Convention, he had a second experience which confirmed for him that the Pentecostal gift was for all believers and that the gift was received by a simple trust that self-discipline could never attain.[88]

The rest of Meyer's ministry was spent in London, alternating between Regent's Park Baptist Church and Christ Church, an independent church on Westminster

---

81 Marchant, *Dr. John Clifford*, p. 290.

82 W.Y. Fullerton, *F.B. Meyer* (London: Marshall, Morgan & Scott, 1929), p. 29.

83 Fullerton, *F.B. Meyer*, pp. 31-32.

84 Fullerton, *F.B. Meyer*, pp. 46-53.

85 Fullerton, *F.B. Meyer*, pp. 54-55.

86 M. Jennie Street, *F.B. Meyer: His Life and Work* (London: Partridge, 1903), pp. 60-61; Heasman, *Evangelicals*, p. 58; Fullerton, *F.B. Meyer*, p. 54.

87 MT, 26.01.1888.

88 Street, *F.B. Meyer*, pp. 71-76; Fullerton, *F.B. Meyer*, pp. 58-59 & 65; F.B. Meyer, *The Christ-Life for the Self-Life* (Chicago: Moody, 1897), pp. 94-95.

Bridge Road.[89] When the London Baptist Association launched its own Forward Movement in September 1889, Hugh Price Hughes was exultant that, 'All the English Churches already feel the throb of this new departure.'[90] Meyer was appointed the honorary Director and the results, while not staggering in scope were not inconsequential. A Baptist Deaconess Institute was formed and this soon grew into a miniature Mildmay with an attached Medical Mission. A 50-bed hostel for men was subsequently obtained off High Holborn.[91]

Though Meyer was far from being as socially and politically involved as Clifford, he was committed to working out the social implications of the gospel. He believed that, 'One of the most promising signs of the time is the energy with which men are attending to social conditions and building the wastes of many generations.'[92]

Meyer supported Dr Paton's Lingfield farm colony from its inception and as the first President of the Central South London Free Church Council led the work against bad housing and prostitution.[93] He stood with Clifford in opposition to the Boer War, personally organising the Peace Manifesto which was signed by over 800 Free Church Ministers.[94] Temperance, sanitary laws and social purity were key issues for forward-looking Nonconformists and Meyer was no exception. In addition to these a booklet on, *Religion and Race Regeneration* he added the relative merits of the nature/nurture debate and eugenics.[95]

As Secretary of the Free Church Council in September 1911 he initiated a public protest against the planned boxing match between the 'flash nigger' Jack Johnson, the world heavyweight champion, and Bombardier Billy Wells, the British challenger. Fearing a repetition of racial violence that followed Johnson's American victories the Nonconformist Conscience was mobilised effectively for the last time as part of a broader coalition. The protest succeeded, an injunction was taken out and the fight cancelled.[96]

What Meyer looked for was a church-led movement of social reconstruction. In his address to the Baptist Union Spring Assembly in 1906 he said,

> Yes, Christ is Immanent in the life of the world as well as Transcendent over it . . . He is moving towards an end which He had in view from all eternity . . . But since the

---

[89] Regent's Park, 1888-1892 and 1909-1915; Christ Church, 1892-1909 and 1915-1921.

[90] MT, 03.10.1889.

[91] Street, *F.B. Meyer*, pp. 84-85; LeBarbour, *Victorian Baptists*, p. 270; Payne, *The Baptist Union*, p. 151.

[92] F.B. Meyer, *Religion and Race Regeneration* (London: Cassell, 1912), p. 61.

[93] Fullerton, *F.B. Meyer*, p. 156; Street, *F.B. Meyer*, pp. 111-12.

[94] Street, *F.B. Meyer*, p. 154.

[95] F.B. Meyer, *Reveries and Realities* (London: Morgan & Scott, nd), pp. 24-25; Meyer, *Race Regeneration*, pp. 17, 22, 40 & 53. N.B. Mews mistakenly names the boxer as Matt Wells who, coincidentally, won the British Lightweight Championship in 1911.

[96] Stuart Mews, 'Puritanicalism, Sport and Race: A Symbolic Crusade of 1911', in G.J. Cumming & Derek Baker (eds), *Studies in Church History*, vol. 8 - Popular Belief and Practice (Cambridge: CUP, 1972), pp. 304-31.

> world discerns Him not, it is for the Church to read His handwriting on the wall, to bear witness to Christian Ideals, to aid Him in the work of reconstruction, and to secure, . . . freedom instead of slavery, peace instead of battalions and warships, self-sacrifice instead of self-interest, for such is the Kingdom of Heaven.[97]

Meyer, however, had grave reservations about the effectiveness of social reconstruction on its own. He believed that the need for a spiritual transformation was paramount. He used the analogy of a pig in a parlour. It remains a pig, but the parlour was soon transformed into a sty.

There had to be a transformation of the inner, as well as the outer-life.[98] His commitment to evangelism remained his first priority and was focussed both within the churches he led and more further afield. He collaborated with Moody both in Britain and in the United States and, through the Free Church Council's Simultaneous Mission at the beginning of the twentieth century, he contributed more to its organisation than anyone else.[99]

Like many of his Nonconformist contemporaries Meyer had begun to explore the doctrine of entire sanctification as a common experiential centre to his evangelistic and social expression of the gospel, but his was no theoretical development. Personal experiences gave his advocacy content, fervour and commitment. Indeed, the references to entire sanctification and the work of the Spirit are relatively sparse in Clifford when compared to the abundance to be found within Meyer's published work.

Having visited Moody's Northfield Conference in America in 1897, he was impressed at how the American churches were rediscovering Pentecost and the work of the Holy Spirit. He longed for the same to happen in England. '[T]here is nothing more urgently necessary than that everyone of us should get back to the enduement of the Holy Ghost. . . . The Church has had her former rain and God is about to give her the latter rain. But it must begin with us.'[100]

For Meyer the Spirit was received by faith in the same manner as the forgiveness of sins.[101] This involved a complete yielding of the individual to the purposes of God,[102] and it resulted in the formation of the character of the Son of God in the life of the believer.[103] He compared the baptism in the Spirit with drinking too much wine, as happened on the Day of Pentecost and as Paul exhorted the Ephesians, 'Be not drunk with wine, . . . but be filled with the Spirit' (Ephesians 5:18). Drunks sing, cannot stop talking and have the bravado to take on all-comers. Likewise the filling of the Spirit brought joy and singing, it loosened a man's tongue to tell of all that

---

[97] LeBarbour, *Victorian Baptists*, p. 226.

[98] Meyer, *Reveries*, p. 25.

[99] Street, *F.B. Meyer*, pp. 113-14.

[100] Fullerton, *F.B. Meyer*, pp. 44-45.

[101] Meyer, *Reveries*, p. 21; For Meyer's experience at Keswick that followed this pattern see Fullerton, *F.B. Meyer*, p. 66.

[102] Meyer, *Reveries*, p. 33.

[103] Meyer, *Christ-Life*, pp. 46-51.

God had done for him and it filled him with power so that he felt as though he could stand against all the world.[104]

The coming of the Spirit was literally 'power from on high', which Meyer believed would equip the church for the work of the gospel.[105] He likened the power of the Spirit to the electricity that lay hidden in nature until its discovery, and such was the power of the Spirit in the church until it was discovered.[106]

While being careful to warn against making the Holy Spirit the head of a movement, he did believe that before attempting any ministry the church must be anointed by the Spirit.[107] What Jordan was to the Head, Pentecost is to the body.[108]

> It is perfectly true that the Holy Spirit is the Executor and Administrator of the Divine plan; and where He is recognised in a community, He will work through its members on the line of least resistance - by which I mean, that those who yield most utterly to Him will be led out most fully into various and fresh manifestations of Christian usefulness.[109]

Just in case any of his listeners or readers were in any doubt about what he was saying he often held an imaginary conversation with the Holy Spirit on the subject of social reform sermons. The Spirit refused to have any part of the sermon until Jesus was restored to his rightful place. 'You may begin where you like, you may deal with any historical subject you like, but you must end with the Lord Jesus Christ.'[110]

Clifford and Meyer were the two pre-eminent leaders in the development of social gospel thinking and practice among the Baptists, and it is significant that neither of them were strongly influenced by Calvinism.

Other Baptists who were active in developing the ideas of Social Christianity include ARCHIBALD BROWN whose ministry of evangelism and philanthropy at the East London Tabernacle in Stepney included the creation of orphanages, low rent housing, the distribution of food, clothing and tools. A contemporary paper found the narrowness of his theology and the broadness of his social concern a strange irony.[111]

CHARLES AKED ministered at Pembroke Chapel in Liverpool (1890-1906) and was probably one of the most radical Baptists of the period. He embraced the developments of 'the new theology' and thought that all wars were the result of capitalist machinations. He was a professed Fabian and a lecture tour of the United

---

[104] Meyer, *Christ-Life*, pp. 98-99.
[105] F.B. Meyer, *Five 'Musts' of the Christian Life* (London: Marshall, Morgan & Scott, nd), p. 82.
[106] Meyer, *Race Regeneration*, p. 58.
[107] Meyer, *Five 'Musts'*, p. 73.
[108] Meyer, *Christ-Life*, pp. 87-88.
[109] Meyer, *Reveries*, p. 33.
[110] Meyer, *Christ-Life*, p. 112.
[111] LeBarbour, *Victorian Baptists*, p. 268.

States brought him a D.D. He later emigrated to take up the pastorate at Fifth Avenue Baptist Church for a reputed stipend of £5,000 per annum.[112]

The great Baptist preacher in Manchester, ALEXANDER MACLAREN, influenced thousands of his generation. He was intelligently aware of the problems of modern science and history, urging Baptists not to see evil demons in the scientific spirit. However, he seems deliberately to have chosen never to speak on social or political matters in the pulpit.[113]

Addresses made under the auspices of the Baptist Union often provided a channel to explore the concerns that were on the minds of forward thinkers within the denomination. In 1885, SAMUEL GREEN addressed the Christian's political responsibility for the welfare of mankind, and, in 1889, T.W. BUSHILL spoke on, 'The Relations of Employer and Employed in the Light of the Social Gospel.' In the autumn of 1889, following the London dock strike, W.T.WIGNER expressed the conviction that Christian citizenship entailed a duty to help heal the conflict between capital and labour. LeBarbour believes that J.C. GREENHOUGH's attempt to find a middle way between personal and social salvation reflects accurately advanced thinking in the early 1890s within the Union, if not representing the convictions of the vast majority.[114]

Both the Bloomsbury and Regent's Park churches developed Domestic Missions, and satellite mission chapels under the care of a lay pastor were quite common in Baptist circles. The only instance of a Baptist Central Hall besides Melbourne Hall in Leicester, was the West Ham Central Mission that ROBERT ROWNTREE CLIFFORD opened in connection with his work at the Barking Tabernacle.[115]

RICHARD MUDIE-SMITH, a deacon at Westbourne Park and the author of the exhaustive survey of London churches in 1904, concluded that it was only those churches who had adopted an Institutional Church or Central Hall type approach that were succeeding.[116] Indeed he saw the features of strong preaching, comfortable modern halls, open-air evangelism and an engagement with social issues to be the common denominator for a thriving church life.[117]

---

[112] Bebbington, *The Nonconformist Conscience*, p. 123; LeBarbour, *Victorian Baptists*, p. 226; P.J. Waller, *Democracy and Sectarianism: A Political and Social History of Liverpool, 1868-1939* (Liverpool: Liverpool University Press, 1981), p. 476.

[113] LeBarbour, *Victorian Baptists*, pp. 200-201; Underwood, *A History*, p. 233.

[114] LeBarbour, *Victorian Baptists*, pp. 227-28 (Green), p. 270 (Bushill), p. 270 (Wigner), p. 228 (Greenhough).

[115] Heasman, *Evangelicals*, p. 57.

[116] Mudie-Smith, *The Religious Life*, p. 10.

[117] Mudie-Smith, *The Religious Life*, pp. 8-14.

Chapter 8

Salvation Army Philanthropists

In many ways the birth of the Salvation Army in the late nineteenth century led directly to its embodiment of the twin preoccupations of evangelicals in this era. Reaching the masses outside of the church with the gospel and responding to the appalling levels of need that society had thrown up came to animate their life and programme of activity. Sketching an historical overview of the early history of the Army is the necessary basis on which to study their special emphasis more closely.

William Booth, the founder of the Salvation Army, was born and brought up in and around Nottingham and was a product of Victorian urban England. It was there in the early 1840s that like many others of his generation he came under the spell of the Chartist movement. Having listened to O'Connor he considered himself a Chartist, though never a revolutionary.[1] Cobden and Bright also attracted him and later he was to confess that 'When a mere child the degradation and helpless misery of the poor stockingers of my native town . . . kindled in my heart yearnings to help the poor which have continued to this day and which have had a powerful influence on my life. At last I may be going to see my longings to help the workless realised.'[2]

These early convictions were soon suppressed as his Christian faith and evangelistic passion came increasingly to the fore. He became a Wesleyan Minister, but a desire for greater personal freedom to engage in evangelism led him out of Wesleyanism, first to the Methodist New Connexion and then ultimately to resign the ministry altogether in June 1862 to begin his own evangelistic organisation.[3]

The early work of his 'Christian Mission' began with a tent crusade at Whitechapel in 1867. The work there assumed a permanent character and a hall was secured. He saw this work in clearly evangelistic terms. It was to be accomplished by a) insisting on a definite confession of Christ; b) watching over and instructing converts; c) training them and setting them to work to save others.[4] Their work

---

1 Harold Begbie, *William Booth, Founder of the Salvation Army*, vol. 1 (London: Macmillan, 1920), pp. 49-50; K.S. Inglis, *Churches and the Working Class in Victorian England* (London: Routledge, 1963), p. 177.

2 General Booth, *Darkest England and the Way Out* (London: Salvation Army, 1890), p. 1.

3 Robert Sandall, *The History of the Salvation Army*, vol. 1, 1865-1878 (London: Thomas Nelson, 1947), pp. 5-11.

4 John Kent, *Holding the Fort: Studies in Victorian Revivalism* (London: Epworth,

under these terms of reference was strictly adhered to. While Booth was a teetotaler and temperance man he did not want his workers diverted into temperance advocacy, so he instructed that there were to be no temperance meetings 'without God in them'.[5]

By 1868 he was in control of 13 preaching stations and in 1870 he fixed a liberally Methodist constitution in which women were equal from the start.[6] Elijah Cadman, an ex-Primitive Methodist preacher, joined Booth and among other things introduced him to the idea of Hallelujah Bands. Increasingly the Mission encountered violent opposition at its street meetings and Booth responded by adopting war metaphors. The Annual Meeting of 1878 was termed 'The War Conference' and across the platform was a banner which read, 'The Salvation Army'.[7] The 'battle' at times was ferocious. At Guildford in September 1882 the wife of the local Captain was kicked unconscious outside the local police station and another woman died of injuries only days after a similar beating. On this particular occasion it took the intervention of the local Vicar, appealing to the Home Secretary, to get the local authorities to uphold the peace.[8]

Under this persecution the Army grew rapidly and by 1886 they had 1006 corps and 2260 officers.[9] Inglis believes that much of their success was due to the fact that they were the one organisation that met the working class at their own cultural level.[10] Indeed Catherine Booth was still upholding this principle in her last sermon when she proclaimed, 'Christ came to save the world, not to civilise it . . . you cannot reform man morally by his intellect; this is the mistake of most social reformers. You must reform man by his soul!'[11]

While the Army's primary task of evangelism was never compromised Booth did lead them into an unexpected field of work when he launched his own social programme, *In Darkest England and the Way Out*, in 1890. As the Army's social work began to grow and their exposure to urban poverty increased, so they began to become more socially conscious. What little philanthropic work there had been up to this point had only played a minor role in their overall strategy, but Booth's understanding was developing. In January 1889 he stressed that salvation, 'meant not only [being] saved from the miseries of the future world but from the miseries of

---

1978), p. 106; Sandall, *The History*, 1. p71.

5 Sandall, *The History*, 1. p. 197.

6 Owen Chadwick, *The Victorian Church (Part II)* (London: A&C Black, 1970), p. 289; Andrew M. Eason, *Women in God's Army* (Waterloo, Ont.: Wilfrid Laurier University Press, 2003), pp. xi-xii, makes the observation that although early Salvation Army documents state that they 'refuse to make any difference between men and women', effectively a complementarian view of gender effectively led to ministry practiced in different spheres.

7 Chadwick, *The Victorian Church*, p. 290.

8 Sandall, *The History*, 1. pp. 178-79.

9 Chadwick, *The Victorian Church*, p. 293.

10 Inglis, *Churches and the Working Class*, pp. 187-88.

11 Inglis, *Churches and the Working Class*, p. 175

this [world] also'.[12] 'As Christ came to call not saints but sinners to repentance, so the New Message of Temporal Salvation, of salvation from pinching poverty, from rags and misery, must be offered to all.'[13]

The *Darkest England* scheme brought social work into the mainstream of the Army's life and the book sold over 200,000 copies and raised £128,000 towards a £1 million target in the first twelve months following publication.[14]

While the *Darkest England* scheme marked a significant shift in Booth's comprehension of salvation[15] it was not the success that it at first promised to be. Certainly it changed the face of the Army and a whole plethora of social schemes were introduced, but the £1 million was never achieved. In addition, one of the leading advocates of the Army's development in this direction, Commissioner Frank Smith, left under a cloud because the General would not give the freedom to the City Colony proposals of the *Darkest England* programme that he considered necessary. Smith had previously been in charge of the Army in the United States and on returning to England had headed up the Social Reform Wing. He was well versed in sociology and had pressed Booth for three years to bring about a scheme like *Darkest England.* Such was the stir that was caused in the press by his resignation that the Army was forced to produce a rebuttal in the *War Cry* and W.T. Stead sent a letter to *The Star*. Following Smith's resignation in 1891 Booth appointed Elijah Cadman in his place. This was a safe appointment as Cadman had neither the sociological expertise nor the social reforming convictions of his predecessor. To some at least this has raised a question regarding Booth's own motives at the very beginning of the campaign.[16]

Reaction to the scheme was mixed. Many within the denominations welcomed it and Hugh Price Hughes was exultant at the 'hearty adoption of the principles of Social Christianity by the most successful revivalist of the age . . . We need scarcely say how greatly we rejoice over so mighty a convert to one of the essential principles of the Forward Movement and the London Mission.'[17]

Others were less positive. The contemporary commentator R.A. Woods maintained that the switch was made because purely emotional religion had failed to win converts. There may be more than an element of truth in this as Kent has demonstrated that between 1886 and 1903 the attendance at Salvation Army services in London had declined from 53,591 to 38,896.[18] Many believed that most

---

[12] Andrew M. Eason & Roger J. Green (eds), *Boundless Salvation: the Shorter Writings of William Booth* (New York: Peter Lang, 2012), pp. 8-9.

[13] General Booth, *Darkest England*, p. 36.

[14] Inglis, *Churches and the Working Class*, pp. 205 & 210.

[15] Roger J. Green, 'Theological roots of *In Darkest England And The Way Out*', *Wesleyan Theological Journal*, 25.1 (1990), pp. 84.

[16] Robert Sandall, *The History of the Salvation Army*, vol. 3, 1883-1953 (Social Reform and Welfare Work) (London: Thomas Nelson, 1955), pp. 101-02 & 324-26; Inglis, *Churches and the Working Class*, pp. 202 & 209.

[17] MT, 23.10.1890.

[18] Kent, *Holding the Fort*, pp. 299-300.

of Booth's converts were actually dissatisfied denominationalists like himself. Indeed, even Hughes estimated that up to 80,000 disillusioned Methodists had joined the Army.[19] Booth made no attempt to cover his motives behind the scheme,

> My only hope for the permanent deliverance of mankind from misery, either in this world or the next, is the regeneration or remaking of the individual by the power of the Holy Ghost through Jesus Christ. But in providing for the relief of temporal misery I reckon that I am only making it easy where it is now difficult . . . for men and women to find their way to the cross of our Lord Jesus Christ.[20]

It is interesting to note that while Booth himself left both Wesleyanism and the New Connexion because they would not give him the freedom he felt he needed, he did not extent to others the freedom of action that he had longed for himself. Lady Frances Balfour commented that he was 'autocratic and dominant, with a manner bordering on the severe and dictatorial'.[21] Following a concerted effort by the agnostic biologist T.H. Huxley to discredit Booth and his scheme *Punch* nicknamed the General 'Field-Marshall von Booth', while others called him 'a sensual, dishonest, sanctimonious and hypocritical scoundrel', 'a brazen-faced charlatan' and 'a pious rogue'.[22]

The Salvation Army stood squarely in the middle of the late nineteenth-century Revivalist/Holiness tradition.[23] The 'Blood and Fire' of the Army's motto referred to Christ's 'blood' for cleansing at conversion and the 'fire' of the Holy Spirit for entire sanctification. The Booths had come under the influence of the American revivalist Phoebe Palmer in 1859 and she had taught them 'the shorter way' to holiness with her 'altar theology'. Catherine Booth wrote in correspondence,

> William said, 'Don't you lay all on the altar?' I replied, 'I am sure I do.' Then he said, 'And isn't the altar holy?' I replied in the language of the Holy Ghost, 'The altar is most holy, and whatsoever toucheth it is holy.' Then he said, 'Are you not holy?' I replied with my heart full of emotion and some faith, 'Oh, I think I am.' Immediately, the word was given to me to confirm my faith . . . and from that moment I have dared to reckon myself dead indeed unto sin, and alive unto God through Jesus Christ my Lord.[24]

This teaching and experience became a regular feature of Salvation Army life and was widely disseminated through the popular writing of Samuel Logan Brengle. His was a simple and easily understood explanation of the relationship between the

---

19 MT, 03.08.1893.

20 General Booth, *Darkest England*, p. 4.

21 T. Nelson & Sons (Publishers), (contributions by various friends), *The Life of General Booth* (London, nd), p. 115.

22 Richard Collier, *The General Next to God* (London: Collins, 1965), p. 194.

23 Kent, *Holding the Fort*, pp. 325-32; Bebbington, *Evangelicalism in Modern Britain (London: Routledge, 1989)*. pp. 164-65.

24 Kent, *Holding the Fort*, p. 328.

Pentecostal blessing and holiness.[25] The foundation deed of the Army also enshrined the doctrine by upholding that 'We believe that it is the privilege of all believers to be "wholly sanctified"'.[26] The experience of holiness was instantaneous,[27] and came not by 'purgatorial fires, but by Holy Ghost fire', into which the believer was 'baptised' and purged of 'unholiness' just as gold is purged of dross in the fire.[28] They maintained that it was the obligation of every believer to be 'filled with the Spirit' in this way,[29] so that the character and mind of Christ can be formed in the believer through his agency.[30] While the Army acknowledged a second function of the Spirit in giving power for service and perseverance in duty, they believed that what a man 'is' in Christian service is more important than what he 'does'.[31] Thus, they never took up R.W. Dale's challenge to the Methodists to develop the doctrine and experience of entire sanctification in the realm of their social work at any serious depth. More often holiness demonstrated itself among them as a prohibition on drinking, smoking, indulging in worldly pleasures, following after worldly fashions and having godless friends.[32]

It was the arrival of the Pearsall Smiths in 1875 that appears to have brought this facet of the Booth's belief system back to the centre of their ministry in the Christian Mission. Their renewed enthusiasm was accompanied by laughing, jumping, rolling on the floor and other manifestations of the Spirit's presence.[33] By the turn of the century such phenomena had become uncommon and when asked whether he still preached entire sanctification, William Booth replied, 'When a man talks about full consecration, we say to him, "Go and do something."'[34]

While no explicit links were made between their understanding of entire sanctification, the baptism of power through the Holy Spirit and their developing social ministries, it is obvious that one did feed into the other.

It was the impression of the Congregationalist R.J. Campbell that Booth was 'The mightiest force of his time in bringing the gospel of Jesus into living touch with the needs of the poorest and most degraded elements in the community'.[35] Certainly the whole emphasis on evangelism and winning souls was of continuing importance to Booth. For this reason he had left Methodism and under this banner

---

[25] Samuel Logan Brengle, *The Guest of the Soul* (London: Marshall, Morgan & Scott, 1934), pp. 43-57; Samuel Logan Brengle, *Heart Talks on Holiness* (London: Salvationist Publishing, 1960), pp. 46-48; Samuel Logan Brengle, *Helps To Holiness* (Salem: Schmul, 1965), pp. 49-53.

[26] Kent, *Holding the Fort*, p. 328.

[27] Brengle, *Heart Talks*, pp. 4-5; Brengle, *Helps*, p. 125.

[28] Brengle, *Heart Talks*, pp. 13 & 15.

[29] Brengle, *Helps*, p. 126.

[30] Brengle, *Guest*, p. 64.

[31] Brengle, *Guest*, p. 52-54 & 46.

[32] Bramwell Booth, *These Fifty Years* (London: Cassell, 1929), p. 190.

[33] Kent, *Holding the Fort*, pp. 333-34; Inglis, *Churches and the Working Class*, pp. 180-81.

[34] Bebbington, *Evangelicalism*, p. 178.

[35] Nelson's *Life of Booth* (R.J. Campbell), p. 138.

the Christian Mission had been established. In November 1889 Booth wrote a lengthy article on how to win 100,000 souls. He said,

> If a man has a money-making spirit he will probably make money. If a man has an ambitious spirit, he will possibly vault to some higher grade of life than that in which he was born. If a man has a soul-saving spirit, he will certainly save souls. It matters little what his circumstances may be. Therefore, the business of every one of us is to come into the possession of an absorbing passion for the salvation of men.[36]

To this end Booth would sponsor whatever methods were useful as long as they did not contravene his strict ideas on holiness. For example, having proved Cadman's suggestion of the Hallelujah Bands in attracting a crowd for open-air work he declared in the *War Cry* of 27.3.1880 that as many officers and soldiers as possible should learn to play instruments.[37] Experience also taught Booth another truth. This was that 'No-one gets a blessing if they have cold feet, and nobody ever got saved while they had toothache!'[38] This particular insight helped to lead him along the road towards the social work that was to play so large a part in the future ministry of the Army.

The early philanthropic work of the Christian Mission was not at all extensive. In 1867 they had only distributed £300 worth of relief to the poor, distributing on average 240 tickets for bread and meat a week. Visitors would meet weekly to discuss cases of distress they had encountered in order to best work out their response. With the development of Soup Kitchens and other agencies the money available for relief became insufficient to sustain this growing aspect of their work and Booth, therefore, made the decision not to give help to strangers. In 1868 they were attacked by the *Saturday Review* for trying to tempt the poor to worship with the bait of breakfast and coal tickets.[39] These accusations persisted and were borne by the Army, however, at no time did they insist on attendance at meetings or profession of faith as a condition to receive help. Yet one of the Mission's visitors candidly confessed,

> How could I hope to impart any spiritual help if I could not do something to alleviate the dreadful poverty? Would they not call it a mockery to talk about their souls whilst their bodies were perishing with hunger? But when I give them a loaf of bread or a pound of meat hearts are opened, and I can preach Christ with some hope of success.[40]

The Army was always prepared to lobby on matters of morality with the Criminal Law Amendment Act, the Poor Law, prostitution and the Children's Charter all being issues on which they brought their weight to bear. Their work on the first of

---

[36] Arch. R. Wiggins, *The History of the Salvation Army*, vol. 4, 1886-1904 (London: Thomas Nelson, 1964), p. 163.

[37] Robert Sandall, *The History of the Salvation Army*, vol. 2, 1878-1886 (London: Thomas Nelson, 1950), p. 102

[38] Collier, *The General*, p. 58.

[39] Sandall, *The History*, 1. pp. 292-93.

[40] Sandall, *The History*, 1. p. 91.

these was carried out with other groups including the campaigner Josephine Butler. One particular attempt to expose the trade in young women resulted in Bramwell Booth and W.T. Stead being prosecuted for the abduction of Eliza Armstrong.[41] In 1885 they used their citadels and halls to organise a petition on the issue and in three weeks they had obtained 393,000 signatures.[42]

The 1880s were a very important time for General Booth and the Army. Their continual exposure to social need did not leave them untouched. Booth came to see that the average man was locked into a circle of homelessness, want of food and friendlessness that left him invariably weakened in will and character to the point where there was little hope for him spiritually. Booth concluded that help was needed to give such men the opportunity to escape by their own exertion from the pressure of constant anxiety. What the General hated more than anything else was the pauperising effect that charity frequently had.

In 1887 Booth revealed that the development of his own thinking with regard to social work had roughly three steps. At first he had seen such work as trivial and contemptible. Experience though had led him to his second position, that in some cases material help was necessary for salvation. The third stage followed shortly afterwards, what he called the 'continual observance of the sacrament of the good Samaritan'. It appears that an early morning ride across London had deeply shocked him with regard to the number of people sleeping out. The following day Bramwell Booth was dispatched to do something about it. The result was that a warehouse was taken in Limehouse as a centre for their new work.[43] While at this stage he appears to have forgotten his early Chartist impressions as a child in Nottingham, those same sympathies were to all intents and purposes being rekindled and the influence of his personal experience and the good offices of Frank Smith brought the pressure to bear which finally resulted in his feeling the way free to establish the scheme, *In Darkest England and the Way Out*.

In the preface to *Darkest England*, Booth laments the inadequacy of much Christian philanthropy and the few who were truly rescued. 'Alike, therefore, my humanity and my Christianity, if I may speak of them in any way as separate one from the other, have cried out for some more comprehensive method of reaching and saving the perishing crowds.'[44]

'Darkest Africa' had arrested the attention of the 'civilised world' that summer as Stanley had told of his journeys across that continent. Booth concluded that this was an appropriate title for his work as he sought to reveal dark truths from closer to home.[45] He recognised that it would be a new departure for his 'soldiers', calling

---

41 Sandall, *The History*, 3. pp. 25-28 & 264-68

42 Sandall, *The History*, 3. p. 36.

43 Sandall, *The History*, 3. pp. 67-68; see also H. Rider Haggard, *Regeneration* (London: Longman, Green & Co., 1910), pp. 12-13, for a separate account.

44 General Booth, *Darkest England*, p. 2.

45 General Booth, *Darkest England*, p. 9.

them to develop new faculties, knowledge and gifts.[46] The scheme had a number of underlying principles:

1. Anything that is done must change the nature of the man.
2. The remedy to be effectual must change the circumstances of the individual. For, most often, they are the cause of his wretched condition and lie beyond his control.
3. Any remedy worth consideration must be on a scale commensurate with the evil with which it proposes to deal.
4. The indirect features of the scheme must not be such as to produce injury to the persons whom we seek to benefit. It is no use conferring six pennyworth of benefit on a man if at the same time we do him a shillings-worth of harm.[47]

Commissioner George Scott Railton admitted that the programmes the scheme outlined were those that were proving effective in other parts of the world. Indeed, Booth did not deny it, claiming that 'In miniature many of them are working already.'[48] For Lady Balfour the scheme made Booth the practical interpreter of Thomas Carlyle.[49] It was together with Stead that the scheme was written, while Stead himself makes it clear that he was only helping with an idea that was wholly the General's. Smith's work with the Social Wing had done much to shape the General's thinking, but the title, content and execution of the scheme were Booth's, and Booth's alone.[50]

The scheme to help the 'submerged tenth' had three main elements:

1. The outcast must have food, shelter and warmth to meet his most urgent needs.
2. He must have temporary work and training to fit him to gain a permanent livelihood.
3. He must receive a definite chance of turning his training to account.[51]

This theory was then implemented through three 'colonies': the City Colony; the Farm Colony and the Overseas Colony.[52] In the City Colony shelter was provided for the homeless in exchange for a small amount of labour. Booth maintained that they did not attempt to pay wages, only enough to allow a man to live, get on his feet and find waged employment outside.[53] Various trades and industries were

---

46 General Booth, *Darkest England*, pp. 283-84.
47 Begbie, *William Booth*. 2, p. 99
48 Nelson's *Life of Booth* (George Scott Railton), p. 78; General Booth, *Darkest England*, p. 4; Inglis, *Churches and the Working Class*, pp. 203-204.
49 Nelson's *Life of Booth* (Lady Frances Balfour), p. 116.
50 Sandall, *The History*, 3. pp. 324-26; Estelle W. Stead, *My Father* (London: Heinemann, 1913), p. 86.
51 Nelson's *Life of Booth* (W.H. Beveridge), p. 174.
52 General Booth, *Darkest England*, pp. 90-92.
53 Haggard, *Regeneration*, pp. 15-16, 28-29 & 65-70.

undertaken in 'elevator' factories associated with the City Colony such as tin-smithery and carpentry. A Labour Bureau was also established. The Farm Colony was purchased in 1891 but it was not until 1912 that permanent buildings were erected.[54] Insurmountable difficulties prevented the Overseas Colony from being established at all. This was later seen as a special providence as there was not enough cash.[55]

The *Darkest England* Scheme was a partial success. During the early years the Army published figures that made it look successful and to a certain extent it was, but never in terms of the overall vision of Booth's grand scheme. With the failure of the Overseas Colony even help with emigration was held back until 1905.[56] The Farm Colony was only a qualified success. It did help those who used it, but the number was small and insignificant. It was in the cities that the greatest work was done. 210,000 free meals were served in the first winter and 8,000 quarterns of bread and 40 tons of cheese were distributed a day. But figures can be deceptive. *The Methodist Temperance Magazine* reported on the first year of the programme that 50,000 beds were provided and 16,000 men had sought help from the Labour Bureau,[57] yet these grand figures actually amounted to 137 beds a night and around 50 enquiries a day. Achievements yes, but hardly the kind of impact that was expected, but the Magazine considered the scheme was worthy of support for two special reasons,

> The first is its clear recognition that the disease is at root an economic one, requiring an economic remedy. The second is the perception that the close and intricate relations existing between the various material and moral forms of social disease require a multiform remedy applied simultaneously at the different points.[58]

The scheme very quickly ran into problems. After two years the General had to launch another appeal for a further £65,000 because the public had failed to contribute the £30,000 per year that he had emphasised would be needed to carry out the work.[59] What Booth had discovered was that it was very easy to raise money for dramatic schemes of immediate relief like midnight feeding, but it was a wholly different matter to find long-term support for the treatment of the problem.

Booth also found that the 'submerged tenth' were not as numerous as he had thought, but that they were even more completely submerged and more difficult to rescue too. Out of this experience the Army had itself come to urge compulsory detention for proven vagrants, supporting the Bill introduced by Sir John Gorst. The Shelters which Booth maintained should never become places of permanent residence or repeated sojourn became just that.[60]

---

[54] Sandall, *The History*, 3. pp. 137-41.
[55] Sandall, *The History*, 3. p. 153.
[56] Sandall, *The History*, 3. pp. 154-58.
[57] MTM, February 1892, p. 24.
[58] MTM, February 1892, p. 24.
[59] Wiggins, *The History*, 4. pp. 221-22.
[60] Nelson's *Life of Booth* (W.H. Beveridge), p. 204.

The most damning failure of all was that the scheme should affect the whole man: 'To change the nature of the individual, to get at the heart, to save his soul, is the only real, lasting method of doing him any good.'[61] Without this, what the General feared most was that the work would slide into being merely palliative. Twenty years into the scheme W.H. Beveridge, the Director of the Labour Exchanges Department with the Board of Trade was of the impression that this was what had happened and that the sheltering, feeding and clothing of the body had come more and more to the fore in the City Colony. While sympathetic to Booth's work Beveridge wrote, 'The redemptive institutions of the social scheme have thus not merely lagged behind the palliative ones in development, they have . . . themselves become merely palliative in their action.'[62]

Booth's explicit objectives that he had held for many years were not borne out by the fruit of his labours. As early as 1869 he had said,

> Legislation may do much to counteract the mischief, but the spread of religious feeling will do more. The true Christian is the real self-helper. In bringing the truth of religion before the suffering masses we are also assisting in the great work of social reform . . . when we have taught the people to be religious half the battle has been won.[63]

Booth considered that to really help someone you needed to offer them Christ. Social reformation, though important, would not change the nature of sinful people. Thus, unlike many of the forward-looking contemporaries of the Salvation Army, he spurned political involvement. At the introduction of the Home Rule Bill in 1886, when many Nonconformists were supporting the controversial proposals for Ireland, Booth said, 'We are Salvationists and whatever we think or do individually as citizens we cannot as a religious organisation mix ourselves up with one or other of the political parties.'[64]

The *Darkest England* scheme was apolitical by design, and during the 1900 General Election a ban was imposed on Army Officers and equipment being used in the campaign.[65]

Booth certainly saw legislation and government action as complementing the work of the gospel, but he gave it a lower profile than fellow Nonconformist leaders like John Clifford or Hugh Price Hughes. In 1868, as the Christian Mission encountered starvation in London, he used the local press to make known his views that only government intervention would remedy the situation.[66] On laissez-faire he said, 'It is a religious cant, which rids itself of the importunity of suffering humanity by drawing unnegotiable bills payable on the other side of the grave.'[67]

---

[61] Nelson's *Life of Booth* (W.H. Beveridge), p. 174.
[62] Nelson's *Life of Booth* (W.H. Beveridge), p. 201-02.
[63] Sandall, *The History*, 1. p. 119.
[64] Sandall, *The History*, 3. p. 263.
[65] General Booth, *Darkest England*, p. 18; Sandall, *The History*, 3. p. 263.
[66] Sandall, *The History*, 1. p. 118.
[67] Collier, *The General*, p. 192.

T.H. Huxley accused Booth of, 'Socialism in disguise, masked in its theological exterior.'[68] This criticism was certainly unjustified. The only exemption for his no politics rule was if some great religious principle were at stake.

There is no doubt that the Army evoked a response from people. Many forward-thinking Nonconformists were positive and supportive of its work. Hugh Price Hughes had sought William Booth's advice in the early days of the Forward Movement,[69] though he personally felt that their services lacked reverence and often fell into the opposite temptation to cold formalism, emotional extravagance.[70] Yet he mourned their loss to Methodism as a 'disastrous suicidal folly' that ranked alongside the Church of England's rejection of Wesley. He hoped for an 'affiliation' between the Army and Methodism that was never to be,[71] not least because Bramwell Booth as the power-broker of the Army towards the end of the century, had been scandalized by Hughes' comment that the Forward Movement was a 'respectable Salvation Army'.[72] However, when the *Darkest England* scheme came under attack, Joseph Parker, Charles Berry, John Clifford, W.F. Moulton and William Arthur all rallied to its defence in a jointly signed letter.[73] Indeed, while Spurgeon disliked Booth's teaching and was critical of his methods, John Clifford opened his pulpit at Westbourne Park to Salvationist preachers.[74] R.W. Dale was supportive, as was the Anglican social reformer Josephine Butler.[75] W.T. Stead had a very close personal and working relationship with the General[76] and Cardinal Manning added his benediction to the movement.[77] Others were not so charitable and the evangelical Anglican, the Earl of Shaftesbury, called them 'the anti-Christ!' at one point.[78] However, some Anglicans approved of Booth and his methods and Carlile's Church Army was a complementary imitation, while the negotiations at one stage for Booth and his followers to become associated with the Church of England further illustrate this.[79]

Even though the *Darkest England* scheme did not accomplish all that had been hoped of it, the work of the Salvation Army continued to grow. Rider Haggard investigated their social agencies in 1910 and reported that world-wide they were established in 56 countries with 28,000 people nightly in their institutions, while they maintained: 229 food depots; 157 labour factories; 17 homes for ex-criminals;

---

68 Sandall, *The History*, 3. p. 82.
69 Bramwell Booth, p186.
70 MT, 12.02.1885; 20.10.1887.
71 MT, 22.12.1892.
72 Bramwell Booth, *These Fifty Years*, pp. 186-90.
73 Sandall, *The History*, 3. p. 88.
74 Inglis, *Churches and the Working Class*, p. 190.
75 Sandall, *The History*, 1. p. 89; Sandall, *The History*, 2. p. 161; Wiggins, *The History*, 4. pp. 322-23; Inglis, *Churches and the Working Class*, pp. 104-105, 190 & 205.
76 Sandall, *The History*, 3. p. 77.
77 Sandall, *The History*, 3. p. 79.
78 Collier, *The General*, p. 110.
79 Inglis, *Churches and the Working Class*, pp. 188-89; Kent, *Holding the Fort*, p. 271.

37 homes for children; 116 industrial homes for women; 60 Labour Bureaux; 521 Day Schools, 'and so on almost ad infinitum'.[80]

The Salvation Army was unique; there had never been anything quite like them before, especially with their uniforms and brass bands. Indeed, in many ways the Army with its theology, music, pageantry and approach to gender was a creation of the urban context in which they ministered.[81] They successfully fused and blended many different aspects of Christian concern. Open-air evangelism had been more or less a constant feature of English life since the time of the Evangelical Revival, and in the early days of the Army their social work and philanthropy only reflected what many Christians were already involved with elsewhere. The *Darkest England* scheme may have been the first integrated scheme to be popularised among the churches, but it was in no way innovative. It is probably best, therefore, to view the Army as an integral part of the readily discernible movement in the latter part of the nineteenth century.

R.J. Campbell believed that Booth never realised how far he had travelled in the direction of a more liberal and humanitarian gospel. He concluded that Booth was too busy to be able to rethink his doctrinal position, but that he somehow broke through its implications. He quotes Booth in a parable about heaven to illustrate the position that he had come to adopt.

> It was just the conventional heaven about which Christians pray and sing. There were white-winged angels, crowns and harps, and all the furniture of blessedness as described in the ordinary language of devotion. But there seemed to be something wanting; there was a certain sadness or dissatisfaction evident on every countenance. At length the mystery was explained. Christ stood forth before the adoring multitude and told them that the cause for which his life was given had not yet been won; mankind was still writhing on earth in the fetters of ignorance, vice and pain. Who would renounce heaven, go back to the world below, and resume the battle with the forces of hell? Without a moment's hesitation the whole of that glorious company rose like one mighty being, flung aside their crowns and rose and volunteered with eagerness for the arduous service.[82]

Campbell's perceptive observation bears scrutiny. The influences at work throughout his life, Chartism, his experience as a missioner with the poor, his son Bramwell, Frank Smith, and the general climate among his Nonconformist supporters had all worked together to effect a change in him, but William Booth was a stubborn man. Such stubbornness had led him out of the Wesleyan and New Connexion Conferences on the issue of evangelism, and this evangelism formed the raison d'être of his new movement. More than this it became a shibboleth for all that they did. Booth neither had the time or the theological freedom to fully recognise

---

[80] Haggard, *Regeneration*, pp. 9-10.

[81] Pamela J. Walker, *Pulling the Devil's Kingdom Down: The Salvation Army in Victorian Britain* (Berkley: University of California Press, 2001), pp. 5-6.

[82] Nelson's *Life of Booth* (R.J. Campbell), pp. 147-49.

and appropriate the position that he had ultimately arrived at. Yet he never went as far as those Nonconformists who were more socially and politically articulate. Like the economic proposals in the *Darkest England* scheme itself Booth remained essentially conservative.[83] As mere philanthropy their work was enlightened, but they lacked the progressive edge in economic and political substance that would have brought them more fully into the sphere of the Social Christianity.

[83] Kent, *Holding the Fort*, p. 335.

Chapter 9

Anglican Evangelicals and Sacramentalists

To trace the fortunes of Anglican Evangelicals in the nineteenth century is to chart a rise and fall in prosperity and influence. The momentum resulting from the Evangelical Revival of the eighteenth century seems to have continued with them well into the middle of the next, yet they appear to have been losing ground at just the point when the evangelicals in the Nonconformist churches were coming alive to a new age and to new challenges. It is the Anglo-Catholic party who provide interesting parallels with Nonconformity in this period, especially when considering their concerns for evangelism, social care and excursions into political activity.

The roots of Anglican Evangelicalism in the Evangelical Revival had a profound effect on the Church of England as the Evangelical party owed their origin and strength to the Revival. At the turn of the nineteenth century they were strong and growing stronger. The victory on the slavery issue further boosted their confidence and marked the beginnings of maturity with the Clapham Sect, who had been behind much of the agitation for change, representative of a generation of evangelicals eager to serve Christ in the world. Their theocratic view of the State meant that they were concerned that the authorities should be made aware of their responsibilities as an instrument in the hands of God.[1] They were confident enough to challenge the government and vested interests uncompromisingly on a matter that they believed had to do with the requirements of the law of God and were also marked by a generosity that gave freely of time and money in various philanthropic endeavours for those who were less fortunate than themselves.

As early as 1815 evangelicals were the most powerful group within the established Church and their influence continued to increase until the late 1860s.[2] The estimated number of evangelical clergy rose from 500 at the turn of the century to around 6,500 in the 1850s, approximately a third of the total number.[3] However, it would be wrong to think of the Anglican Evangelicals as the largest group within the Church, because they were not as the great mass of the clergy remained 'low and slow'.[4]

---

1 Stephen Neill, *Anglicanism* (London: Penguin, 1958), pp. 239-40.
2 Neill, *Anglicanism*, p. 234.
3 Bebbington, *Evangelicalism in Modern Britain* (London: Routledge, 1989), p. 106.
4 Eugene Stock, *The English Church in the Nineteenth Century* (London: Longmans,

In the early years of the nineteenth century the evangelicals were channelling their energies into the formation of a plethora of charitable and evangelistic societies. The most striking feature of this area of their work was its sheer dimensions as there were societies of all sorts and descriptions to meet a widespread variety of needs. Indeed, Kathleen Heasman has estimated that up to three-quarters of voluntary charitable organisations from 1850-1900 were evangelical in character and control.[5] Within the Church of England some were large like the Church Pastoral Aid Society (CPAS) or the Church Missionary Society (CMS), others were small; some were run by committee, others were entirely under the control of a particular individual; some were nation-wide, others were completely local. It would be difficult to point to a need that was not catered for in one way or another. Societies dealing with children and young people vied with those helping the sick and aged. There were organisations to cope with criminals, prostitutes and drunkards while others worked to make life more bearable for the handicapped or in the interests of soldiers, sailors, working men and women, railwaymen, policemen, flatboatmen and others. Lord Shaftesbury was probably right when he maintained that most of the great philanthropic movements of the century had sprung from the evangelicals.[6] Within Anglicanism the CMS acted as a barometer for the prospects of evangelicalism, and during the second half of the century it entered a period of decline.[7]

The Earl of Shaftesbury inherited the reformist mantle of Wilberforce and was a very important figure for the Anglican Evangelicals. He had a high profile and sought to use that to advantage by being involved in philanthropic work and by agitating for legislative reform in the House of Lords. Factory Reform and the appointment of Lunacy Commissioners were two particular areas of Shaftesbury's concern.[8] When his step-father-in-law Lord Palmerston became Prime Minister, the advice he sought from Shaftesbury ensured previously rare evangelical appointments in the House of Bishops became more numerous.[9] In himself Shaftesbury ought to have been a great rallying point for the evangelical party, and he had expected this to be the case, only to be disappointed. At the end of the 1860s he admitted that he had lost faith in them, finding them to be utterly intolerant, cold and insincere. He bemoaned the fact that they had degenerated as a group and no longer had a concern for charity and justice.[10]

Green & Co., 1910), pp. 16-19.

5 Kathleen Heasman, *Evangelicals in Action* (London: Geoffrey Bles, 1962), p. 14.

6 Edwin Hodder, *The Life of Lord Shaftesbury*, vol. 2 (London: Cassell, 1886), p. 3.

7 Neill, *Anglicanism*, p. 266.

8 G.R. Balleine, *A History of the Evangelical Party in the Church of England* (London: Longmans, 1933), p. 191; J.T. Inskip, *Evangelical Influence in English Life* (London: Macmillan), pp. 170-89.

9 George W.E. Russell, *A Short History of the Evangelical Movement* (London: Mowbray, 1915), pp. 106-107; though Bebbington, *Evangelicalism*, p.107, disagrees.

10 Desmond Bowen, *The Idea of the Victorian Church: A Study of the Church of England, 1833-1889* (Montreal: University of Toronto Press, 1968), p. 382.

While it appeared that evangelical vitality was exhausted all was not completely dead. William Weldon Champneys had been appointed Rector of Whitechapel in 1837 with the aid of the CPAS and stayed there for thirty years. He developed a ministry to the neighbourhood by subdividing his parish, building new buildings, opening day schools and Sunday schools, forming Mothers' meetings, a Savings Bank, a Coal Club, a Shoeblack Brigade and a Young Men's Institute. Champneys was very much the pioneer of this type of arrangement among Anglicans. At one point his parish staff consisted of thirteen members.[11] In 1853 William Cadman was appointed to St George's, Southwark and he followed Champneys' pattern by dividing his 35,000 strong parish into six districts and appointing a curate, Scripture Reader and Deaconess or Bible woman to each.[12] Bishop Thorold concluded that evangelicals were not settling back into conservatism, but were rather being innovative and audacious. Open-air preaching, evening communions, women workers, services in unconsecrated buildings, children's meetings and involvement in the evangelistic campaigns of Moody were just some of the activities that he cited. Unfortunately, men like Champneys and Cadman were rare. Evangelical clergy tended to concentrate on Bible-preaching and would therefore leave the tougher, poorer areas to go where they were likely to enjoy a larger congregation.

The Church Army was perhaps one of the few positive things to come out of the evangelical constituency in the latter part of the century. It was founded in 1882 by Wilson Carlile who was at that time a curate in Kensington. It was an unashamed copy of the Salvation Army, but completely within the structure of the established Church. They ran shelters for the homeless, prison visitation, open-air preaching and evangelistic work, lodging houses, shelters, relief-depots, an emigration department and a farm colony at Newdigate in Surrey, among a range of other agencies.[13] Many Anglicans were shocked at these developments, especially as Carlile maintained that, 'Surely it is better for a sinecure City church to be a live centre than dead with respectability, propriety, and starch!'[14]

Having been influenced by the work of Pastor von Bodelschwingh in Germany, Carlile set about a reclamation work with the 'Our Tramps' project in November 1889. A pamphlet published in March 1890 outlined the proposed city, farm and overseas colonies a full six months before General Booth's *Darkest England* scheme was launched.[15] The project was never intended to be on the same scale as Booth's work, and they only claimed to have helped some 9,000 in 1896 while the

---

[11] Michael Hennell, *The Early Years of the Church Pastoral Aid Society* (unpublished paper, nd), p. 8; Bowen, *The Idea of the Victorian Church*, p. 291; Balleine, *A History of the Evangelical Party*, pp. 237-38.

[12] Hennell, *The Early Years*, pp. 9-10; Balleine, *A History of the Evangelical Party*, pp. 238-39.

[13] Stock, *The English Church*, pp. 109-10.

[14] Edgar Rowan, *Wilson Carlile and the Church Army* (London: Church Army Bookroom, 1926), p. 211.

[15] Rowan, *Wilson Carlile*, pp. 126-28; Sidney Dark, *Wilson Carlile* (London: James Clarke, 1944), pp. 91-94.

Salvation Army had sold 3.25 million meals, provided shelter for 1 million and employed 4,000 to 5,000 in their elevator enterprises.[16]

Holiness revivalism also touched the Church of England. William Pennefather began organising conferences in his parish at Barnet in 1856, and then at Mildmay Park from 1864.[17] While they covered many topics, the role of the Holy Spirit was central, as was talk of entire consecration. No link appears to have been made between the issues of holiness and social work, yet they always set aside a day to consider contemporary social problems.[18] Pennefather never seems to have preached 'the second blessing', yet members of the Mildmay circle were closely linked with the Pearsall Smiths' visit of 1875. Also in 1875, flowing out of the Moody campaign, the Vicar of Keswick, T.D. Harford-Battersby, an acquaintance of Pennefather, called the first Keswick Holiness Convention. At Keswick the full teaching of holiness 'by faith alone' was proclaimed.[19]

The Pennefathers were also responsible for founding a deaconess order at Mildmay in 1860, following the Lutheran pattern from Kaiserwerth and Strasbourg. This indication of interest in the social aspect of ministry was reinforced by Mrs Pennefather who kept up with developments by keeping in constant touch with evangelical social workers of all types.[20]

Ultimately, the evangelicals did not hold onto their pre-eminent position within the Church as they slipped into decline. A correspondent for *The Times* in 1879, was led to comment on their fall from power, noting that the remains of evangelicalism in the establish Church appeared as a decaying monument to their past activity and now forgotten warfare.[21]

With evangelicalism within Nonconformity renewing itself and making significant progress it is rather ironic that the strength and influence of evangelicals within Anglicanism did not provide them with a platform for similar development and advance within the established church. Shaftesbury believed that they had degenerated into a mere 'theological expression' and were no longer concerned for charity and justice[22] and there is certainly some truth in this. Theologically they did not see the necessity of thinking through their faith for a new situation and, as a result they continued to teach what was by then the tired dogma and doctrine of the eighteenth century. They also failed to respond to, and challenge, some of the questionable theories and philosophies that underlay the industrial era.[23] Their philanthropy was rather the result of a combination of Christian altruism and enlightened self-interest, with their fear of the masses as a contributory factor and

16 Heasman, *Evangelicals in Action*, p. 60.

17 Bebbington, *Evangelicalism*, p. 159; Kent, *Holding the Fort*, p. 105.

18 Heasman, *Evangelicals in Action*, p. 22.

19 Bebbington, *Evangelicalism*, pp. 160-61.

20 S.C. Carpenter, *Church and People, 1789-1889* (London: SPCK., 1937), p. 412; Heasman, *Evangelicals in Action*, p. 22.

21 Balleine, *A History of the Evangelical Party*, p. 271.

22 Bowen, *The Idea of the Victorian Church*, p. 382.

23 Neill, *Anglicanism*, pp. 242-43.

motivating force in their social work.[24] More fundamentally they had no overall social vision except for the maintenance of the status quo and they remained good Tories like Shaftesbury. The net result was that they failed to engage with the social problems of their age in any other than a paternalistic manner, and they were increasingly marginalised and tended to stand aloof. Bebbington also believes that their growing premillennialist inclinations gave them an added immunity to the spread of the social gospel which was animating the evangelicals within Nonconformity and therefore further cut them off from their natural allies.[25]

This increasing isolation was exaggerated by three further factors. First, the momentum of any group in decline is one of contraction and is both demoralising and debilitating. This was so with the evangelicals and, having failed to give a firm theological and philosophical foundation to their social and philanthropic work, the consequences were inevitable. The work languished and Shaftesbury despaired.[26]

The second factor was theological. On the whole the evangelical Anglicans were mildly Calvinistic,[27] and Hugh Price Hughes believed that this led them to preach a hard gospel that disparaged the gifts of God manifest in contemporary society.

> Church of England evangelicalism has lost ground.... Science, literature, art, and deep seated pity have had a fearful revenge. The authority of science, the innumerable hosts of literature, and the resistless charms of art, and the intense humanitarianism of our time have combined to disparage and denounce evangelicalism.[28]

Among them there had always been a strong puritan element and it had grown stronger during the early part of the nineteenth century. Its pull was towards withdrawal from society and engagement with contemporary issues. Did 'the world' belong to God or the devil? In 1770 they would have been certain that 'the world' belonged to God; by 1870 they were not so sure. A new strictness began to appear.[29] Christians were expected to withdraw from worldly amusements like the theatre, dancing and parties. Sabbath Observance was strictly held and even works like Handel's Messiah were suspect as they were considered by some to be inappropriate subjects for musical entertainment.[30] When Wilberforce's biography revealed that he read novels, great anxiety was expressed by some because of the damage such a bad witness from an influential figure would create among the young.[31] To a group that was already contracting its borders and withdrawing from previous spheres of influence, this new puritanism gave a theological and spiritualized justification to withdraw even further from the world. It is no

---

[24] Bowen, *The Idea of the Victorian Church*, p. 256.
[25] Bebbington, *Evangelicalism*, p. 216.
[26] Bowen, *The Idea of the Victorian Church*, p. 291.
[27] Stock, *The English Church*, p. 16.
[28] MT, 08.04.1886.
[29] Michael Hennell, 'Evangelicalism and Worldliness, 1770 to 1870', in G.J. Cuming & Derek Baker, *Studies in Church History*, vol. 8 (Cambridge: CUP, 1972), p. 229.
[30] Hennell, 'Evangelicalism and Worldliness', pp. 230-33.
[31] Hennell, 'Evangelicalism and Worldliness', p. 233.

coincidence that the Keswick Movement blossomed in the late nineteenth century.[32] Their style of perfectionism insisted on withdrawal from political and social action as well as cultural activity. Evangelicals like J.C. Ryle, the Bishop of Liverpool, were typical of this trend that was articulated in his definitive work on the subject, *Holiness*. It is not insignificant that the other denomination which had a Calvinistic legacy, the Baptists, were also slow to respond to the new movement that was reviving evangelicalism.

The third factor has to do with leadership. Like many Nonconformist evangelicals, Hugh Price Hughes was eager to establish a cross-denominational evangelical federation. Yet when he looked towards Anglicanism he saw them infatuated with the political establishment and lacking the cohesion and courage of their principles to exert the influence of their greater numbers and prosperity. He drew a poignant parallel between their relative timidity compared with the bellicose audacity of the ritualists.[33]

The politicisation of the forward thinkers in Nonconformity was relatively easy to accomplish when compared to the restraint that the close relationship with the ruling powers exerted on Anglicanism. Shaftesbury detested the Trade Unions because he disliked the thought of democracy feeling that it ran counter to God's ordained order for society.[34] Shared evangelical belief was not a sufficient basis for co-operation. Nonconformists did share with their Anglican brethren in certain areas of common interest like the Evangelical Alliance and various philanthropic agencies, but their vastly different backgrounds and experience were a hindrance that was compounded by an historic antipathy. The Church Rate issue divided many and the earlier celebration by many dissenters of the bicentenary of the 1662 ejection of clergy from the Church of England had done nothing to help relationships either.[35] In addition to this the open hostility of some just served to further retrench attitudes. It is remarkable that the open hand of fellowship continued to be proffered by Hughes and his Nonconformist colleagues when the Bishop of London was accused in 1899 of 'fraternising with the malignant enemies of the Church of England' for appearing on a platform to support Stephenson's Children's Home during the Wesleyan conference.[36] Some Nonconformists also cherished the hope that the evangelical clergy would leave the Church of England and join them, but few ever did.[37]

Anglican evangelicals failed to address the contemporary thought and developing social conditions of their age. Their innate conservativism in politics, churchmanship and theology combined with the dynamics of decline, their link with the establishment, the historic antipathy towards dissent and a lack of

[32] Hennell, 'Evangelicalism and Worldliness', p. 236.

[33] MT, 19.01.1893; 11.03.1897; 07.10.1897; 16.02.1899.

[34] Carpenter, *Church and People*, pp. 307-08.

[35] A. LeBarbour, *Victorian Baptists: A Study of Denominational Development,* (Maryland, 1977: unpublished Ph.D. Thesis), p. 242.

[36] MT, 07.09.1899.

[37] Balleine, *A History of the Evangelical Party*, pp. 233-34.

courageous and visionary leadership in stopping them meeting the challenge of the late nineteenth century with their fellow evangelicals in Nonconformity.

Elsewhere in the Church of England evangelism was being fused with a burning passion for social engagement and political change among a group with whom the Nonconformists had previously had very little in common. Michael Hennell comments that, 'By 1870 the Anglo-Catholics had caught the Evangelicals bathing and had borrowed their costumes.'[38]

Like many Nonconformists they had been profoundly influenced by F.D. Maurice and these 'Sacramental Socialists' were Maurice's logical heirs within Anglicanism.[39] Their Socialism represented a commitment and concern to attempt change in society for the benefit of the exploited working classes. Stewart Headlam formed the Guild of St Matthew in 1877 and it embodied this understanding. Headlam was an Anglo-Catholic ritualist who never wore priestly garb. He led unemployment marches and was anti-sabbatarian, anti-puritan, anti-temperance and pro-secular education, advocating a programme of thoroughgoing State Socialism.[40] He also became a personal friend of Henry George and was an enthusiastic advocate of the Single Tax proposals.[41]

The Guilds popularity peaked in 1894-95 with a membership of about 400, but it was never large enough to have any real influence on matters of importance.[42] The Guild's decline in the subsequent years saw the rise of the Christian Social Union (CSU) that had been formed in 1889 by Henry Scott Holland and Charles Gore, who were much admired by Nonconformist leaders like Clifford and Hughes. As with many forward thinkers in the church Scott Holland had also been deeply influenced by the teaching of T.H. Green while he was a student at Oxford.[43] 'It was Green who charged us with the ardour which made him always the champion of the poor.'[44]

Jones views the CSU as the 'occupying army' that followed on from Headlam's 'shocktroopers'. They were not as radical as the Guild and consequently had a far broader appeal and by 1895 they boasted 27 branches and nearly 3,000 members.[45] Other Social Union groups formed among the reformers in other denominations too – the Friends Social Union in 1904; the Wesleyan Social Union in 1905; [Roman]

---

38 Michael Hennell in a letter to Henry Rack, dated 09.05.1986.

39 Peter d'A. Jones, *The Christian Socialist Revival (1877-1914)* (Princeton: Princeton University Press, 1968), p. 6.

40 Carpenter, *Church and People*, p. 328.

41 Jones, *Christian Socialist Revival*, pp. 103 & 117.

42 Jones, *Christian Socialist Revival*, pp. 99-100; Carpenter, *Church and People*, pp. 327-38.

43 John Heidt, 'The King of Terrors: The Theology of Henry Scott Holland', *Contemporary Review* 276, 1610, (2000), p. 123; Denys P. Leighton, *The Greenian moment: T.H. Green, Religion and Political Argument in Victorian Britain* (Exeter: Imprint Academic, 2004), p. 20.

44 Jones, *Christian Socialist Revival*, pp. 85-87.

45 Bowen, *The Idea of the Victorian Church*, pp. 281-82.

Catholic Social Union in 1909.[46] The aims of the CSU were outlined on 14 June 1889:

1. To claim for Christian law the ultimate authority to rule social practice.
2. To study in common how to apply the moral truths and principles of Christianity to the social and economic difficulties of the present time.
3. To present Christ in practical life as the living master and king, the enemy of wrong and selfishness, the power of righteousness and love.[47]

They were moderately successful in what they undertook. In 1893 the Oxford CSU published a white list of firms who paid the union rates to their employees and encouraged discriminating purchasing. In 1894 they had 88 firms on the list, and by 1900 this had risen to 146. Preferential dealing in the Potteries with regard to the leaded glaze technique gradually forced the industry, 'through the power of the purse', to change its practices. In 1898-99 the London CSU demanded a revision of the Factory Acts by Parliament. When the new bill was published the CSU thought that it was inadequate, and following their pressure it was subsequently withdrawn. Their influence over certain MPs was significant too and through them they helped to mould the Factory & Workshops Act, 1901 and the Trades Boards Act, 1909.[48] Yet even with this influence and moderate success the Rev. R.F. Donaldson outlined his perception of the Union's method as being, 'Here's a social evil, let's read a paper on it.'[49] The working classes were never themselves involved in the CSU as it was made up of predominantly Oxbridge, High Church Anglicans, and according to George Haw, 'to them it is as far removed . . . as freemasonry and Mohammedanism'.[50]

It is only when the work of the CSU is placed against the background of the work that was carried out by lesser-known Anglo-Catholic clergy who lived and died among the poor that its true contribution comes into perspective. A significant number of Ritualist clergy committed themselves to ministry in the slums, and in many ways paralleled the activities that were the hallmark of the Forward Movement. George Wilkinson, for example, had a living in the centre of London. He took to holding open-air preaching services and also included his High Church practice of processing the cross. He gave fervent evangelistic sermons and made appeals at the end of them for commitments to Christ. His introduction of extempore prayer along with vivid sacramentalism did much to bring the common people to his services. His reputation for 'High-Church Methodism' was benevolently looked upon by the hierarchy as combining the best elements of Wesleyanism on one side and of High Churchmanship on the other.[51]

---

[46] Jones, *Christian Socialist Revival*, p. 166.
[47] Jones, *Christian Socialist Revival*, p. 177.
[48] Jones, *Christian Socialist Revival*, pp. 183-85.
[49] Jones, *Christian Socialist Revival*, p. 220.
[50] Jones, *Christian Socialist Revival*, p. 217.
[51] Bowen, *The Idea of the Victorian Church*, pp. 288-89.

Robert Dolling was an Ulsterman who, having been inspired by Francis of Assisi and John Wesley, went to minister in the slums of Portsmouth in the late 1880s.[52] He mixed his evangelistic preaching with vivid disclosures of the degradation in the area. His picture of children so hungry as to eat raw meat from the local slaughter house and drinking the blood remains a powerful image.[53] He sought to counter drink and prostitution by forming the Portsmouth Social Purity Organisation with other clergy, Nonconformist ministers, doctors, labour leaders and the town's leading citizens.[54]

George Rundle Prynne of Plymouth was another Ritualist of this type and was typical of the men who quietly went about their work, were appreciated by their parishioners but little known elsewhere.[55] He lived and worked with them for 55 years from 1849-1903, like Arthur Douglas Wagner of Brighton, who was also in his parish for over 50 years.[56] Ritualists such as these and C.F. Lowder at St. George's in-the-East, A.B. Goulden at the Elephant and Castle and A.H. Mackonochie at Holborn,[57] all identified themselves with the lives of the poor in their parish. The problems of the poor became their problems too.

It is easy to conclude that the old English evangelicals within Anglicanism were still to be found exhibiting their 'enthusiasm', albeit within the High Church fold.[58] Certainly this was how some of them saw themselves. A.H. Mackonochie said in the 1860s, 'If you want to find an old Evangelical, you must look for him in the ranks of the extreme High Churchmen.'[59] Hugh Price Hughes makes a similar observation, seeing them as allies in the evangelistic thrust of the gospel.

> The truth is that many excellent priests of the Anglican Communion have succeeded not on account of their Romish doctrines and practices, but in spite of them, because in some illogical way they have strangely combined with them the Evangelical Gospel of JESUS CHRIST.[60]

Even the *Daily Telegraph* saw similarities between Moody and the Anglican Ritualists.[61]

A further pioneering Anglican development was Samuel Barnett's Toynbee Settlement. Barnett was a Broad Churchman and Vicar of St Jude's, Whitechapel.

---

52 Bowen, *The Idea of the Victorian Church*, pp. 303-09.
53 Bowen, *The Idea of the Victorian Church*, p. 308.
54 Bowen, *The Idea of the Victorian Church*, p. 307.
55 Bowen, *The Idea of the Victorian Church*, p. 289.
56 Bowen, *The Idea of the Victorian Church*, p. 290.
57 Bowen, *The Idea of the Victorian Church*, pp. 292-96 (Lowder), p. 299 (Goulder) and pp. 299-303 (Mackonochie).
58 See Yngve Brilioth and Dieter Voll , but John Kent disagrees believing this to be a special form of Anglo-Catholic revivalism, not a reversion to the tradition of evangelicalism. Kent, *Holding the Fort*, pp. 242-44.
59 Bowen, *The Idea of the Victorian Church*, p. 299.
60 MT, 20.10.1898.
61 *Daily Telegraph*, 18.04.1844, quoted by James F. Findlay, Jr., *Dwight L. Moody: American Evangelist, 1837-99* (Chicago: University of Chicago Press, 1969), p. 187.

Taken with the thought of Arnold Toynbee that undergraduates should spend their long vacation working in the slums, he proposed a scheme that was readily taken up by students from Oxford that extended the idea into a fully developed community. Between 1884, when Toynbee Hall was opened, and 1911 a total of 188 residents became members of the community. A broad programme of classes and activities were pursued, along with campaigns of local action as diverse as the formation of a public library and the provision of fresh water in the East End.[62] Convinced that the people of Whitechapel could never just become Christian he set about elevating them through music of a high standard, his parish library, lectures and art. While his primary desire was to bring individuals to God, he was often misunderstood because of what was perceived to be a religiously reductionist approach.[63] Evangelism was not a part of his creed, he also minimised the importance of theology and only a few from the local community attended their worship and prayer meetings. Accepting that, his work was pioneering and copied by many others including Scott Holland with his Oxford House Settlement in Bethnal Green and Scott Lidgett's in Bermondsey.

While Anglican evangelicalism was not dead, it was fast becoming an impotent force in the second half of the nineteenth century. There are a number of identifiable factors which contributed to this trend, and pulled this particular group in a completely different direction to their Nonconformist contemporaries. Unexpectedly the fusion of evangelistic concern, social compassion and political involvement of the Forward Movement was paralleled among the Anglo-Catholics. The Ritualist slum priests on the one hand and thinkers in the CSU on the other, when taken together, accomplished just that. They went into the slums to preach and often had similar agencies at work in their parishes to those the Wesleyans had adopted for their Central Missions. Their liberal use of ceremonial in presenting the gospel was essentially a means to bring colour and vividness into drab lives and worship, in much the same way as brass bands and Sankey hymns fulfilled a similar need elsewhere. Added to this there was a desire to change things politically, although the CSU was a mildly socialist group compared to the majority of Radical Liberals in Nonconformity. Similar intellectual foundations to their ideas were also found in the work of F.D. Maurice, T.H. Green and Henry George.

The evidence seems to indicate that these Anglicans were a part of the same phenomenon that was sweeping Nonconformity. Theologically, they looked exclusively to Maurice's incarnationalism rather than to Wesleyan notions of entire sanctification and enduement with the Holy Spirit. It is perhaps ironic that they may not have properly understood or recognised their closeness at the time because of widespread ecclesiastical pettiness that at times bordered on blind prejudice. Yet it was among the Sacramentalists that the most innovative changes were being wrought in Anglican church life at the end of the nineteenth century.

---

[62] Bowen, *The Idea of the Victorian Church*, pp. 330-33.

[63] Carpenter, *Church and People*, pp. 330-32.

Chapter 10

American Theorists

In the narrative which surrounded the development of Social Christianity in Britain the contribution of Americans like the revivalist D.L. Moody and the political economist Henry George were important and have already been acknowledged. Indeed, some historians of the American Social Gospel movement consider George to be a neglected catalyst or antecedent, if not participant, within the movement.[1] It should therefore be no surprise that a parallel movement was under way there at the same time. The American context, through its comparisons and contrasts sheds further light on the analysis of this late nineteenth century phenomenon.

By the beginning of the twentieth century the Social Gospel was the most conspicuous movement in American Protestantism. The term itself is somewhat misleading as, like their British contemporaries, they centred their thinking on 'Social Christianity'. In the United States this term came to signify a more conservative approach to social action that did not challenge the dominant individualism of American culture and was later dropped. The 'progressives' adopted the Social Gospel so that their more advanced social and theological views might be more easily discerned.[2] As a consequence many fellow evangelicals dubbed them 'liberals', but this too is misleading. Many Social Gospellers still considered themselves to be evangelicals and upheld the importance of evangelism, personal experience and orthodox Christology. Handy concludes that theirs was a 'halfway house', an 'evangelical or Christocentric' liberalism.[3] One of the leading proponents of the Social Gospel, Walter Rauschenbusch, said of his own pilgrimage in 1912,

> I set out with the proposition that social Christianity, which makes the Reign of God on earth its object, is a distinct type of personal religion, and that in its best manifestations it involves the possibility of a purer spirituality, a keener recognition of sin, more durable powers of growth, a more personal evangelism, and a more all-around salvation than the individualistic type of religion which makes the salvation of the soul

---

1 Eileen W. Lindner, 'The redemptive politic of Henry George: a legacy to the Social Gospel', *Union Seminary Quarterly Review*, 42.3 (1988), pp. 1-2.

2 Robert T. Handy, *The Social Gospel in American* (New York: OUP, 1966), pp. 5-6.

3 Mark A. Noll et al (eds.), *Christianity in America* (Tring, Lion, 1983), pp. 312 & 323; Handy, *The Social Gospel*, pp. 6-7.

> its object. I want to add that this new type of religion is especially adapted to win and inspire modern man.[4]

Unlike their British counterparts, the American social gospellers were more theorists than activists. Dombrowski maintains that the movement gained its impetus more from forward-looking professors in theological seminaries than anywhere else, and this is certainly true of the three pre-eminent leaders within the movement.[5] Walter Rauschenbusch spent twenty years in a seminary, firstly teaching New Testament and then Church History. Richard T. Ely had studied economics and politics at the University of Heidelberg before having an influential academic career in America, becoming a professor of economics first at the University of Wisconsin and towards the end of his life at Northwestern University in Chicago.[6] Washington Gladden, often called the 'Father of the Social Gospel', was primarily a pastor though he frequently lectured at universities and was for some years the religious editor of the New York newspaper *The Independent*.[7] While advocating responsible participation in philanthropic and political causes so as to right social wrongs, the social gospellers themselves sought to change views and attitudes, primarily through their writing.[8] A key dimension of the Social Gospel movement in the United States was the legacy it left in adult education as the ideas of the theologian educators at its helm filtered down and influenced other progressive movements through the classroom.[9]

Their starting point was the familiar understanding of the 'Fatherhood of God and the Brotherhood of Man' and the belief that Jesus taught a doctrine of community and fraternity. At the heart of their message was the immanence of God, the goodness and worth of man, and the coming of the Kingdom of God on earth as a possibility in history.[10] This teaching began to arouse interest in the 1870s, received considerable attention in the 1880s, assuming the proportions of a movement in the 1890s. By 1908 it had become a matter of common consensus among the denominations.[11] Henry May sees the movement falling into three political types, radicals (left wing), progressives (centrist) and conservatives (right

---

4 Walter Rauschenbusch, *Christianizing the Social Order* (New York: Macmillan, 1919), p. 117.

5 James Dombrowski, *The Early Days of Christian Socialism in America* (New York: Columbia University Press, 1936), p. 60.

6 Benjamin G. Rader, *The Academic Mind and Reform: The Influence of Richard T. Ely in American Life* (Lexington: University of Kentucky Press, 1966), pp. 110, 212.

7 DCC, p. 827 (Rauschenbusch); Handy, *The Social Gospel*, pp. 173-74 (Ely); DCC, p. 413 (Gladden).

8 William McLoughlin, *Revivals, Awakenings and Reform: An Essay on Religious and Social Change in America, 1607-1977* (Chicago: University of Chicago Press, 1978), p. 175; Handy, *The Social Gospel*, p. 11.

9 Dorothy Lander, 'The Legacy of the Social Gospel in Adult Education', *Journal of Adult Theological Education* 1.1 (2004), p. 79.

10 McLoughlin, *Revivals*, p. 162; Handy, *The Social Gospel*, p. 10.

11 Dombrowski, *The Early Days*, p. 73.

wing), though care needs to be taken for at this stage theological and political classifications do not necessarily correspond. Over time, the social determinism of the left and the philanthropic paternalism of the right were squeezed by the advance of the progressives.[12]

The rise of the Social Gospel in the United States was the product of the rapid industrialisation and urbanisation in the latter years of the century. Child labour, slum housing, and the bloody confrontations between capital and labour during the major industrial depression of the 'gay nineties' were all elements that contributed to the rise of the movement.[13] Not all Christians shared the sentiments of the Social Gospellers though, as the remedy offered by a writer in *The Congregationalist* illustrates, following the labour riots in Chicago in 1886. '[A] gatling gun or two, swiftly brought into position and well served, offers, on the whole, the most merciful as well as effectual remedy.'[14]

For the leaders of the movement the thought of German philosophy and the higher criticism of the Bible were significant especially as the latter stripped traditional belief of many of its fixed points and returned scholarship to the study of the ethical imperatives of the historical Jesus. Ely had studied philosophy at Halle to which he had added economics and politics at Heidelberg. Rauschenbusch was of German Lutheran extraction and had begun his formal education there. His father, having converted to Baptist views, became professor of the German Department at Rochester Theological Seminary.[15] Besides their German influences these leading thinkers also acknowledged their debts to English influence through F.D. Maurice, Charles Kingsley and Henry Scott Holland. Washington Gladden was particularly affected by the Christocentric liberalism of F.W. Robertson of Brighton, alongside the teaching of the Congregationalists A.M. Fairbairn and R.J. Campbell.[16] The notion of the perfectibility of man inherent in Social Darwinism was widespread too which, when added to their theological emphases outlined above, 'composed the liberal theological soil that nurtured the Social Gospel'.[17] The teaching and activism of Henry George also impacted upon the movement, most dramatically on Walter Rauschenbusch. 'I owe my own first awakening to the world of social problems to the agitation of Henry George in 1886, and wish here to record my lifelong debt to this single-minded apostle of a great truth.'[18] He aligned himself

---

[12] Paul A. Carter, *The decline and revival of the social gospel: social and political liberalism in American Protestant churches, 1920-1940* (New York: Cornell University Press, 1956), p. 12.

[13] Noll, *Christianity in America*, pp. 318-19; Carter, *The decline and revival of the social gospel*, p. 10.

[14] Noll, *Christianity in America*, p. 311.

[15] Carter, *The decline and revival of the social gospel*, p. 14; Handy, *The Social Gospel*, p. 174 (Ely) and p. 253 (Rauschenbusch).

[16] Handy, *The Social Gospel*, pp. 13, 26, 44, 51 & 260-61.

[17] Emory Stevens Bucke (ed.), *The History of American Methodism*, vol. 3 (Nashville: Abingdon, 1964), p. 389.

[18] Rauschenbusch, *Social Order*, p. 394.

with George's unsuccessful campaign to become Mayor of New York[19] and, in 1907 he described *Progress and Poverty* as 'brilliant' and contended that the main points of George's thought had never been answered.[20]

To the accepted and orthodox understanding of the origins of the movement Smith added another believing that scholars had neglected the contribution of one of the most persistent and socially significant religious themes of the nineteenth century, revivalism, with its accompanying emphasis on entire sanctification and perfectionism. He holds that it was in the revivals of the mid-nineteenth century, rather than with Social Darwinism and the new sociology, that the Social Gospel was born.[21] Historians neglected revivalism as a possible source because they felt that in the second half of the century it was in decline and could therefore be eliminated. However, while revivalism may have been in decline, the doctrine of perfection and the methods of mass evangelism became ever more important as the years passed. In explaining his conclusions Smith writes,

> [My] thesis . . . is that, whatever may have been the role of other factors, the quest for perfection joined with compassion for poor and needy sinners and a rebirth of millennial expectation to make popular Protestantism a mighty social force.[22]

The mild Calvinistic revivalism of Charles Finney was suffused with perfectionism, and through his extensive revivalistic work and appointment as Professor of Theology at Oberlin College, Ohio, in 1835, his emphasis gained a wide audience. He told his hearers that they were 'saved for service', and encouraged them to participate in the movements for temperance, peace, prison reform, the abolition of slavery and women's rights.[23] Methodist revivalism hit a similar theme and was given added weight in 1856 with the publication in America of William Arthur's popular *Tongue of Fire* in the United States. Thus revivalism came to stand not only for personal salvation, but also for a belief in God's immanence and his readiness to transform the present world through the outpouring of the Holy Ghost. Arthur argued that there was salvation for the body here as well as the soul in eternity, and that a holy community was to be created not only in heaven, but also on earth.[24]

In 1841 Albert Barnes wrote in *The National Preacher* that sin and evil were interlocked, confederated and sustained by one another in every city. It was only by the power of the Spirit that such alliances could be broken.[25] Smith concluded,

---

19 Barbara A. Lundsten, 'The Legacy of Walter Rauschenbusch: A Life Informed by Mission', *International Bulletin of Missionary Research* (April, 2004), p. 76.

20 Walter Rauschenbusch, *Christianity and the Social Crisis* (New York: Macmillan, 1907), p. 299n.

21 Timothy L. Smith, *Revivalism and Social Reform : American Protestantism on the Eve of the Civil War* (Nashville: Abingdon), pp. 237 & 103.

22 Smith, *Revivalism*, pp. 148-49.

23 Smith, *Revivalism*, p. 154; Carter, *The decline and revival of the social gospel*, p. 8.

24 Smith, *Revivalism*, pp. 155 & 157.

25 Smith, *Revivalism*, pp. 152.

> They saw with surprising clarity the social implications of their prized ideals of righteous living, brotherly love, and the immanence of God through the outpoured Holy Spirit. They moved rapidly towards a systematic elaboration of Christian humanitarian doctrine. Perfectionists like Finney and William Arthur, who added to these ideals a passion for full personal consecration and freedom from all sin, actually led the way.[26]

They believed that as individuals actually manifested the likeness of Christ in their own lives through the agency of the Spirit, so these transformed individuals would help to renovate society. This perfectionism protected American revivalism from a Calvinistic quietism that would have left the Almighty to accomplish his own judgements. Their perfectionism was also directed along the avenue of social service rather than towards mystical experience. So when the widespread spiritual awakening occurred in 1858 it led many to believe that the conquest of social and political evil was near at hand.[27]

Evangelicals who were working in the slums to convert the poor were the best placed to know at first hand the appalling conditions that were developing. Phoebe Palmer, the holiness revivalist, is perhaps the best known slum missioner of the period. With Methodist help she founded the Five Points Mission in 1850 and engaged in pioneering the social ministries that would be repeated elsewhere throughout the century. The Rev. Lewis Pease opened the Five Points House of Industry next door to the mission at the same time, and by 1854 they were supporting 500 women by employment in much the same way as Booth's 'elevator' factories worked in the *Darkest England* scheme in the 1890s.[28] Before the turn of the century these mission-orientated revivalists had established the Christian and Missionary Alliance. This federation served hundreds of like-minded groups across America and Canada who held to the four-fold emphasis of evangelism, sanctification, divine healing and the second coming of Christ.[29]

Movements like the YMCA, and the United States Christian Commission were dominated by people who had revivalist and perfectionist sentiments. Alfred Cookman, in his 1869 Anniversary Sermon for the YMCA encouraged his hearers to be 'Entirely consecrated to service, and then filled with God . . . A co-worker with omnipotence. I challenge the world to supply a more sublime ideal of character, of experience, of life.'[30]

The baptism in the Spirit was seen to purify the heart and by faith to connect them to the self-denying love of Christ. Having this understanding, John Humphrey Noyes predicted that, 'the next phase of National history will be that of Revivalism and Socialism harmonised and working together for the Kingdom of Heaven'.[31]

---

[26] Smith, *Revivalism*, p. 161.
[27] Smith, *Revivalism*, pp. 161, 157, 175-76 & 153.
[28] Noll, *Christianity in America*, p. 317; Smith, *Revivalism*, pp. 169-70.
[29] Noll, *Christianity in America*, p. 317.
[30] Smith, *Revivalism*, p. 176.
[31] Smith, *Revivalism*, p. 162.

Smith holds that as late as 1910 the central feature of the Christian social method in America remained the dedication of the individual and their resources to the will of God. This further confirms his thesis of the significant contribution to the rise of the Social Gospel in America of perfectionist revivalism.[32] However, it is important to remember that in its more liberal theology and advocacy of wholesale structural change in law, government policy and in the formal and informal institutions of society, the Social Gospel movement went much further than any of its revivalist predecessors.[33]

Building on the work of Richard T. Ely's American Economic Association which was formed in 1885, and on the popular impact of two urban exposes – Jacob Riis, *How the Other Half Lives* (1890); W.T. Stead, *If Christ Came to Chicago* (1894) – the number of ministers sympathetic to the movement grew. Riis's work on New York and Stead's on Chicago – the latter timed to coincide with the opening of the World's Fair in that city, selling over 100,000 copies – shocked middle-class American sensibilities.[34]

In 1893 it was estimated that a mere 660 of the 100,000 American ministers were deeply interested in the labour problem. In 1934, 95% of the 21,000 who responded to a questionnaire favoured a 'co-operative commonwealth' over against the capitalist system. [35] Indeed, the hegemony of Social Gospel ideals over Protestantism is clearly illustrated in the formation of the Federal Council of Churches of Christ in America in 1908 with its 33 denominational members pledged to 'social service' through their adoption of a social creed at its inception.[36]

The Social Creed

We deem it the duty of all Christian people to concern themselves directly with certain practical industrial problems. To us it seems that the churches must stand - for equal rights and complete justice for all men in all stations of life.

For the right of all men to the opportunity for self-maintenance, a right ever to be wisely and strongly safeguarded against encroachments of every kind.

For the right of workers to some protection against the hardships often resulting from the swift crises of industrial change.

For the principle of conciliation and arbitration in industrial dissensions.

---

[32] Smith, *Revivalism*, p. 151.

[33] Noll, *Christianity in America*, p. 319.

[34] Noll, *Christianity in America*, pp. 311-12; W.T. Stead, *If Christ Came to Chicago* (London: Review of Reviews, 1894), p. vi; Handy, *The Social Gospel*, pp. 9-10; C. Howard Hopkins, *The Rise of the Social Gospel in American Protestantism* (New Haven: Yale University Press, 1940), p. 146.

[35] McLoughlin, *Revivals*, p. 172.

[36] Carter, *The decline and revival of the social gospel*, p. 11; Noll, *Christianity in America*, p. 319; Rauschenbusch, *Social Order*, p. 15.

> *For the protection of the worker from dangerous machinery, occupational disease, injuries, and mortality.*
>
> *For the abolition of child labor.*
>
> *For such regulations of the conditions of toil for women as shall safeguard the physical and moral health of the community.*
>
> *For the suppression of the 'sweating system'.*
>
> *For the gradual and reasonable reduction of the hours of labor to the lowest practicable point, and for that degree of leisure for all which is a condition of the highest human life.*
>
> *For a release from employment one day in seven.*
>
> *For a living wage as a minimum in every industry, and for the highest wage that each industry can afford.*
>
> *For the most equitable division of the products of industry that can ultimately be devised.*
>
> *For suitable provision for the old age of the workers and for those incapacitated by injury.*
>
> *For the abatement of poverty.*
>
> *For the toilers of America and to those who by organised effort are seeking to lift the crushing burdens of the poor, and to reduce the hardships and uphold the dignity of labor, this Council sends the greeting of human brotherhood and the pledge of sympathy and of help in a cause which belongs to all who follow Christ.*[37]

Such vigorous advocacy of social emphases brought criticism from conservatives within the denominations, so, in 1912 the Federal Council balanced the commission on social service with one on evangelism. The same year saw the culmination of one of the last great united crusades of the era, riding the high tide of interest in the Social Gospel. 'The Men and Religion Forward Movement' was a highly organised series of eight day events in sixty cities. Its aim was to win men and boys to Christ and the church. Along with the usual emphasis on evangelism went a new stress on social service and mobilisation to action. The missions gave the impression of being highly over-planned and did not live up to expectations. Billy Sunday, a rising evangelist of the traditional school, believed that the failure of the Men and Religion Forward Movement was because denominationalists were trying to make a religion out of social service. 'We've had enough of this godless social service nonsense,' he said.[38]

Many consider it an enigma that in the pioneering work of the Social Gospel in America the Methodists were notable by their absence. It was not until the early twentieth century that they began to have a significant presence within the

---

[37] Rauschenbusch, *Social Order*, pp. 14-15.

[38] Noll, *Christianity in America*, pp. 313-14; Handy, *The Social Gospel*, p. 14.

movement, and the Methodist Federation for Social Service was not formed by Francis McConnell, Frank Mason North, Worth Tippy and others until 1907.[39] The explanation of this is most probably to be found in the social make-up of American Methodism. The Church consisted largely of artisans and small shopkeepers, the bastions of frugality and hard work. Many converts were also from among the farming and wealthier business classes who were naturally more conservative. Added to this, the influence of the Social Gospel was first felt most strongly among the industrial workers and the advanced intellectuals, and neither of these groups was highly represented in Methodism. Furthermore, Methodist theology at the time was highly individualistic and the revivalist influence was strong. Personal sin was seen to be a sufficient explanation for social evil.[40] In Britain, by contrast, Methodism had had a long association with the working class and the struggle for political change and where, by the end of the century the old men of the denomination had been shaped by their experience of Chartism and the struggle against the Corn Laws fifty years earlier. In American Methodists were far more economically prosperous and conservative in both social and political senses.

The three key individuals in developing Social Gospel thinking in the United States also bear scrutiny in shedding light onto the development and substance of the movement.

WASHINGTON GLADDEN had been brought up a Presbyterian but had failed to have the emotional experience of God's favour that he had been taught was necessary for salvation. Away from home he was converted under the ministry and mild Calvinism of an associate of Finney and became a Congregationalist.[41] As a pastor in Columbus, Ohio his preaching on Sunday mornings always concerned personal religion as he believed this to be the core of the faith. Divine grace was the helper in a believer's infirmities, the promoter of better thoughts and a quickening influence of all that is best, enabling the believer to be strong and overcome all that was opposed to the rule of God. The topics of his Sunday evening addresses were wide-ranging, touching on social and biographical subjects as well as religion and theology.[42]

Gladden believed that the individual and social gospels were inseparably bound together. While affirming the importance of evangelism, he believed that the gospel was imperfectly heard if only personal salvation was proclaimed. Therefore he supported wholeheartedly the Men and Religion Forward Movement, but refused to lend his support to Billy Sunday when the latter led a revivalistic campaign at Columbus in 1912.[43]

---

[39] William Warren Sweet, *Methodism in American History* (Nashville: Abingdon, 1953), p. 359.

[40] Henry F. May, *Protestant Churches and Industrial America* (New York: Harper), pp. 189-90.

[41] Handy, *The Social Gospel*, p. 19.

[42] Handy, *The Social Gospel*, pp. 24 & 27.

[43] McLoughlin, *Revivals*, pp. 173-74.

A dream of seeing the United States as a united, holy and 'socialised' nation, that fulfilled Protestant hopes for the coming of the Kingdom of God kept him involved in the whole of the nation's life. He was no socialist, but a firm commitment to the progressive cause brought him into close relationship with Theodore Roosevelt and reformist politics. He argued for fixed proportion profit-sharing; reduced hours; co-operative manufacturing and merchandising; worker's compensation; unemployment/health insurance and government intervention to curb the worst excesses of urban industrialisation and laissez-faire. In 1895, following great disruption caused by the rail strikes, he advocated public ownership of the machinery of transportation, though he thought that it would be sufficient for the people to own the tracks, leasing them to operating syndicates.[44] In this way Gladden sought to develop his understanding of the primacy of the Fatherhood of God, indeed he held that all America's national problems were problems of brotherhood.[45]

> If God is the Father of all men, all men are brethren; and there can be but one law for home and school and shop and factory and market and court and legislative hall. One child of the common Father can not enslave another nor exploit another; the strong and the fortunate and the wise can not take advantage of the weak and the crippled and the ignorant, and enrich themselves by spoiling their neighbors; each must care for the welfare of all . . . This is the law of brotherhood which directly follows from Christ's doctrine of the Fatherhood [of God] . . . which is . . . the only solution of the problems of society.[46]

He had been very much influenced by the work of A.M. Fairbairn and his emphasis on the Kingdom. Indeed in 1887 he gave his Lyman Beecher lectures, *Tools and the Man*, at Mansfield College, Oxford having previously given them at Yale.[47] Walter Rauschenbusch considered that Gladden, with Richard T. Ely and Josiah Strong, had produced the mature thought which had kindled and compelled his own social thought and that of other second generation social gospellers.[48]

RICHARD T. ELY was also brought up with a strict Presbyterian background. Unable to accept predestination he went over to the Protestant Episcopal Church.[49] Dombrowski believes that prior to 1890 nobody did more than Ely to turn the attention of organised religion to the ethical implications of the industrial revolution, especially in his books, *Social Aspects to Christianity*, and *Introduction*

---

[44] Handy, *The Social Gospel*, p. 31; May, *Protestant Churches*, p. 174; McLoughlin, *Revivals*, p. 174.

[45] David Fisher, 'Washington Gladden: Salvation in the Public Square', *International Congregational Journal* 8.2 (2009), pp. 65.

[46] Noll, *Christianity in America*, p. 323; Thompson, *Social Gospel*, p. 268.

[47] Handy, *The Social Gospel*, p. 26.

[48] Rauschenbusch, *Social Order*, p. 9.

[49] Handy, *The Social Gospel*, p. 173.

to Political Economy.[50] In the former he related how widespread sermons addressing Social Christianity were with even 'Mr. Moody's Church' in Chicago receiving one from Charles E. Goss, though some complained that they wanted 'simple gospel sermons' rather than hearing about the trials and temptations of working girls and their remedy.[51]

Ely believed that Christianity was reducible to loving God and loving your neighbour. The first led to theology the second to sociology. Love to God was piety, love to the neighbour was philanthropy. He maintained that time in seminary should be equally divided between the two.[52] While he held that it was absurd for a minister to exhort his congregation to love God on Sunday if he did not also encourage them to love their neighbour during the week, he understood that love to God was primary. It was the only way that Christians would receive the grace to succeed.[53] 'It is true that we get at the second commandment through the first; and we must first love God, in order to serve as we should our fellow men.'[54] On this subject he had been particularly inspired in the summer of 1887 by Mark Guy Pearse who was visiting Chautauqua from the West London Mission and publicly acknowledged his appreciation in print, two years later.[55]

Because Ely perceived that evolutionary progress was a natural law operating as much in the social and economic process as in natural selection, he only advocated a programme of mild reform.[56] However, 'Positive righteousness' involved an unceasing attack on wrong institutions until the earth became 'the new earth' and cities were transformed into 'cities of God'.[57] As human health, development and fulfilment were the means to this end he therefore resisted the notion that labour was a commodity in the production process and campaigned for workers' compensation; the abolition of child labour; the eight-hour day; boards of arbitration; women's rights; parks and playgrounds; slum renovation; public health clinics; old age and health insurance and a public works programme. Yet he too was no socialist.[58] 'I condemn alike that individualism which would allow the state no room for industrial action and that socialism which would absorb in the state the functions of the individual.'[59]

WALTER RAUSCHENBUSCH was the son of a German Lutheran Missionary who emigrated to the United States and was subsequently converted to a Baptist position. Rauschenbusch had a conversion experience in 1879 which led him to

---

50 Dombrowski, *The Early Days*, p. 50.
51 Handy, *The Social Gospel*, p. 196.
52 Dombrowski, *The Early Days*, pp. 52-54.
53 Handy, *The Social Gospel*, pp. 187 & 192.
54 Handy, *The Social Gospel*, pp. 192-93.
55 Handy, *The Social Gospel*, p. 187.
56 Dombrowski, *The Early Days*, p. 54.
57 C. Howard Hopkins, *The Rise of the Social Gospel in American Protestantism* (New Haven: Yale University Press, 1940), p. 109.
58 McLoughlin, *Revivals*, p. 170.
59 McLoughlin, *Revivals*, p. 171.

baptism on profession of faith. He always held to the centrality of this event, which he later described as that 'tender, mysterious experience'. He undertook his first pastorate in the Hell's Kitchen on New York's West Side intending 'to save souls in the ordinarily accepted religious sense'.[60] But, confronted by the appalling social problems that surrounded him his theological conservatism was challenged. He faced the problem of how to relate his evangelical passion for saving souls with his growing conviction of the imperative need for social action.

> [T]hey didn't fit . . . 'I went ahead, although I had to set myself against all that I had previously been taught. I had to revise my whole study of the Bible . . . all my scientific studying of the Bible was undertaken to find a basis of the Christian teaching of a social gospel.'[61]

He found the basis for drawing together his social vision with his evangelical concern for individuals in the doctrine of the Kingdom.[62] Arguing that the Kingdom held a social dimension that had been lost following the days of the early church, a dimension that encompassed the whole aim of Jesus, Rauschenbusch held that just as justification by faith alone was to Luther and the sovereignty of God was to Jonathan Edwards, so the Kingdom was to Social Gospellers.[63]

Rauschenbusch lamented that while evangelicalism was rich in men of piety and evangelistic fervour, it was singularly poor in the prophetic gift.[64] Hopkins believes that he was that 'spiritual prophet' which evangelicalism so desperately needed.[65] This spiritual emphasis was often explicit in Rauschenbusch as he called for more religion and not less,[66] and often drew on allusions to the help of divine grace (*sic*, the Holy Spirit) as the sustaining power in all the believer's endeavours.

> I affirm my faith in the reality of the spiritual world . . . I rejoice to believe in God . . . I affirm my faith in the Kingdom of God and my hope in its final triumph . . . I desire to minister God's love to men and to offer no hindrance to the free flow of his love through me. . . . I accept the limitations of my own life. . . . Through the power of Christ which descends on me, I know that I can be more than conqueror.[67]

This is characteristic of his combination of evangelical and social themes and such a fusion was the doorway to the successful communication of his convictions. Martin

---

60 Lundsten, The Legacy of Walter Rauschenbusch', p. 76.

61 Handy, *The Social Gospel*, p. 255.

62 Janet R. Nelson, 'Walter Rauschenbusch and the social gospel: a hopeful theology for the twenty-first century economy', *Cross Currents* 59.4 (2009), p. 445.

63 Walter Rauschenbusch, *A Theology for the Social Gospel* (New York: Macmillan, 1917), p. 131.

64 Rauschenbusch, *Social Crisis*, p. 338.

65 Hopkins, *The Rise of the Social Gospel*, p. 218.

66 Rauschenbusch, *Social Order*, pp. 464-65.

67 Walter Rauschenbusch, *Prayers of the Social Awakening* (Boston: Pilgrim Press, 1925), pp. 148-49.

Luther King, Jr said, 'Rauschenbusch gave to American Protestantism a sense of social responsibility that it should never lose.'[68]

Rauschenbusch believed that the prophetic religion of the Old Testament and the teaching of Jesus all pointed to 'the reconstruction of the whole of human life in accordance with the will of God and under the motive power of religion'.[69]

In facing this issue afresh he said that Social Christianity built on the traditional individualist gospel of evangelicalism, with its evangelism, and, 'holds to all the real values in the old methods, but rounds them out to meet all the needs of human life'.[70] To accomplish this Rauschenbusch attempted to construct a bridge between modern biblical scholarship, the theology of the Social Gospel and the analysis of contemporary problems.[71]

Religious experience was the non-negotiable foundation of the Social Gospel. Speaking of his own experience, he said,

> I have no doubt there was a great deal in it that was foolish, that I had to get away from, and that was untrue. And yet, such as it was, it was of everlasting value to me. It turned me permanently, and I thank God with all my heart for it.[72]

The primacy of religious experience did not negate social righteousness. Some had charged that the Social Gospel movement was detracting from prayer meetings and evangelistic efforts. Rauschenbusch strongly disagreed. He believed that evangelism was the cutting edge of the church and in 1887 and 1888 he had participated in Moody's summer revival meetings in Northfield Massachusetts, giving himself unreservedly and receiving a 'rich blessing' and in an article for the *Christian Inquirer* spoke in high praise of both Moody and Hudson Taylor.[73] He was also taken by the focus on the work of the Holy Spirit and Evans speculates that the influence of William Arthur might also have been at work in Northfield.[74]

In an article for *The Independent* on 12 May 1904 Rauchenbusch called for 'A New Evangelism' to bring people into touch with the social and economic sins of industrialised society. This was not the end of the Old Evangelism, rather its transformation. 'The tongue of fire will descent on men and give them great faith, joy and boldness, and then we shall hear the new evangel, and it will be the Old Gospel.'[75]

Rauschenbush felt that if spiritual life was sapped by devotion to social work, then it was a calamity 'second to none' for the church should not have to choose

---

68 Handy, *The Social Gospel*, p. 259.
69 Rauschenbusch, *Social Crisis*, p. 343.
70 Rauschenbusch, *Social Order*, p. 114.
71 Cushing Strout, *The New Heavens and the New Earth: Political Religion in America* (New York: Harper & Row, 1973), p. 240.
72 Handy, *The Social Gospel*, pp. 264-65.
73 Lundsten, 'The Legacy of Walter Rauschenbusch', p. 76; Christopher H. Evans, *The Kingdom is Always but Coming* (Waco: Baylor University Press, 2010), p. 71.
74 Evans, *The Kingdom*, pp. 71-72.
75 Evans, *The Kingdom*, p. xvii.

between social righteousness and communion with God. The two went together and strengthened one another. Evangelism, for example, was driven by the accumulated weight of the moral capital behind it.[76] To illustrate this he referred to the impact of Garibaldi on Moody and the humanitarian spirit of a gypsy on Evan Roberts, one of the leaders of the Welsh Revival of 1904.[77]

Based upon the personal religious experience of the believer, the Social Gospel movement would then be sure of its true development as believers opened themselves continually to the inspiration of the Spirit of Jesus and the life of contemporary society. These two would form a 'vital union in our personalities' from which the Christian life flows in its fullest and broadest sense,[78] for the inspired man is the channel through which the Spirit of God enters humanity. 'Therefore the most immediate and constant need in christianizing the social order is for more religious individuals.'[79]

In his last book, *A Theology of the Social Gospel* (1917), Rauschenbusch attempted to complete his refashioning of orthodox theology to incorporate the understanding of the Social Gospel. Thus original sin symbolised the inability of humanity to overcome the cultural sins of race, class, nation, creed and sex without divine help. Sin, as such, was transmitted from generation to generation and was acquired by a process of socialisation, and conversion was the way that selfish motives for profit and cultural prejudice were turned to brotherhood and co-operation.[80] Repentance and faith, salvation, regeneration, conviction of sin, the Kingdom of God and other theological concepts were all subject to Rauschenbusch's re-interpretive work.[81] He saw this re-interpretation as of vital importance in preparing men for a righteous society as well as for individual salvation, and in so doing was keen to bridge the growing divide between proponents of the Social Gospel and more conservative evangelicals.[82] 'The old theology must develop social relevance; the new social movement must discover religious depth.'[83]

Reinhold Niebuhr considered Rauschenbusch the real founder of Social Christianity in the United States and 'it's most brilliant and generally satisfying exponent'.[84]

---

76 Rauschenbusch, *Social Order*, pp. 103-05; Handy, *The Social Gospel*, p. 326.

77 Rauschenbusch, *Social Crisis*, p. 337.

78 Handy, *The Social Gospel*, p. 330.

79 Rauschenbusch, *Social Order*, p. 460

80 McLoughlin, *Revivals*, p. 177.

81 Rauschenbusch, *Social Crisis*, pp. 345, 349, 351 & 354; Rauschenbusch, *Social Order*, pp. 1 & 458.

82 Strout, *The New Heavens*, p. 240; Lundsten, 'The Legacy of Walter Rauschenbusch', p. 78.

83 Paul M. Minus, *Walter Rauschenbusch: American Reformer* (New York: Macmillan, 1988), p. 187.

84 W. Morgan Patterson, 'Walter Rauschenbusch: Baptist exemplar of social concern', *Baptist History and Heritage* 7.3 (1972), p. 135.

The notion that the Social Gospel was an indigenous American movement is widespread. Even among those who recognise the developing world-wide interest in Social Christianity.[85] Obviously the expression of the Social Gospel that was encouraged by men like Gladden, Ely and Rauschenbusch was uniquely tailored to the American context. Yet the parallels between the American Social Gospellers and the wider British Forward Movement are interesting to draw; the problems of urbanisation, the influence of evangelicalism and a shared interest in the works of Maurice, Kingsley, William Arthur, Scott Holland, Henry George and others which provided the pool of thought from which they drew. Some have even begun to see the movement, in part, as a consequence of the first historic wave of Globalisation.[86] Mark Guy Pearse's visit to Chautauqua, Washington Gladden's time in Oxford and the influence of the English CSU in the establishment of its American counterpart[87] are indicative of how travel and communication was leading to a cross-fertilisation of ideas across the Atlantic. Indeed Gladden received a favourable review of *Who Wrote the Bible?* in *The Methodist Times*.[88]

Like their British counterparts, those American Social Gospellers who began their spiritual life under Calvinistic influence found that they had to increasingly soften or dilute its influence to progress further along this line of theological development. The most interesting parallel of all with the British movement is Smith's assessment of the contribution made by the revivalist holiness movement, with its 'second blessing' teaching concerning the baptism of the Spirit and its relationship to Christian perfection which touches exactly the same spot as R.W. Dale's request to the Wesleyan Methodist Conference of 1879 to develop the social dimension of Wesley's doctrine of entire sanctification, which Hugh Price Hughes attempted to fulfil. It is also interesting to note that quite early on, appeals to the Fatherhood of God and the Brotherhood of man began to overshadow references to holiness and the divine aid afforded by the Holy Spirit.

---

85 Hopkins, *The Rise of the Social Gospel*, p. 326; Noll, *Christianity in America*, p. 320; Handy, *The Social Gospel*, p. 4.

86 Gary Dorrien, 'Society as the Subject of Redemption: The Relevance of the Social Gospel', *Tikkun* 24.6 (2009): http://www.tikkun.org/article.php/nov_dec_09_dorrien [accessed, 25.08.2014].

87 Phyllis Amenda, 'One name, two unions: the Christian Social Union in the United States and England', *Journal of the Canadian Church Historical Society* 44.1 (2002), pp. 108.

88 MT, 24.09.1891.

Chapter 11

Conclusion

Bebbington is right in denying that the Social Gospel was an alternative to the evangelical approach.[1] The evidence is quite clear that the Social Christianity was in fact not only grounded in late Victorian Nonconformist evangelicalism but was also an integral part of it. In the wake of the Welsh Revival, F.B. Meyer expected great things and proclaimed in his Presidential address to the National Free Church Council in 1904 that 'Every great revival of religion has issued in social and political reconstruction.'[2]

Lloyd George's patronage of Evan Roberts, a leader in the revival, showed him to be alert to this inter-relationship, too. Another leading Baptist holding Free Church office, the Rev. J.H. Shakespeare also looked for the influence of the revival to be repeated in London, 'as has been the experience in Wales through the great outpouring of the Holy Spirit'.[3]

The relationship between evangelicalism and the emerging Social Gospel flows directly out of an understanding of Christian experience. This was the foundation of both their understanding and motivation and upon which they attempted to construct an experiential theology of personal and social holiness, based upon Wesley's doctrine of entire sanctification. Central to this was the experience of the baptism in the Holy Spirit which, following the increasingly influential 'Second Blessing' teaching from the United States, was understood as essential for personal holiness.

Their own experience of conversion and sanctification through the activity of the Holy Spirit gave them a passionate desire for others to share the blessings of salvation and holiness too, hence their commitment to evangelism and entire sanctification. Yet there was more than this, they also recognised the necessity of working for the conversion and sanctification of society too. The experience and empowering of the Holy Spirit were just as crucial for believers who sought to change society as they were for believers who sought to change their own lives.

---

1 David W. Bebbington, *Evangelicalism in Modern Britain* (London: Routledge, 1989), p. 211.

2 Stephen Koss, *Nonconformity in Modern British Politics* (London: Batsford, 1975), p. 45.

3 Shakespeare was President of the Metropolitan Federation, Koss, *Nonconformity*, pp. 43-45.

Their Christian experience therefore led them to engage with contemporary thought alongside working for social and political change. Their openness to the progressive social and intellectual movements of their generation was in no small way born of their experience of, and involvement with, the Chartists and the Anti-Corn Law League earlier in the century.

This developing emphasis was widespread amongst evangelicals in the last quarter of the nineteenth century, however, it was the Wesleyans with their Arminian theology, connexional structure and history of commitment to the doctrine and experience of entire sanctification, who were best placed to benefit from this 'Forward Movement'.

The contribution of R.W. Dale to these developments in evangelical social concern is highly significant, not least in the example of his own life. However, his desire to strengthen the experiential foundation of Christian service through the application of the doctrine of the Holy Spirit was potentially a far more significant contribution. His failure to see this adequately articulated was highly damaging to the emergent movement. Hugh Price Hughes faithfully responded to Dale's exhortation to Methodists to develop the ethical implications for society of Wesley's doctrine of entire sanctification, which Dale had said would produce 'an ethical revolution which would have had a far deeper effect on the thought and life - first of England, and then of Christendom - than the Reformation of the sixteenth century'.[4]

Yet Hughes was never a theologian of the stature of Dale, and his reformulations never properly took hold. Indeed, some have had difficulty in seeing how the old and the new tie together in his theology. 'The resultant clash of ideas in Hughes' mind reflected the mental and social confusion of the late nineteenth century.'[5] For others Hughes is a paradox, holding together at the same time the older emphasis on personal regeneration with the newer emphasis on social reconstruction.[6]

The confusion is caused by Hughes using the same religious language in two different ways, both personally and societally, and often in the same breath. He can maintain that Jesus Christ came to save society as well as to save individuals and also talk in a similar terms about social holiness and personal holiness. While he hints at the presence of corporate sin, he does not quite get there, although it must be implicit in an idea of social holiness. When T.H. Green speaks of self-sacrifice for others and the transformation of the world for the better through religious self-realisation, Hughes automatically sees this in terms of the Methodist understanding of entire sanctification. Just as the converted individual found in God's will his ultimate self-expression and happiness, so the converted community also found fulfilment in being obedient to God's will.

---

[4] MT, 20.12.1894.

[5] John Kent, 'Hugh Price Hughes and the Nonconformist Conscience' in G.V. Bennett & J.D. Walsh (eds), *Essays in Modern Church History* (New York: OUP, 1966), p. 185.

[6] King, 'Hugh Price Hughes', p68.

Hughes was open to Dale's theology because of its appeal to experience, for this was the link that brought together, and provided the substantive connection between these apparently disparate elements in Hughes' life and teaching. Without doubt his evangelism is of the old Methodist 'warmed heart' variety, albeit that field preaching had been supplanted by 'outdoor meetings with roofs on', as the Central Halls had been called. With this went the Methodist desire for something more, perfection in love and entire sanctification, and his experiences at Dover, Brighton and Oxford were clearly determinative for his words and actions that followed in later years.

An individual was converted or saved when he came into contact with the living Christ and was persuaded to accept the Christian way. Hughes came to see that not only was evangelism right and proper on an individual level, it also had an important corollary. That was that society too could be persuaded to accept the Christian way. The result was not only morally changed individuals but a socially reconstructed and transformed society.[7]

Green's altruistic, self-sacrificing, self-realising and socially transformed world has already been noted, especially its correlation to Methodist holiness doctrine. What Hughes discerned was that he was able to apply the traditional Methodist understanding of religious experience to social and political life as well as to that of the individual. Two sermons illustrate this. In the first he addresses the social gospel in Joel with a passage normally used for pietistic interpretations of holiness. He stresses that biblical holiness always refers to the vision of a righteous and just society. In the second he focusses on the Pentecostal Blessing which he re-interprets to mean the reconstruction of human society in every land and every department of life.[8] Hughes stays true to Wesley and attempts to make Christianity credible within his contemporary context of the late nineteenth century as well as within his Wesleyan tradition.

His daughter noticed how these two elements in his teaching, the personal and the social, became more and more merged in his preaching and teaching over the years.[9] The West London Mission's third annual report states:

> We combine evangelistic and social work. Every attempt at social work that had not been sustained by an evangelistic spirit has failed . . . On the other hand General Booth has discovered that the spiritual problems of the great cities cannot be solved by purely evangelistic agencies.

Or again, in *The Methodist Times* of 25 April 1901:

---

7 C.E. Gwyther, *The Methodist Social and Political Theory and Practice, 1848-1914; with special reference to The Forward Movement* (Liverpool, 1961: unpublished M.A. Thesis), p. 120.

8 Hugh Price Hughes, *Essential Christianity* (London: Isbister, 1894), pp. 160-61 & 169-70.

9 D.P. Hughes, *The Life of Hugh Price Hughes* (London: Hodder & Stoughton, 1903), pp. 80-81.

> The business of all good men is to seek first the Kingdom of GOD and His righteousness. But it is a fatal error to suppose that we can effectively promote the Kingdom of GOD while we neglect the promotion of personal righteousness; or, on the other hand, to imagine that personal righteousness can be effectively promoted while we neglect the Kingdom of GOD, which is a social reconstruction on the principles of our LORD JESUS CHRIST.

However, Hughes feared 'naturalism', that is, an increasing dependence upon human agency rather than 'supernatural and miraculous power'. It was only the doctrine and activity of the Holy Spirit that would prove to be the antidote to this condition.

> The Spirit of GOD is the sole agent . . . Neither social improvement nor intellectual culture . . . will secure salvation for man. The most highly-educated are as absolutely dependent as the most ignorant upon the miraculous agency of the Holy Spirit . . . When we realise this fundamental truth of the Christian era we are no longer in danger of substituting social reform or education for Pentecostal power.[10]

Yet for all his advocacy and attempts to develop Dale's request, Hughes fails to embed this experiential theology sufficiently within Wesleyanism, and more generally in Nonconformity, for it to be passed on to the rising generation. As a consequence this theological theme silently slips from sight soon after his death, and Pentecostal power came to signify another new movement which also drew its life from the old roots of Wesleyan 'second blessing' teaching, Pentecostalism.

Many observers have felt that the Fatherhood theology and immanentalism of nineteenth century Nonconformists led to a rather vague, diffuse theology of humanitarianism.[11] Norman singles Hughes out and is particularly scathing about him having an unoriginal mind and failing to have properly understood and assimilated Green, Maurice, Ruskin or Morris.[12] This assessment fails to appreciate Hughes on a number of important points.[13] Advocates of Social Christianity were primarily activists, often in pastoral charge of a large congregation, and theological treatises were neither possible nor likely to be key elements of their vocation. Most

---

[10] MT, 23.05.1895.

[11] David Thompson, 'John Clifford's Social Gospel', *The Baptist Quarterly*, 31.5 (January 1986), pp. 255-56.

[12] E.R. Norman, *Victorian Christian Socialists* (Cambridge: CUP, 1987), pp. 145-49.

[13] Norman misreads and consequently misunderstands Hughes on a number of important issues. He is wrong in his perception of Hughes' unwillingness to enter the debates about disestablishment and education (*Victorian Christian Socialists*, p. 161), and his assertion that the provincial Wesleyan Missions copied the London model (p. 146). He seems unaware that Liverpool and Manchester antedated London and together provided the model. He also maintains that Hughes had no alterations to suggest to the ecclesiastical structure (p. 158), when Hughes spent a considerable amount of time lobbying for a great number of structural reforms for Wesleyanism. He also contends that Hughes did not comprehend Green's philosophy (p. 147), whereas it is clear that he did, and was most grateful for its contribution in his re-emphasis of Wesleyan entire sanctification.

often their theology was haphazard, rhetorical and populist, representing the sermons from which it was drawn. But vague and diffuse it was not, for an uncertain call to battle against the evils in society would have achieved little response from their congregations.

Hughes was particularly concerned with the eclipse of Calvinism. It has been previously noted that on both sides of the Atlantic, where Calvinism was strong the support for Social Christianity was correspondingly weak, and vice versa. Following a series of articles in *The Times* on 'The Decay of Evangelicalism', Hughes commented that evangelical failure was the responsibility of Calvinism which resulted in a harsh, austere and selfish form of Christianity which was intolerable in a democratic society. The sovereignty of God and surrender to his will were important truths, but it was better to have God first as Father, not judge, otherwise Christians were produced resembling Elijah rather than the apostle John. Hughes believed that Methodists had yet to understand how grateful they should be to Wesley for standing against the harshness of 'old-style' Calvinism.[14]

The path of Social Christianity was fraught with dangers too. Munson comments on the series of steps which led from evangelical Christianity to a legitimate social and political concern, only then to develop into an obsession in which there was a decreasing reference to the Christian criterion of analysis, the gospel. The attempt to see the Christian message in the secular world ended up with seeing the secular world in the Christian message, and then confusing the two.[15]

Evangelicalism in Britain increasingly lost touch with the Social Gospel as the twentieth century progressed, and Nonconformity itself encountered a period of substantial and unarrestable decline. Various explanations have been given for this separation of evangelicalism from the Social Gospel to which it gave birth.

Bebbington believes that this is the British parallel to a phenomenon identified in America as 'The Great Reversal', that is, the repudiation of evangelicals of their earlier engagement with social issues so that conservative theology became associated with conservative politics and liberal theology with progressive politics.[16] In Britain, political disillusionment set in following the failure of co-ordinated Nonconformist action on the Education Act. Even a sympathetic Liberal administration was unable to deliver its promises.[17] In addition to this Bebbington also believes that recognition of the secularising effect of politics upon the church, theological worries about the developing theology of the Social Gospel and the division caused within Nonconformity by the rise of the Labour movement

---

[14] MT, 01.03.1888; 26.01.1899.

[15] James Munson, *The Nonconformists: In Search of a Lost Culture* (London: SPCK, 1991), p. 115.

[16] Bebbington, *Evangelicalism*, pp. 214-17; Noll, *Christianity in America*, p. 313.

[17] Bebbington, *The Nonconformist Conscience*, p. 157.

also contributed significantly.[18] Indeed, R.F. Horton had himself foreseen the latter.[19]

Nonconformist optimism which had flowed from their espousal of Social Darwinism received a series of minor blows prior to the devastating impact of World War One. Contemporary commentators and later scholars have agreed on the catastrophic impact of the war. Yet between 1901 and 1933 the four main Nonconformist churches continued registered a modest increase in membership, even when war casualties are factored into the figures.[20]

It is only possible to speculate about what would have happened if Hugh Price Hughes had not died prematurely in 1902 aged 55 years. As the key voice and prophetic spokesmen of the movement with unparalleled influence, had he lived longer and facilitated a succession, maybe making connections with the embryonic Pentecostal movement, all kinds of possibilities might have emerged. However, there is evidence that he was already sensing the some of the momentum running out of the movement. In an interview just before he died he related,

> In my young days . . . we were enthusiastic. We believed in enthusiasm, we thronged to hear Gladstone and Bright when they denounced oppression. Mazzini and Garibaldi could fire our thoughts. But to-day – well, to-day the people read *The Daily Mail*.[21]

His passing was symbolic of a transition to a new century in more ways than one. While Hughes was happy to use the 'Fatherhood of God, brotherhood of man' theology, it was always in addition to the experiential theology that was his default position. This was not the case in John Scott Lidgett who concentrated on 'the Fatherhood of God' and for whom it was the defining centre of his understanding. The role of leading thinker within Congregationalism had changed too. R.W. Dale had died in 1895 leaving A.M. Fairbairn as the unrivalled teacher on the progressive wing of the denomination. Like Lidgett, his emphasis was also far more centred on Maurician themes and, in this way, the impetus of Social Christianity passed gradually from a liberal evangelicalism to a younger and more theologically liberal generation, and from Nonconformity to Anglicanism. By 1910 the voice of the Nonconformist Conscience was also all but silent.

This is not to say the influence of Forward Movement disappeared overnight. Indeed some hold that it is possible to see an ongoing legacy from evangelical Nonconformity in contemporary British life. Munson sees an 'indelible mark' on

---

[18] Bebbington, *The Nonconformist Conscience*, pp. 159-60; Bebbington, *Evangelicalism*, pp. 215-16.

[19] Munson, *The Nonconformists*, p. 234.

[20] Wesleyans 414,049 to 443,786 (+7.18%); Primitive Methodists 185,000 to 189,843 (+2.62%); Baptist Union 243,534 to 254,618 (+4.55%); Congregational Union 258,434 to 276,384 (+6.95%). A decline between 1914-1919 of 26,843 for the combined totals of the four denominations was probably the result of war deaths and the influenza epidemic that swept Britain in 1918-19. Munson, *The Nonconformists*, p. 294.

[21] MT, 20.10.1902.

the national character which, while at time a touch sanctimonious, aspires to standards of behaviour in public and private life and has direct continuity with the Nonconformist Conscience. Or again, from the welfare state to food banks and the education system to initiatives like Street Pastors and campaigning against people trafficking, life in Britain continues to be built upon and re-express values that were, at least in part, pioneered by the Forward Movement. Through a seeping, sublimal 'permeation by filtration' the influence and activism of the Victorian evangelicals and the Forward Movement continue to affect contemporary Britain.[22]

William Temple was to become the most visible leader of the movement in its next phase. His incarnational theology was to typify the Conference on Christian Politics, Economics and Citizenship (COPEC) which he chaired in 1924, and the developing movement that it spawned. COPEC traced its own history through the Brotherhood, Settlement, Wesleyan Mission and Anglo-Catholic 'Slum Priest' movements, viewing the work of the Congregationalist J.B. Paton as the first to catch the 'COPEC' vision of Church Reunion and implementation of the Social Gospel.[23]

Back in 1888 Hugh Price Hughes felt that the Forward Movement and its emphasis on Social Christianity was well understood by the little girl's comment on Bunyan's, *Pilgrim's Progress*. She had said that she preferred Christiana to Christian for she took the children with her. True Christianity involved a commitment not only to the salvation of others, but also to their moral and physical welfare.[24]

---

[22] Munson, *The Nonconformists*, p. 5; Boyd Hilton, *The Age of Atonement* (Oxford: Clarendon, 1991), p. 26.

[23] J.F. Laun, *Social Christianity in England* (London: SCM. 1929), pp. 86-90.

[24] MT, 08.03.1888.

Bibliography

Primary Sources - Manuscript

The Papers of William Montgomery Crook, 1883-1944 (Bodleian Library, Oxford), Ref: MSS. Eng. Hist. d365-404.
Dover Methodist Circuit archives material.
National Methodist Archives, University of Manchester Library (Deansgate), for Charles Garrett & Hugh Price Hughes correspondence.
West Croydon Baptist Church archive material.

Primary Sources - Printed

Arthur, William, *The Tongue of Fire: Or, The True Power of Christianity* (London: Hamilton Adams, 1856).
Bennett, Canon, *Father Nugent of Liverpool* (Liverpool: Catholic Children's Protection Society, 1949).
Berry, Charles A., *Vision and Duty* (London: Sampson Low Marston, 1893).
Booth, Bramwell, *These Fifty Years* (London: Cassell, 1929).
Booth, Charles, *Life and Labour of the People of London* (3rd. Series, Religious Influences) vol 7 (London: Macmillan, 1902).
Booth, General, *In Darkest England and the Way Out* (London: Salvation Army, 1890).
Brash, W. Bardsley, *The Story of our Colleges, 1835-1935* (London: Epworth, 1935).
Brengle, Samuel Logan, *The Guest of the Soul* (London: Marshall, Morgan & Scott, 1934).
—. *Heart Talks on Holiness* (London: Salvationist Publishing, 1960).
—. *Helps To Holiness* (Salem: Schmul, 1965).
British Weekly, The.
Broadbent, James W., *The People's Life of Charles Garrett* (Leeds: James Broadbent, 1900).
Champness, E.M., *The Life Story of Thomas Champness* (London: Charles H. Kelly, 1907).
Clifford, John, *Is Life Worth Living?* (London: E. Marlborough, 1884).
—. *The Inspiration and the Authority of the Bible* (London: James Clarke, 1892).

—. *Socialism and the Teaching of Christ* (London: The Fabian Socity, 1897).
—. *Typical Christian Leaders* (London: Marshall, 1898).
—. *The Ultimate Problems of Christianity* (London: Kingsgate Press, 1906).
—. *Socialism and the Churches* (London: The Fabian Society, 1908).
—. *The Gospel of Gladness* (Edinburgh: T&T Clark, 1912).
Colwell, John *Progress and Promise* (London: T. Woolmer, 1887).
Contemporary Review, The.
Crozier, Forster, *Methodism and the Bitter Cry of Outcast London* (London: np, 1885).
Crusader, The
Dale, A.W.W., *The Life of R.W. Dale of Birmingham* (London: Hodder & Stoughton, 1898).
Dale, R.W., *The Ten Commandments* (London: Hodder & Stoughton, 1872).
—. *The Evangelical Revival* (London: Hodder & Stoughton, 1880).
—. *The Old Evangelicalism and the New* (London: Hodder & Stoughton, 1889).
—. *Fellowship with Christ* (London, Hodder & Stoughton, 1891).
—. *Christian Doctrine* (London: Hodder & Stoughton, 1894).
—. *The Atonement* (London: Congregational Union of England & Wales, 1902).
—. *Laws of Life for Common Life* (London: Hodder & Stoughton, 1903).
—. *The Living Christ and the Four Gospels (Fifteenth edition)* (London: Hodder & Stoughton, 1905).
Drummond, James S., *Charles A. Berry, D.D.* (London: Cassell, 1899).
Fairbairn, A.M., *Studies in Religion and Theology* (London: Hodder & Stoughton, 1910).
Garrett, Charles, *Loving Counsels* (London: Charles H. Kelly, 1887).
General Baptist Magazine, The.
Haggard, H. Rider, *Regeneration* (London: Longman, Green & Co., 1910).
Hall, Charles J., *The Phrenological Characteristics of the Rev. Charles Garrett* (Maidstone: G.H. Graham, 1873).
Horne, C. Silvester, *The Soul's Awakening* (London: Passmore and Alabaster, 1902).
—. *A Popular History of the Free Churches* (London: James Clark, 1903).
—. *Pulpit, Platform and Parliament* (London: Hodder & Stoughton, 1913).
—. *The Romance of Preaching* (London: James Clarke, 1914).
Horton, R. F., *Inspiration and the Bible,* (London: T. Fisher Unwin, 1888).
—. *Revelation and the Bible* (London: T. Fisher Unwin, 1892).
—. *An Autobiography (Second edition)* (London: George Allen & Unwin, 1918).
Hughes, D.P., *The Life of Hugh Price Hughes* (London: Hodder & Stoughton, 1903).
Hughes, Hugh Price, *Social Christianity* (London: Hodder & Stoughton, 1889).
—. *Essential Christianity* (London: Isbister & Co., 1894).
Hughes, Katherine Price, *The Story of My Life* (London: Epworth, 1945).
Keeble, S.E. (ed.), *The Citizen of To-morrow* (London: C.H. Kelly, 1906).

Lidgett, J. Scott, *The Fatherhood of God (Second edition)* (London: Charles H. Kelly, 1913).
—. *Reminiscences* (London: Epworth, 1928).
—. *My Guided Life* (London: Methuen, 1936).
Liverpool Courier, The
Liverpool Daily Post, The
Liverpool Methodist Mission, *Exploits of a Hundred Years: a brief history,* (Liverpool: Liverpool Methodist Mission, 1975).
Liverpool Review, The
London Journalist, *A Visit to the Liverpool Wesleyan Mission* (London: Wesleyan Methodist Book-Room, 1896).
London Wesleyan Mission: *Summary of its Purpose, Policy and Work* (London, nd).
McClure's Magazine.
Methodist Recorder, The
Methodist Temperance Magazine, The
Methodist Times, The
Meyer, F.B., *The Christ-Life for The Self-Life* (Chicago: Moody, 1897).
—. *Religion and Race Regeneration* (London: Cassell, 1912).
—. *Reveries and Realities* (London: Morgan & Scott, nd).
—. *Five 'Musts' of the Christian Life* (London: Marshall, Morgan & Scott, nd).
Minutes of the Wesleyan Methodist Conference.
Moody, W.R., *The Life of D.L. Moody* (London: Morgan & Scott, c.1900).
Moulton, W. Fiddian, *The Story of the Manchester Mission* (London: np, nd).
Mudie-Smith, R., *The Religious Life of London* (London: Hodder & Stoughton, 1904).
Nelson & Sons (Publishers), (contributions by various friends), *The Life of General Booth* (London, nd).
Orchard, B. Guinness, *Liverpool's Legion of Honou,* (Birkenhead: B. Guinness Orchard, 1893).
Parker, Joseph, *A Preacher's Life* (London: Hodder & Stoughton, 1899).
Porcupine, The
Proceedings of the First Ecumenical World Methodist Conference 1881, The (London : Wesleyan Conference Office, 1881).
Rauschenbusch, Walter, *Christianity and the Social Crisis* (New York: Macmillan, 1907).
—. *Christianizing the Social Order* (New York: Macmillan, 1919).
—. *A Theology for the Social Gospel* (New York: Macmillan, 1917).
—. *Prayers of the Social Awakening* (Boston: Pilgrim Press, 1925).
Report of the Metropolitan Methodist Lay Mission, 1873.
Reports of the Liverpool Wesleyan Mission (annual), 1876-95.
Sackett, Walter, *Saving Wonders, being incidents in the Manchester Mission* (London: Charles H. Kelly, 1891).
Smith, Samuel, M.P., *My Life-Work* (London: Hodder & Stoughton, 1902).

Spurgeon, C.H., *Autobiography; compiled from his diary, letters, and records by his wife and his private secretary* (London: Passmore and Alabaster, 1900).
Stead, Estelle W., *My Father* (London: Heinemann, 1913).
Stead, W.T., *If Christ Came to Chicago* (London: Review of Reviews, 1894).
Taylor, William George, *Taylor of Down Under* (London: Epworth, 1921).
Telford, John (ed.), *The Letters of John Wesley*, vol 8 (London: Epworth, 1960).
Thompson, Rosalie Budgett, *Peter Thompson* (London: Charles H. Kelly, 1910).
Wesleyan Methodist Magazine, The

Secondary Sources

Amenda, Phyllis, 'One name, two unions: the Christian Social Union in the United States and England', *Journal of The Canadian Church Historical Society*, 44.1 (2002), pp. 107-121.
Andelson, Robert V., *Critics of Henry George: A Centenary Appraisal of Their Strictures on Progress and Poverty* (London: Associated University Presses, 1979).
Ausubel, Herman, *John Bright, Victorian Reformer* (London: John Wiley & Sons, 1966).
Bagwell, Philip S., *Outcast London: A Christian Response. The West London Mission of the Methodist Church, 1887-1987* (London: Epworth, 1987).
Balleine, G.R., *A History of the Evangelical Party in the Church of England* (London: Longmans, 1933).
Barker, Charles A., *Henry George* (Oxford: Oxford University Press, 1955).
Bateman, Charles T., *John Clifford* (London: Partridge, 1902).
Beasley, John D., *The Bitter Cry Heard and Heeded (The Story of the South London Mission, 1889-1989)* (London: South London Mission, 1989).
Bebbington, D.W., 'Conscience and Politics' in Lesley Husselbee & Paul Ballard (eds), *Free Churches and Society: The Nonconformist Contribution to Social Welfare 1800-2010* (London: Continuum, 2012), pp. 45-64.
—. 'The City, the Countryside and the Social Gospel in Late Victorian Nonconformity' in D. Baker (ed.), *The Church in Town and Countryside* (Studies in Church History, 16) (Oxford: Blackwell, 1979), pp. 415-426.
—. *The Nonconformist Conscience* (London: George Allen & Unwin, 1982).
—. *Evangelicalism in Modern Britain* (London: Routledge, 1989).
—. 'The Baptist Conscience in the Nineteenth Century', in *The Baptist Quarterly* 34.1 (January 1991), pp. 13-24.
Begbie, Harold, *William Booth, Founder of the Salvation Army* (London: Macmillan, 1920), vols 1&2.
Binfield, Clyde, *So Down to Prayers* (London: J.M. Dent, 1977).
Binyon, Gilbert Clive, *The Christian Socialist Movement in England* (London: SPCK, 1931).
Bowen, Desmond, *The Idea of the Victorian Church: A Study of the Church of England, 1833-1889* (Montreal: University of Toronto Press, 1968).

Briggs, Asa, *The Age of Improvement* (London: Longman, Green & Co., 1957).
—. (ed.), *Chartist Studies.,* (London: Macmillan, 1962).
—. *Victorian Cities.,* (London: Odhams, 1963).
Briggs, John & Ian Sellers, *Victorian Nonconformity* (London: Edward Arnold, 1973).
Briggs, J.H.Y., 'Evangelical Ecumenism: The Amalgamation of General and Particular Baptists in 1891', in *The Baptist Quarterly* 34.3 (July 1991), p. 99-115.
Brink, David O., *Perfectionism and the Common Good* (Oxford: Clarendon Press, 2007).
Brown, Richard, *Chartism: Rise and Demise* (United Kingdom: Authoring History, 2014).
Brose, Olive J., *Frederick Denison Maurice* (Ohio: Ohio University Press, 1971).
Bucke, Emory Stevens (ed.), *The History of American Methodism*, vol. 3 (Nashville: Abingdon, 1964).
Burnett, R.G., *These My Brethren, The Story of the London East End Mission* (London: Epworth, 1946).
Byrt, G.W., *John Clifford, A Fighting Free Churchman* (London: Kingsgate, 1947).
Cacoullos, Ann R., *Thomas Hill Green: Philosopher of Rights* (New York: Twayne, 1975).
Carpenter, S.C., *Church and People, 1789-1889* (London: SPCK, 1937).
Carter, Matt, *T.H. Green and the Development of Ethical Socialism* (Exeter: Imprint Academic, 2003).
Carter, Paul A., *The Decline and Revival of the Social Gospel: social and political liberalism in American Protestant churches, 1920-1940* (New York: Cornell University Press, 1956).
Cash, Bill, *John Bright* (London: I.B. Tauris, 2012).
Chadwick, Owen, *The Victorian Church* (Part II) (London: A&C Black, 1970).
Chase, Malcolm, *Chartism: a new history* (Manchester: Manchester University Press, 2007).
—. *Early Trade Unionism: Fraternity, Skill and the Politics of Labour* (London: Breviary Stuff, 2012).
Coffey, John, 'Democracy and Popular Religion: Moody and Sankey's Mission to Britain, 1873-1875', in Eugenio F. Biagini (ed.), *Citizenship and Community: Liberals, radicals and collective identities in the British Isles 1865-1931* (Cambridge: Cambridge University Press, 1996), pp. 93-119.
Collier, Richard, *The General Next to God* (London: Collins, 1965).
Coleman, Bruce, 'Religion in the Victorian City', *History Today*, 30.8 (1980), pp. 25-31.
Colwell, James, *A Century in the Pacific* (Sydney: William H. Beale, 1914).
Cord, Steven B., *Henry George: Dreamer or Realist?* (Philadelphia: University of Pennsylvania Press, 1965).
Currie, Robert, 'Were the Central Halls a Failure?' *New Directions* (Spring 1967), pp. 21-24.

—. *Methodism Divided* (London: Faber, 1968).
Dark, Sidney, *Wilson Carlile* (London: James Clarke, 1944).
Davey, Cyril J., *The Methodist Story* (London: Epworth, 1955).
—. *A Man for All Children* (London: Epworth, 1968).
Davies, Rupert (ed.), *John Scott Lidgett, A Symposium* (London: Epworth, 1957).
—. A. Raymond George & Gordon Rupp (eds), *A History of the Methodist Church in Great Britain*, Volume 3 (London: Epworth, 1983).
Dieter, M.E., 'From Vineland and Manheim to Brighton and Berlin : the holiness revival in nineteenth-century Europe', *Wesleyan Theological Journal* 9 (March 1, 1974), pp. 15-27.
Dimova-Cookson, Maria, & William J. Mander, *T.H. Green* (Oxford: Clarendon Press, 2006).
Dombrowski, James, *The Early Days of Christian Socialism in America* (New York: Columbia University Press, 1936).
Dorrien, Gary, 'Society as the Subject of Redemption: The Relevance of the Social Gospel', *Tikkun*, 24.6, (2009), pp. 43-74.
Douglas, J.D. (ed.), *The New International Dictionary of the Christian Church* (Second edition) (Exeter: Paternoster, 1978).
Eason, Andrew M., *Women in God's Army* (Waterloo, Ont.: Wilfrid Laurier University Press, 2003).
—. & Roger J. Green (eds), *Boundless Salvation: the Shorter Writings of William Booth* (New York: Peter Lang, 2012).
Eastwood, David, 'Peel and the Tory party reconsidered', *History Today*, 42.3 (1992), pp. 27-33.
Edwards, Maldwyn, *Methodism and England* (London: Epworth, 1944).
—. *S.E. Keeble: Pioneer and Prophet* (London: Epworth, 1949).
Edwards, Michael S., *S.E. Keeble: The Rejected Prophet* (Chester: Wesley Historical Society, 1977).
Exploits of a Hundred Years: A Brief History of the Liverpool Methodist Mission, (Liverpool, 1975).
Evans, Christopher H., *The Kingdom is Always But Coming* (Waco: Baylor University Press, 2010).
Findlay, James F., Jr., *Dwight L. Moody: American Evangelist, 1837-99* (Chicago: University of Chicago Press, 1969).
Fisher, David, 'Washington Gladden: Salvation in the Public Square', *International Congregational Journal*, 8.2 (2009), pp. 63-72.
Fullerton, W.Y., *F.B. Meyer* (London: Marshall, Morgan & Scott, 1929).
Goodwin, Charles H., 'An evangelical pastorate: the unresolved dilemma in Wesleyan concepts of ministry and church growth, *Wesleyan Theological Journal*, 34.2 (1999), pp. 222-251.
Grant, J.W., *Free Churchmanship in England* (London: Independent Press, 1955).
Green, Roger J., 'Theological roots of *In Darkest England And The Way Out*', *Wesleyan Theological Journal*, 25.1 (1990), pp. 83-105.

Greengarten, I.M., *Thomas Hill Green and the Development of Liberal-Democratic Thought* (Toronto: University of Toronto Press, 1981).
Greet, Kenneth G., *Jabez Bunting* (Peterborough: Foundery Press, 1995).
Gwyther, C.E., *The Methodist Social and Political Theory and Practice, 1848-1914; with special reference to The Forward Movement* (Liverpool, 1961: unpublished M.A. Thesis).
Halliday, Stephen, *The Great Filth: Disease, Death and the Victorian City* (Stroud: History Press, 2011).
Handy, Robert T., *The Social Gospel in America* (New York: Oxford University Press, 1966).
Hardesty, Nancy, 'Hannah Whitehall Smith found the secret', *Daughters of Sarah*, 10.5 (1984), pp. 20-22.
Harrison, Brian, *Drink and the Victorians* (London: Faber & Faber, 1971).
—. '"Kindness and Reason": William Lovett and Education', *History Today* 37.3 (1987), pp. 14-22.
Hart, Philip R., 'John Clifford: An English Social Reformer in the Pastorate', *Perspectives in Religious Studies*, 16.3 (1989), pp. 225-244.
Heasman, Kathleen, *Evangelicals in Action* (London: Geoffrey Bles, 1962).
Heidt, John, 'The King of Terrors: The Theology of Henry Scott Holland', *Contemporary Review*, 276, 1610, (2000), pp. 121-126.
Hempton, David, 'For God and Ulster: Evangelical Protestantism and the Home Rule Crisis of 1886' in Keith Robbins (ed.), *Studies in Church History, Subsidia 7* (Oxford: Blackwell, 1990), pp. 225-254.
Hennell, Michael, 'Evangelicalism and Worldliness, 1770 to 1870', in G.J. Cuming & Derek Baker, *Studies in Church History*, Vol. 8 (Cambridge: Cambridge University Press, 1972), pp. 229-236.
—. *The Early Years of the Church Pastoral Aid Society* (Unpublished paper, nd).
Hennessey, Una Pope, *Canon Charles Kingsley* (London: Chatto & Windus, 1948).
Higham, Florence, *Frederick Denison Maurice* (London: SCM. Press, 1947).
Hilton, Boyd, *The Age of Atonement* (Oxford: Clarendon Press, 1991).
Hodder, Edwin, *The Life of Lord Shaftesbury* (London: Cassell, 1886).
Hooker, Mary R., *Adventures of an Agnostic, the Life and Letters of Reader Harris, Q.C.* (London: Marshall, Morgan & Scott, 1959).
Hopkins, C. Howard, *The Rise of the Social Gospel in American Protestantism* (New Haven: Yale University Press, 1940).
Howe, Anthony & Simon Morgan, *Rethinking Nineteenth-Century Liberalism*, (Aldershot: Ashgate, 2006).
—. 'Richard Cobden and the Crimean War', *History Today*, 54.6 (2004), pp. 46-51.
Hunt, E.H., *British Labour History, 1815-1914* (London: Weidenfeld & Nicolson, 1981).
Hunt, Tristram, *Building Jerusalem: The Rise and Fall of the Victorian City* (London: Weidenfeld & Nicholson, 2004).

Husselbee, Lesley & Paul Ballard (eds), *Free Churches and Society: The Nonconformist Contribution to Social Welfare 1800-2010* (London: Continuum, 2012).
Inglis, K.S., *Churches and the Working Class in Victorian England* (London: Routledge, 1963).
Inskip, J.T., *Evangelical Influence in English Life* (London: Macmillan, 1933).
Jackson, George, *Collier of Manchester* (London: Hodder & Stoughton, 1923).
Jones, D., *Chartism and Chartists* (London: Allen Lane, 1975).
Jones, Peter d'A., *The Christian Socialist Revival (1877-1914,* (Princeton: Princeton University Press, 1968).
Jones, R. Tudor, *Congregationalism in England (1662-1962)* (London: Independent Press, 1962).
Jordan, E.K.H., *Free Church Unity* (London: Lutterworth Press, 1956).
Kent, John, 'Hugh Price Hughes and the Nonconformist Conscience', in G.V. Bennett & J.D. Walsh (eds), *Essays in Modern Church History* (New York: Oxford University Press, 1966), pp. 181-205.
—. *Holding the Fort: Studies in Victorian Revivalism* (London: Epworth, 1978).
King, William McGuire, 'Hugh Price Hughes and the British "Social Gospel"', *Journal of Religious History* (June, 1984), pp. 66-82.
Noll, Mark A., et al (eds), *Christianity in America* (Tring, Lion 1983).
Konvitz, Josef W., *The Urban Millennium: The City Building Process from the Early Middle Ages to the Present* (Illinois: Southern Illinois University Press, 1985).
Koss, Stephen, *Nonconformity in Modern British Politics* (London: Batsford, 1975).
Lambert, D.W., *The Testament of Samuel Chadwick, 1860-1932* (London: Epworth, 1957).
Lander, Dorothy, 'The Legacy of the Social Gospel in Adult Education', *Journal of Adult Theological Education*, 1.1 (2004), pp. 79-90.
Laun, J.F., *Social Christianity in England* (London: SCM. Press, 1929).
Lawrence, E.P., *Henry George in the British Isles* (Michigan: Michigan State University Press, 1957).
Lawton, Richard (ed.), *The Rise and Fall of Great Cities: Aspects of Urbanisation in the Western World* (London: Bellhaven, 1989).
LeBarbour, A., *Victorian Baptists: A Study of Denominational Development,* (Maryland, 1977: unpublished Ph.D. Thesis).
Leighton, Denys P., *The Greenian Moment: T.H. Green, Religion and Political Argument in Victorian Britain* (Exeter: Imprint Academic, 2004).
Lees, Andrew, *Cities Perceived: Urban Society in European and American Thought, 1820-1914* (Manchester: Manchester University Press, 1985).
Lindner, Eileen W., 'The redemptive politic of Henry George: a legacy to the Social Gospel', *Union Seminary Quarterly Review*, 42.3 (1988), pp. 1-8.
Longmate, Norman, *The Breadstealers* (London: Maurice Temple Smith, 1984).

Lundsten, Barbara A., 'The Legacy of Walter Rauschenbusch: A Life Informed by Mission', *International Bulletin of Missionary Research* (April, 2004), pp. 75-79.

Macilwee, Michael, *The Gangs of Liverpool* (Wrea Green, Lancs: Milo, 2006).

McBeth, H. Leon, *The Baptist Heritage* (Nashville: B&H Academic, 1987).

McLeod, Hugh, *Class and Religion in the Late Victorian City* (London: Croom Helm, 1974).

McLoughlin, William, *Revivals, Awakenings and Reform: An Essay on Religious and Social Change in America, 1607-1977* (Chicago: University of Chicago Press, 1978).

Marchant, James, *Dr. John Clifford: Life, Letters and Reminiscences* (London: Cassell & Co., 1924)

Marlow, Joyce, *The Tolpuddle Martyrs* (St. Albans: Panther, 1971).

May, Henry F., *Protestant Churches and Industrial America* (New York: Harper, 1949).

Mee, Josiah, *Thomas Champness as I Knew Him* (London: Charles H. Kelly, nd).

Mews, Stuart, 'Puritanicalism, Sport and Race: A Symbolic Crusade of 1911', in G.J. Cumming & Derek Baker (eds), *Studies in Church History*, Vol. 8, Popular Belief and Practice (Cambridge: Cambridge University Press, 1972), pp. 303-331.

Milne, R.G., *The History of the British Workman Public House Company Ltd. (The Liverpool 'Cocoa Rooms')* (unpublished Dip. Local History, Liverpool University, Dept. Extra-Mural Studies, 1982).

Minus, Paul M., *Walter Rauschenbusch: American Reformer* (New York: Macmillan, 1988).

Morris, Jeremy, (ed.), *To Build Christ's Kingdom: F.D. Maurice & his Writings* (Norwich: Canterbury Press, 2007).

—. *F.D. Maurice and the Crisis of Christian Authority* (Oxford: Oxford University Press, 2008).

Munson, James, *The Nonconformists: In Search of a Lost Culture* (London: SPCK, 1991).

Musson, A.E., *Trade Union & Social History* (London: Routledge, 1974).

Nead, Lynda, *Victorian Babylon: People, Streets and Images in Nineteenth Century London* (New Haven: Yale University Press, 2005).

Neill, Stephen, *Anglicanism* (London: Penguin, 1958).

Nelson, Janet R., 'Walter Rauschenbusch and the social gospel: a hopeful theology for the twenty-first century economy', *Cross Currents*, 59.4 (2009), pp. 442-456.

Norman, E.R., *Victorian Christian Socialists* (Cambridge: Cambridge University Press, 1987).

Oldstone-Moore, Christopher, *Hugh Price Hughes* (Cardiff: University of Wales Press, 1999).

Oxford Dictionary of National Biography (Oxford: Oxford University Press, 2004).

Patterson, W. Morgan, 'Walter Rauschenbusch: Baptist exemplar of social concern', *Baptist History and Heritage*, 7.3 (1972), pp.130-136.

Payne, Ernest A., *The Baptist Union* (London: Carey Kingsgate Press, 1959).

Peart, Ross, *Hugh Price Hughes and the Origins of the Forward Movement* (unpublished paper).

Peel, Albert & John Marriott, *Robert Forman Horton* (London: George Allen & Unwin, 1937).

Pelling, Henry, *A History of British Trade Unionism*, (Fourth edition) (London: Penguin, 1987).

Pickering, Paul A. & Alex Tyrrell, *The People's Bread: a History of the Anti-Corn Law League* (London: Leicester University Press, 2000).

Pollock, John, *Moody without Sankey* (London: Hodder & Stoughton, 1963).

Porter, John F. & William J. Wolf, *Toward the Recovery of Unity* (New York: Seabury Press, 1964).

Prichard, John, *Methodists and their Missionary Societies 1760-1900* (Farnham: Ashgate, 2013).

Rack, H.D., *The Future of John Wesley's Methodism* (London: Lutterworth Press, 1965).

—. 'Domestic Visitation: A Chapter in Early Nineteenth Century Evangelism', *Journal of Ecclesiastical History* 24 (1973), pp. 357-376.

Rader, Benjamin G., *The Academic Mind and Reform: The Influence of Richard T. Ely in American Life* (Lexington: University of Kentucky Press, 1966).

Read, Donald, *Cobden and Bright: A Victorian Political Partnership* (London: Edward Arnold, 1967).

Read, Gordon & David Jebson, *A Voice in the City* (Liverpool: Liverpool City Mission, 1979).

Review of the Churches, The.

Richter, Melvin, *The Politics of Conscience: T.H. Green and his Age* (Cambridge, Mass.: Harvard University Press, 1964).

Robbins, Keith, 'The Spiritual Pilgrimage of the Rev. R.J. Campbell', *Journal of Ecclesiastical History,* 30 (1979), pp. 261-276.

Rowan, Edgar, *Wilson Carlile and the Church Army* (London: Church Army Bookroom, 1926).

Russell, George W.E., *A Short History of the Evangelical Movement* (London: Mowbray, 1915).

Sails, George, *At The Centre* (London: Methodist Church Home Mission Dept., 1970).

Sandall, Robert, *The History of the Salvation Army*, Vol. 1, 1865-1878 (London: Thomas Nelson, 1947).

—. *The History of the Salvation Army*, Vol. 2, 1878-1886, (London: Thomas Nelson, 1950).

—. *The History of the Salvation Army*, Vol. 3, 1883-1953 (Social Reform and Welfare Work) (London: Thomas Nelson, 1955).

Selbie, W.B., *The Life of Andrew Martin Fairbairn* (London: Hodder & Stoughton, 1914).
—. *The Life of Charles Silvester Horne* (London: Hodder & Stoughton, 1920).
Sellers, Ian, 'Nonconformist Attitudes in Later Nineteenth Century Liverpool', in *Transactions of the Historical Society of Lancashire and Cheshire*, Vol. 114 (1962), pp. 215-239.
—. *Liverpool Nonconformity (1786-1914)* (Keele, 1969, unpublished Ph.D Thesis).
—. 'Charles Garrett and the Liverpool Mission', *Journal of the Lancashire and Cheshire Branch of the Wesley Historical Society* 4.1 (January 1980), pp. 5-11.
Shaw, Ian J., 'Thomas Chalmers, David Nasmith, and the Origins of the City Mission Movement', *Evangelical Quarterly*, 76.1 (2004), pp. 31-46.
Shiman, Lilian Lewis, *Crusade Against Drink in Victorian England* (London: St Martin's Press, 1988).
Sidgwick, Henry, *Lectures on the Ethics of T.H. Green, Mr. Herbert Spencer and J. Martineau,* (London: Macmillan, 1902).
Smith, Timothy L., *Revivalism and Social Reform: American Protestantism on the Eve of the Civil War* (Nashville: Abingdon,1957).
Sowton, Stanley, *Pathfinders for Modern Methodism* (London: Epworth, 1933).
Spall, Richard Francis, 'The Anti-Corn-Law League's opposition to English Church establishment', *Journal of Church & State* 32.1 (1990), pp. 97-123.
Spencer, Carole Dale, 'Hannah Whitall Smith and the Evolution of Quakerism: An Orthodox Heretic in an Age of Controversy', *Quaker Studies*, 18.1 (2013), pp7-22.
Stock, Eugene, *The English Church in the Nineteenth Century* (London: Longmans, Green & Co., 1910).
Street, M. Jennie, *F.B. Meyer: His Life and Work* (London: Partridge, 1903).
Strout, Cushing, *The New Heavens and the New Earth: Political Religion in America* (New York: Harper & Row, 1973).
Sweet, William Warren, *Methodism in American History* (Nashville: Abingdon, 1953).
Thomas, Geoffrey, *The Moral Philosophy of T.H. Green* (Oxford: Oxford University Press, 1987).
Thompson, David, 'John Clifford's Social Gospel', *The Baptist Quarterly*, 31.5 (January 1986), pp. 199-217.
Thompson, David M., 'The Emergence of the Nonconformist Social Gospel in England', in Keith Robbins (ed.), *Studies in Church History, Subsidia 7* (Oxford: Blackwell, 1990), pp. 255-280.
Townsend, W.J., H.B. Workman & G. Eayrs, *A New History of Methodism*, 2 volumes (London: Hodder & Stoughton, 1909).
Turberfield, Alan, *John Scott Lidgett: Archbishop of British Methodism?* (Peterborough: Epworth, 2003).
Turnbull, Richard, *Shaftesbury: the Great Reformer* (Oxford: Lion, 2010).
Underwood, A.C., *A History of the English Baptists* (London: Carey Kingsgate, 1947).

Walker, Pamela J., *Pulling the Devil's Kingdom Down: The Salvation Army in Victorian Britain* (Berkley: University of California Press, 2001).
Walker, R.B., 'Religious Change in Liverpool in the Nineteenth Century', *Journal of Ecclesiastical History* 19 (1968), pp. 195-211.
Waller, P.J., *Democracy and Sectarianism: A Political and Social History of Liverpool, 1868-1939* (Liverpool: Liverpool University Press, 1981).
Walters, Arthur, *Hugh Price Hughes: Pioneer and Reformer* (London: Robert Culley, 1907).
Wearmouth, Robert F., *Methodism and the Working Class Movements of England, 1800-1850* (London: Epworth, 1947).
Wempe, Ben, *T.H. Green's Theory of Positive Freedom* (Exeter: Imprint Academic, 2004).
Wiggins, Arch. R., *The History of the Salvation Army*, vol. 4, 1886-1904 (London, 1964).
Williamson, Jeffrey G., *Coping with City Growth during the British Industrial Revolution* (Cambridge: Cambridge University Press, 2002).
Wilson, A.N., *The Victorians* (New York: Arrow, 2003).
Wohl, Anthony S., *The Bitter Cry of Outcast London by Andrew Mearns with other selections and an introduction by Anthony S. Wohl* (Leicester: Leicester University Press, 1970).
Wright, Don, *Mantle of Christ: A History of the Sydney Central Methodist Mission* (Brisbane: University of Queensland Press, 1984).
Wrintmore, F.H., *God Speaks to London* (London: London City Mission, 1954).

Author Index

Scripture Index

Persons Index

Subject Index